11 New Fetter Lane
London EC4P 4EE
Telephone: 071-583 9855
Fax: 071-583 4519

We have much pleasure in sending you
the accompanying book for review

Title:
**The Limits of Medical
Paternalism**

Author: **Hayry**

ISBN: Hb **0 415 06320 5**
     Pb

Publication Date: **12.12.91**

Published Price: £ **30.00**   Hb

              £   Pb

A copy of the review would be greatly appreciated.
Reviews should not appear in the press prior to the
date of publication.
For further information please contact:

James Powell

THE LIMITS OF MEDICAL
PATERNALISM

SOCIAL ETHICS AND POLICY SERIES
Edited by Anthony Dyson and John Harris
Centre for Social Ethics and Policy,
University of Manchester

EXPERIMENTS ON EMBRYOS
Anthony Dyson and John Harris (eds)

THE LIMITS OF MEDICAL PATERNALISM
Heta Häyry

PROTECTING THE VULNERABLE
Autonomy and Consent in Health Care
Margaret Brazier and Mary Lobjoit (eds)

THE LIMITS OF
MEDICAL
PATERNALISM

Heta Häyry

London and New York

First published 1991
by Routledge
11 New Fetter Lane, London EC4P 4EE

Simultaneously published in the USA and Canada
by Routledge
a division of Routledge, Chapman and Hall, Inc.
29 West 35th Street, New York, NY 10001

© 1991 Heta Häyry

Typeset in 10/12 Garamond by
Falcon Typographic Art Ltd, Edinburgh & London
Printed in Great Britain by
T J Press (Padstow) Ltd, Padstow, Cornwall

British Library Cataloguing in Publication Data
Häyry, Heta
The limits of medical paternalism. – (Social ethics and society).
1. Medicine. Ethics
I. Title II. Series
174.2

Library of Congress Cataloging in Publication Data
Häyry, Heta.
The limits of medical paternalism / Heta Häyry.
p. cm – (Social ethics and policy)
Includes bibliographical references and index.
1. Medical personnel and patient. 2. Paternalism. 3. Medical
personnel – Psychology. I. Title. II. Series.
R727.3.H38   1991
610'.69—dc20   91–9501

ISBN 0–415–06320–5

CONTENTS

PREFACE

Whilst studying the problems of medical ethics after completing my MA thesis on the morality of euthanasia, in 1984, the fact gradually began to dawn on me that paternalism, or control over people's lives, allegedly in their own best interest, is the common denominator of many ethical dilemmas and pseudo-dilemmas in today's medicine and health care. There were several happy coincidences which contributed to this realization. First, in the spring of 1986 I received with the help of Professor Timo Airaksinen a generous three-year grant from the Emil Aaltonen Foundation to prepare a book on 'The coercive and non-coercive modes of social interaction'. I had applied for several other scholarships and posts at the same time, and my research plans varied from social philosophy to the history of European aesthetics. That I turned my attention to the questions of coercion and constraint at all was, at that point, a matter of chance. Second, in May 1986 I attended an IVR Special Nordic Conference in Reykjavik, Iceland. For that conference, I had earlier prepared a paper entitled 'Voluntary euthanasia and medical paternalism', which now connected my fresh research interest with the previous preoccupation I had had with medical ethics.* And third, a book which I had co-authored with Matti Häyry on the moral issues related to abortion and euthanasia was published during the same summer.† The public debate following the release of the book amply showed that the majority of medical professionals in Finland

---

* The paper has been published in Finnish as 'Tahdonalainen eutanasia ja lääkärin paternalismi' (1989) *Ajatus* 45: 154–66. It is also forthcoming in English in *Praxiology* (Warsaw: Polish Academy of Sciences).
† *Rakasta kärsi ja unhoita: Moraalifilosofisia pohdintoja ihmiselämän alusta ja lopusta*, first edition, Reports from the Department of Philosophy, University of Helsinki Nr. 2/1986, second revised edition, Helsinki: Kirjayhtymä, 1987.

at least consider it self-evident that 'the doctor always knows best', even in cases where the patient's own wishes and beliefs are at stake. While things have probably improved since then there is no doubt that here as elsewhere in Europe and in the United States the habit of medical paternalism is still deeply ingrained and widely accepted as right by health professionals.

Throughout the period which might be called euphemistically 'preliminary research' – i.e., the first one and a half years of the scholarship during which I mainly leant back in my chair and pondered – the debate on euthanasia went on, and silently reshaped the research plan. The official records of the Emil Aaltonen Foundation show that in February 1987 I was preparing the book on 'The ethics of constraint and coercion, with special emphasis on the problems of euthanasia and paternalism', while only a month later the research plan was in another context entitled simply 'Euthanasia and paternalism'. It was not until the second year of the scholarship was drawing to a close in January 1988 that the topic was finally fixed as 'The ethical problems of medical paternalism'.

The book was for the most part written during three shortish periods of inspiration. The first version of chapters 4 and 5, as well as parts of chapter 2, came first. The main motivation for the effort was that I had to prepare a presentation for a conference which was held in August in Murikka, Finland, on The Legitimacy of Law.* I then rearranged these parts, and wrote chapter 3 and most of chapter 6. The results of this work were presented and discussed in Professor G. H. von Wright's research seminar. Finally, I completed the manuscript by writing chapters 1, 2 and 7, and rewriting the rest.

The title *The Limits of Medical Paternalism* does not completely indicate the dual aim which the study has. On the one hand, I wanted to give a detailed account of different types of paternalism, and of their respective moral statuses. On the other hand, it seemed to me essential to apply this analysis to the most important cases of paternalistic intervention within medical practice and health care.

My warm thanks are due to Professor Timo Airaksinen, without whom I would have had neither the financial means nor the inclination to prepare this study. His support and critical insights have contributed enormously to the book. I also thank

---

* At the conference, I presented an extremely compressed version of chapter 4, which is forthcoming in *Rechtstheorie* (Berlin), under the title 'Liberalism, utilitarianism, paternalism and moralism: J. S. Mill vs. J. F. Stephen'.

the Emil Aaltonen Foundation for financing most of the work. My sincere thanks are due to Mark Shackleton, Lecturer in English, University of Helsinki, who patiently revised the many versions of the manuscript, and to Professor Matti Sintonen, whose helpful comments on the completed manuscript I greatly appreciated. My very special thanks are due to Jyrki Uusitalo, who in his comments on the winter 1988–9 version of the manuscript introduced several topics related to freedom and constraint which I had up to that time completely overlooked. And finally, I want to thank Matti Häyry for his constant emotional and intellectual support throughout the completion of the study.

I dedicate this book to my parents, whose support has made my work possible.

Heta Häyry
Helsinki, 28 December 1990

1

THE PROBLEM OF PATERNALISM IN MODERN MEDICINE AND HEALTH CARE

It is an old tradition in medicine and health care to suppose that since 'the doctor always knows best', it is not the patients' business to interfere with her or his professional choices. It has, indeed, been customary that in the doctor–patient relationship patients have been seen as quasi-children seeking help from their medical quasi-parents, or – to use a classic term introduced by the sociologist Talcott Parsons – as persons reduced to playing the 'sick role' to gain the acceptance of their social environment and the attention of the health care personnel.[1] Accordingly, the authority and power relations between the doctor and the patient have quite understandably been coined 'paternalistic', or to substitute a non-sexist metaphor which some authors prefer, 'parentalistic'.[2]

An unquestioned subordination to medical authority is not as self-evident today, however, as it may have been in the times from which the tradition of widespread social and political paternalism dates. There was an era in Western history when individuals could see themselves primarily as occupants of fixed social roles, elements in a predetermined political order, rather than separate persons and makers of their own lives and worlds.[3] In those days it was natural to obey the monarch and the patriarch, who were more or less thought of as omnipotent and omniscient representatives of God on Earth. However, the rise of liberalism and the new liberal society marked the end of most blind obedience on a large scale. The new individual, armed with Reason and Natural Rights, emerged to challenge the old order in most areas of social and political life.[4] In fact, as John Kleinig has stated the matter in his informative account entitled simply *Paternalism*, by the latter part of the nineteenth century the situation was already much the same as it is today in that 'though in some areas patriarchal perspectives and practices persist, liberal reconceptualization [had already or at least now has] articulated a new *bête noire* – paternalism.'[5]

However, beast or no beast, medicine and health care are practices which have managed to preserve the patriarchal spirit to a large extent even in our own days. On reflection this is not very surprising when one recalls that medical professionals can by and large claim self-evident *epistemic authority* over their patients in medical matters: they really 'do know best' in the sense that they do possess more knowledge concerning injuries and diseases and their elimination and alleviation than most patients. It is therefore both intelligible and advisable that those who require medical help should succumb to this epistemic authority.

But the problem here is that epistemic authority does not necessarily justify all the patriarchal practices that doctors and nurses are accustomed to carrying out in its name. There are moral, social, political and ideological aspects to most authoritative directives which require separate legitimization, quite apart from the superior factual knowledge of the (alleged) authority. In particular, in questions of life and death or illness and health these extra-epistemic considerations become pressing, since the (alleged) authority's knowledge concerning the subject's values and expectations – which are clearly relevant to the issue – can always be challenged.

This, in short, is the background against which the problems of paternalism and moralism in modern medicine become visible.

The aims of the present study are, first, to analyse and explicate the concept of paternalism, as well as related concepts such as freedom, constraint and coercion; second, to distinguish between ethically acceptable and unacceptable modes of paternalism; third, to defend this distinction against the most important types of counterargument presented in the literature; and fourth, to apply the distinction to some of the central problems of modern medicine and health care.

My presentation will proceed in five stages. (a) I shall begin in this chapter by introducing some of the most persistent fortresses of paternalism in health care. The examples will, it is to be hoped, go some considerable way towards showing how the physician's epistemic authority related to the patient's physical condition tends to be transformed into other forms of (alleged) authority in current medical practices. (b) In chapter 2, the conceptual background issues concerning freedom, constraint and coercion are defined. Using

J.S. Mill's anti-paternalism as the starting point, I shall unearth the main descriptive, normative and axiological aspects of liberty and its restrictions by law and social policy. (c) The axiological conclusions of chapter 2 will then be carried over to the third, where types of paternalism are distinguished. As a corollary to the classification, I shall state which modes of paternalism can be regarded as legitimate within the liberal theory and which cannot. (d) In chapters 4, 5 and 6 this normative view will be defended against three prominent counterarguments. The core of the defence is that despite the many claims to the contrary, individual liberty and autonomy should always be given priority over welfare calculations, public morality and abstract rationality in matters which solely or primarily concern the individuals themselves. (e) Chapter 7 concludes the examination by analysing and assessing the main practices nurturing possibly illegitimate medical paternalism.

A word of warning is appropriate at this point. Since the justificatory problems in the issue at hand are complex and deep, it is not my intention to actually put forward any solutions in this first chapter. Rather, the occasional arguments introduced here should be seen only as examples of the lines of thinking generally employed in the issue of medical paternalism. Fuller accounts on the normative and axiological basis of the matter, as mentioned above, will be provided in later chapters.

VARIETIES OF PATERNALISM IN DAY-TO-DAY MEDICAL PRACTICE

Acting in the patient's best interest is one of the most important prerequisites of all medical practice. In their work, doctors and nurses regularly have to do unpleasant things to their patients: they push needles into them, cut them with knives, expose them to toxic substances and harmful radiation, and restrict their freedom. Surely these activities would merit moral condemnation and legal prosecution if they were to take place in the absence of mitigating circumstances. Medical practitioners are, however, immune to such charges on the grounds that what they do is, by the codes of their explicit professional ethics, always directed towards helping those in need of aid. From the Hippocratic Oath onwards one can read in various professional codes for physicians and nurses echoes of the line of the Oath,

'Whatever houses I may visit, I will come for the benefit of the sick.'[6]

But the 'benefit of the sick' is sometimes an ambiguous matter indeed, and this is where problems arise. The following six cases represent some of the categories in which it is not entirely clear where the patient's best interest lies – or whether appeals to it could be used to justify decisions.

(1) *The Case of the Dying Mother*
Mrs A is lying in a hospital bed, dying. Collecting the last of her strength, she calls for her doctor, and asks if there is any word about her son, whom she has not seen or heard of during the last few months. The doctor has just learned that the son was killed a few days ago trying to escape from prison after having been indicted for multiple rape and murder. Thinking that it is in the best interest of Mrs A, the doctor tells her that the son is doing well.[7]

(2) *The Case of the Man with Lung Cancer*
When a man aged 75 was examined for respiratory infection a shadowed area was detected in the chest x-ray. This was thought to indicate cancer of the lung. The patient recovered from the infection, and the only complaint he afterwards suffered from was intermittent claudication due to atherosclerosis. The patient was not informed about the suspected lung cancer – the doctor, however, followed up the progress of the shadow through chest x-ray examinations every few months, and noticed that it was growing very slowly. The patient was content and died suddenly two and half years later owing to occlusion of the cerebral artery.[8]

(3) *The Case of the Fatal Urography*
An experienced radiologist decided that what Mrs E needed was intravenous urography. He knew that with this procedure there would be a very small yet nevertheless a potential risk on the patient's life – however, he had himself done 6,000–8,000 urograms during the preceding thirteen years and no patient had ever had a fatal reaction. To facilitate things, and acting on the strong conviction that a warning would in the end do Mrs E absolutely no good, he withheld the information from her.

The urography was performed, Mrs E developed a reaction, and died of it.[9]

(4) *The Case of the Determined Doctor*
A middle-aged man comes to see his physician, and asks her to test him extensively to find out if he has contracted any sexually transmissible diseases during his one-year stay in Central Africa. 'It's no use testing for HIV, though,' he continues, 'it doesn't do any good to know as there is no cure for AIDS, anyway. I'd rather remain ignorant about that.' The doctor, however, thinking that it is in the patient's best interest, tests his blood for HIV antibodies, finds the result positive, and informs him of the fact.

(5) *The Case of the Refused Sterilization*
Dr Elizabeth Stanley, a sexually active 26-year-old intern in the field of Internal Medicine, requests a tubal ligation. She insists that she has been thinking about this decision for months, she does not want children, she does not like available contraceptives, and she understands that tubal ligation is irreversible. When the staff gynaecologist on service suggests that Dr Stanley might sometime marry and that her future husband might want children, she indicates that she would either find another husband or adopt children. Although she concedes that she might possibly change her mind in the future, she thinks that this is unlikely and views the tubal ligation as making it impossible for her to reconsider her current decision. She speaks quietly but sincerely. She has scheduled a vacation in two weeks and wants the surgery performed then. The gynaecologist, however, refuses to do the operation, mainly on two grounds: first, because he has known her father during the war and feels she is letting him down by the decision, and second, because he firmly believes that irreversible decisions like this will eventually harm patients if they are made too hastily. Accordingly, he suggests that the matter could be discussed again in a year.[10]

(6) *The Case of the Lady with Mnemic Problems*
A 60-year-old woman, Mrs L, suffered from chronic brain syndrome with arteriosclerosis. As a result, she had periods of confusion and mild loss of memory, interspersed with times of mental alertness and rationality. She was hospitalized

after having been found wandering on a city street; when questioned she could not give her home address. During her third hospitalization, she petitioned for release on the grounds of unlawful deprivation of liberty.

In the hearing a psychiatrist testified that Mrs L showed no tendency to harm either others or herself intentionally. Her commitment was based solely on the need for supervision because of her confused and defenceless state. Mrs L herself also testified at the hearing. She appeared to be fully rational, and stated that she understood her condition and the risks involved in her living outside the hospital. But she preferred to accept these risks rather than endure continued hospitalization.

The petition was, however, denied, and Mrs L died four years later, still confined in a mental hospital.[11]

In all these cases, medical practitioners, experts and judges have thought that it is in the patients' best interest that they are lied to, deceived, insufficiently informed, compulsorily informed, left untreated or forcibly detained against their own expressed wishes. In some of these cases it may, indeed, genuinely be the authority's first consideration to seek the patient's good. In some of them, the decisions may even be justifiable. But since some of the cases nevertheless remain ambiguous, several additional reasons are often given to justify authoritarian medical decisions. These include harm inflicted on other people (a possible consideration in The Case of the Determined Doctor),[12] inconvenience or waste of time (as in The Case of the Fatal Urography), and offence against other people's feelings on moral convictions (apparently a factor in The Case of the Refused Sterilization).

More systematically, it seems that medical professionals employ four standard lines of defence when faced with pertinacious clients such as Elizabeth Stanley, who requested the sterilization in Case (6) above. In conversational terms, these four responses might be put in something like the following forms:

(i) 'But it's for *your own good!*'
(ii) 'It would be *irrational* to do otherwise.'
(iii) 'It would be *immoral* to do otherwise.'
(iv) 'It would *hurt other people* if you were allowed to choose so selfishly.'

The succession of these four arguments – which appeal, respectively, to the person's own good, rationality, morality and offence to others – can be seen in any one of the truly contentious issues within medical ethics; i.e., usually where *sex* or *reproduction* or *death* or a combination of these are involved.

SEX, REPRODUCTION AND THE EMERGENCE OF MORAL UPROAR

The case of the Refused Sterilization, originally presented in 1980 for discussion in a conference on ethics, humanism and medicine, offers an outstanding example. As for the contentiousness of the case, here is how Marc Basson, the editor of the conference proceedings, describes the session in question:

> The question in this topic is a simple one, quiet and undramatic. No one is dying or being forced to live in agony against his will. No ignorant or distraught patient is being overruled or manipulated into an unsafe experiment. The doctor does nothing irreversible to the patient and the patient surely can find someone else to perform the tubal ligation she seeks. Yet the discussion on this topic ranked among the most heated that has ever occurred at one of the conferences in this series. Several times it threatened to degenerate into a shouting match.[13]

In his account, Basson goes on to attribute the heatedness of the discussion to the concepts of 'paternalism' and 'patient rights', which at the beginning of the 1980s were according to him among the 'buzz words of bioethics' in the United States. But the use of these concepts cannot have been the only reason for the vivid response, since they appear in relatively uncontroversial issues as well. Rather, what aroused excitement in the audience must have been, at least partly, the unique combination of sex, childbearing and the battle between the sexes, apparent in the case.[14]

This interpretation is strongly, albeit implicitly, supported by Eric Cassell's presentation given at the conference.[15] He provides an imaginative first person narrative from the viewpoint of a middle-aged male gynaecologist, who obviously does not think much of women's capacity for reasoning or discussing matters calmly. The

7

narrative begins with a background story which Cassell himself seems to consider relevant:

> I knew Elizabeth's father from way back and we were in the Army together in an infantry unit around Salerno that had a bad time for a few days. He died when Liz was still in high school but we had always kept in touch. He was a good man whom I owe a favour, dead or not. . . . So when she came in the first time to talk about the tubal I was totally unprepared. I wanted to tell her about her father and about what we all wanted, and hoped for, and talked about endlessly because we were even younger than she is. You know, the way you would talk to the child of a friend who was old enough to know something and to joke and talk about wars and parents and training programs. Someone who was at the same time your child and not your child. A surgeon and a friend, but a young friend.[16]

After this nostalgic moment, Cassell moves on to contradict the original formulation of the case:

> Anyway that was definitively not Elizabeth Stanley. I got the whole tubal ligation number by the Woman's Movement book. Every objection that I offered was countered not by any content but merely by her telling me about her rights as an individual. . . . So after hearing her out . . . I said that I was sorry, but I was not going to tie her tubes and that was the end of it. She said it was certainly not the end of it. . . . To tell you the honest truth, all the substantive matters about having children or not, reversibility or not, surgical risk or not, the actual factual basis for her desire to become infertile got lost in the yelling that followed my saying NO.[17]

The contradiction with the original case is twofold: first, Elizabeth Stanley replied to the physician's tentative objections with precise and reasonable answers, not with feminist slogans, and second, Cassell has miraculously transformed her 'quiet but sincere' speech into uncontrolled yelling at the practitioner.

What, then, is the point of these alterations in the story? And more generally, what kinds of reasons does Eric, Elizabeth's father's brother-in-arms, present in favour of his refusal? In what follows, I shall endeavour to show that Cassell's way of formulating the issue neatly brings forth the four principles mentioned in the above, namely the principles of: (i) the best interest of the patient; (ii) irrationality; (iii) immorality; and (iv) offence to other people. As the point of the exercise is classificatory rather than genuinely justificatory, I have not followed the possibly more tenable lines of argument which might be developed in favour of paternalism here. These will be tackled in due course at the later stages of the study.

(i) To start with, Cassell questions the motives behind Dr Stanley's decision to have her tubes ligated. He writes:

> I am not about to sterilize Arnold's kid just because as a green no-nothing intern who has had loose bowels, sweaty hands and no sleep for a month, she thinks that is the way she is going to show the world that she is grown-up. Okay, I may not know why she wants to do it but I don't think she does either. There isn't a doctor in the world who does not know that people change their minds.[18]

This, I think, could only be read as saying that the age and experience of the older doctor make him infinitely more competent to judge the younger doctor's own best interests and motives than the younger doctor herself could ever judge them. Especially the irreversible nature of the operation is a definite problem: younger people seem to be unable to grasp the seriousness of that factor.

However, in the original formulation of the case Elizabeth Stanley does explicitly note that the procedure cannot be reversed. In fact, she makes it a part of her argument by welcoming the tubal ligation 'as making it impossible to reconsider her current decision'. And if this is her calm and rational opinion, what more could there be to say?

(ii) As it turns out, Cassell seems to have a lot more to say, though the focus of his argument begins to drift at this point. The next logical step is to point out the patient's irrationality, and in the last passage quoted above this is already anticipated. No less than four separate grounds are given for considering Elizabeth Stanley incompetent to make decisions of this magnitude. These are: first, that for some reason or other she has not been sleeping well lately, and is therefore in a confused state of mind; second, that her primary motive for the sterilization is to 'show the world that she is grown-up', which shows immaturity of thought; third, that she does not herself realize that 'showing the world' is the true motive behind her request; and fourth, that any rational human being would naturally eschew irreversible decisions like this one.

But the relevance of these considerations can be neatly contested by applying them, in turn, to the decisions Eric and Arnold presumably made shortly after they had had their hard times in Salerno. What happened was, in all probability, that coming home as exhausted but high-spirited war heroes they married immediately and, to show the world that they were grown-up, immediately started producing offspring. The mental condition of the young heroes was certainly somewhat confused, their motives rather less than thoroughly considered, and their having children was as irreversible as Elizabeth Stanley's requested sterilization. However, it is far from evident that Cassell would like to condemn himself and Arnold as strongly as he condemns Dr Stanley for her decision.

This is where Cassell's additions to the original story enter the picture: knowing, in the back of his mind at least, that all sorts of compromising comparisons can be made unless they are stopped at the source, he provides the reader with independent proof of Dr Stanley's irrationality. A person yelling uncontrollably and hammering the opponent with ideological slogans instead of giving her own reasons for wishing the operation could hardly be considered rational in any very demanding sense. And perhaps rationality of a demanding kind is required if a person's opinions are to be taken seriously by other people.

(iii) In the case at hand, this line of reasoning has to be abandoned because it perverts the original description – but this by no means exhausts Cassell's resources. The nostalgic story at the outset of his account, with a few additions, now begins to add its weight. Referring to the 'endless discussions in Salerno' he writes:

> Every objection that I offered was countered not by any content but merely by her telling me about her rights as an individual – and also how I had let her down. Never entered her mind for even a moment that she might have let me down – to say nothing of Arnold.[19]

So this is what it all boils down to: it would be wrong to get sterilized, since common morality – at least the morality common to Eric and Arnold – dictates that healthy young people ought to get married and have children. By having her tubes tied instead, Elizabeth would let her (late) father down; he could never have grandchildren, and his comforting feeling that his life could continue after death through Elizabeth's children and their children would be brutally frustrated.

It must be noted, however, that even if moral considerations of this sort were relevant to the issue, it would still be far from evident that Cassell's views are correct. It may indeed be the case that Arnold hoped to have grandchildren; but it is equally possible that he loved and trusted his daughter enough to think that whatever she came to decide for herself would be right. In that case, it would really be Eric the gynaecologist who would be letting his old army buddy down, not Elizabeth.

(iv) This brings us to the final defence, the core of which is already present in the quotation above. As Cassell remarks, it never occurred to Dr Stanley that she could be letting her male colleague down by asking him to perform the tubal ligation. Perhaps this means that the colleague has expected the young intern to have children, and now feels betrayed. Or perhaps he is just feeling awkward and embarrassed about acting as the gynaecologist of the daughter of an old friend. Or maybe it is his own personal opinion that the sterilization of healthy young women is morally to be condemned. Be that as it may, one thing is clear: the practitioner feels offended by Elizabeth's request, and firmly believes that the offence experienced by him is, as such, enough to justify the refusal to operate.

The merits and demerits of this kind of 'gut reaction ethics', as indeed the credits and discredits of all the other lines of argument introduced above, will be discussed in detail in the following chapters. The important thing here is merely to notice how in the course of argumentation the physician's calm and professional references to 'the patient's own best interest' seem to have an almost intrinsic tendency to become transformed into charges of irrationality, immorality and offensiveness.

VOLUNTARY EUTHANASIA AND MEDICAL PATERNALISM

Another example, more dramatic in many respects but void of sex-related elements, will further illustrate my point. The unprecedented development of life-sustaining medical techniques has during the last few decades made it possible to keep many people alive even when the severity of their condition casts doubt on the intrinsic worth of doing so. Some of these people, victims of disease or accidents, have long since permanently lost any kind of conscious contact with other human beings, being now reduced to a persistent vegetative state. In addition, there are severely defective infants and children without the slightest positive prospects in their lives, who live a few painful years at the most and never become conscious of themselves or others as persons. And there are other victims of disease and accidents with intolerable pain and suffering, whose only wish, under such circumstances, is to die as quickly and peacefully as possible.

The members of the last-mentioned group, the conscious sufferers, sometimes ask the medical personnel to hasten their deaths, either by withdrawing treatments or by actively terminating the patient's life. What they are requesting by expressing such wishes is *voluntary euthanasia*. In this combined concept, the latter part, 'euthanasia', is generally taken to mean the easy death of a person for whom death is a better alternative than life, or – and this is probably the main usage nowadays – the conscious inducement of such a death by other persons, either by acting or omitting to act, either directly or indirectly.[20] The attribute 'voluntary', in its turn, refers to the fact that the persons themselves wish to be actively or passively, directly or indirectly euthanatized.[21] With newborn infants and irreversibly incompetent persons only non-voluntary euthanasia can take place, and in the cases of people who do not want to die the term involuntary euthanasia remains a possibility (although 'murder' is a word that perhaps comes to mind more readily).[22]

The active forms of voluntary euthanasia are legally prohibited in most Western countries.[23] A vast majority of medical professionals seem to consider this a blessing, despite the fact that the absolute prohibition in many cases causes much unnecessary pain and anguish. And although the passive forms of euthanasia – roughly, letting patients die peacefully and without aggressive life-prolonging treatment – are by and large legally permissible, physicians sometimes deny their patients even that possibility. The reasons given in support of the denial are often quite similar to those encountered in the sterilization case.

(i) The first step, again, is to state that it is in the patient's own best interest to be treated exactly in the manner that the doctors have decided. After all, it is their job to know about these things – that is what their extensive and expensive training is all about – and it would therefore be absurd to think that the patient's expertise in medical matters could exceed that of the doctor.

Counter to this view it can be noted that physicians, however well trained in medicine they may be, can hardly be expected to be especially knowledgeable concerning each and every patient's wishes, hopes, expectations and values. And surely these psychological and ethical factors are more important in deciding about life and death than the clinical facts undoubtedly mastered by the medical profession.

(ii) But the relevance of individual psychology to the issue can be challenged by referring to rationality. It can be argued, namely, that for every human being her or his own life is a good thing, a valuable item. Death is the end of that good thing, and must accordingly be looked upon as an evil. Therefore, as it is clearly irrational to hope or wish anything evil for oneself,[24] it is irrational to hope for one's own death.

There are many problems in this kind of argument. To begin with, it is not quite true that one could not or should not wish to reach the end of a pleasurable or otherwise personally valuable set of experiences. A good movie or musical performance, for instance, may lead one to think, 'I wish this would never end!' but in reality, of course, one knows that it will and must inevitably come to a conclusion sooner or later. Nor is it an evil that it does: once the story has been told or the theme exhausted, there is simply no point in degenerating into endless repetition. This applies – to a certain degree at least – to human life as well: if the end of the story is clearly in sight anyway, then it does not necessarily seem irrational that the dying person wishes to avoid any further repetition, and hopes to have the merciful curtain drawn instead.[25]

Another angle from which the argument can be attacked is that of casting doubt upon the assignment of positive value to every human life in any circumstances. It does seem an inevitable truth that life usually counts as a good, but does it always? Philippa Foot has given the following account to justify her own contrary view:

> It seems . . . that merely being alive is not a good. . . . The idea
> we need seems to be that of life which is ordinary human life in
> . . . that it contains a minimum of basic human goods. What is
> ordinary in human life . . . is that a man is not driven to work
> far beyond his capacity; that he has the support of a family
> or community; that he can more or less satisfy his hunger;
> that he has hopes for the future; that he can lie down to rest
> at night.[26]

After stating these general conditions, Foot moves on to address the problem in the medical field:

Disease too can so take over a man's life that the normal human goods disappear. When a patient is so overwhelmed by pain or nausea that he cannot eat with pleasure, if he can eat at all, and is out of the reach of even the most loving voice, he no longer has ordinary human life in the sense in which the words are used here. And . . . crippling depression can destroy the enjoyment of ordinary goods as effectively as external circumstances can remove them.[27]

Accordingly, Foot concludes that:

there is a certain conceptual connexion between life and good in the case of human beings as in that of animals and even plants. Here, as there, however, it is not the mere state of being alive that can determine, or itself count as, a good, but rather life coming up to some standard of normality.[28]

I think that what Foot states in these passages makes perfect sense, and casts strong doubts upon the argument that it would always be irrational to wish one's life to be allowed to come to a peaceful and swift end.

(iii) The *prudential* permission to wish one's death will, however, once established, be countered by *moral* prohibitions. A theistic approach is probably the most popular one here. Life is a gift from God, supporters of this view say, and as such it should be respected from its natural beginning to its natural end.[29] It is therefore morally wrong to wish one's life to come to a premature end, let alone to hope it to be deliberately terminated.

Two matters must be kept apart from each other in this moral objection to voluntary euthanasia. First, there is a continuum from the patient's best interest via rationality to morality, which centres upon the idea of the wrongness of *giving up* a life – in the present case, giving up one's own life. By focusing on this idea in their refusals to euthanatize suffering patients, physicians take the clearly paternalistic view that they are the best judges of the patient's good, rationality and morality. Second, however, there is another sense in which morality can enter the matter. Instead of referring to the morality of patients, doctors can also refer to their own ethics, focusing on the widely assumed wrongness of *taking* a life – in this case, taking the life of another human being.

A variety of reasons has been given against taking human lives. The 'traditional theory', for instance, stating that innocent human beings should not be intentionally killed has been backed up by referring to things such as respect for human life, sanctity of life, the (inalienable) right to life, protection of human autonomy, direct harm to the person being killed and indirect harm to other people.[30] In addition, the somewhat stricter view, stating that people should not even be allowed to die if their lives can be sustained somehow, can be argued for by references to suffering as a part of God's plan for us, the impermissibility of 'playing God', and the fear that even the slightest deviation from an absolute respect towards human life would lead mankind to uncontrollable mass murder and holocaust.[31] Now, whether these attempts at justification are valid or not, the fact remains that a doctor's refusal to euthanatize a patient will, in the eyes of the medical profession as well as in the eyes of the general public, be better supported by reasons related to the wrongness of taking the life of another than by reasons related to the alleged wrongness of giving up one's own life. However, in arguments against medical euthanasia these sets of reasons are intermingled to the extent that the assessment of one cannot be completed without an assessment of the other. In fact, it can well be argued that if the paternalistic attitudes were proven untenable, many intuitions against killing suffering patients at their own free, informed and considered request would evaporate by themselves.

In any case, the important point here is that in the euthanasia issue, as in the sterilization issue, the path from the patient's own good to charges of irrationality and immorality is fairly well marked. Even though sex – one of the primary inducements for employing the epithet 'immoral' – is not present, physicians and philosophers alike have been forced to retreat from their original benevolently camouflaged expert positions to the windier battlefields of prudence and morality.

FROM FACE-TO-FACE MEDICAL PATERNALISM TO 'LIBERTICIDE' IN HEALTH CARE?

Armed with the knowledge provided by the cases of sterilization and voluntary euthanasia, it is easy to see how patriarchal attitudes may hold sway in other areas of modern medicine as well. Thus far cases have invariably involved face-to-face clinical contact between physicians and their own patients but, in fact, the deepest patriarchal remnants may be found in more impersonal practices and regulations within public health care and legislation related to it.

First, there are a number of laws in most Western countries, many of them essentially non-medical in content, which clearly aim at protecting the lives and health of citizens against their own ill-advised behavioural tendencies. These laws can, for instance, oblige people to use seat belts while driving a car or crash helmets while riding a motorcycle. They can also prohibit the manufacture, sale and use of risky mechanical equipment, dangerous materials and toxic substances. The production, sale and use of drugs can be regulated so that while some medically indispensable types of pharmaceuticals are available by prescription, others are banned. Additionally, the 'moral sanity' of the people is sometimes protected by laws permitting only certain limited modes of sexual behaviour – ordinarily, 'normal' heterosexual practices between spouses in the privacy of their own bedroom.

Second, there are legal and socio-political principles defining the kind of people who will be permitted to live freely within society, making to some degree at least their own life-plans and decisions. Exclusion from this group of trustworthy citizens can be based either on risk of harm inflicted on others, or on a tendency to harm oneself, accompanied by incompetence, irrationality or immorality. People belonging to the out-group can be incarcerated and isolated for their own protection, or for the protection of others, and they are generally labelled as *criminal* (harm to others, major immorality), *vicious* (minor immorality) or *mad* (harm to self, irrationality). The categories overlap each other, and a person can at the same time be considered mad, vicious *and* criminal. However, the liberalization of criminal laws and penal institutions in the West have recently lead most theorists to ignore the possibility of positive viciousness, as they have tended to treat both criminality and madness as psychiatrically corrigible disorders of the mind.

Third, with the rise of social medicine, first as a practice, then also as an academic discipline, public health authorities have increasingly planned and executed socio-medical programmes, some of which are almost invisible but which nevertheless have a great effect on communal health as a whole. Explicit and more or less efficient social medicine started with vaccinations against communicable diseases in the nineteenth century, and since then many strategies for improving the health of citizens have been developed.

Fluoridation of drinking water is supposed to strengthen people's teeth, food regulations are presumed to eliminate toxications and diseases, and, say, regulations concerning tobacco and alcohol marketing and sale aim at decreasing the prevalence of cancer and other illnesses. All these policies have the twofold goal of both protecting people from themselves *and* – and this may often be more important – saving (other) people's money by preventing diseases from occurring rather than waiting for them to occur and then treating them at multiple financial as well as human cost. In addition, in issues such as regulating tobacco and alcohol sales, one motive can usually be traced to the moral area: as indicators of an 'immoral' lifestyle, smoking and drinking are often thought of as deserving an extra price tag of social condemnation.

And, finally, there are measures which do not necessarily involve explicit sanctions of any sort, such as health education, screening for the most common diseases and the free distribution of medical or paramedical equipment relating to hygiene and the prevention of contagion. Even if no sanctions exist, these practices have their patriarchal aspects in that basic choices are made by medical authorities: they decide about the content of health education, the diseases to be screened, and the equipment to be distributed. To give an example of selective policies, it is quite certain, say, that each and every newly detected risk of smoking will be widely publicized by the health authorities, yet, on the other hand, it is highly unlikely that any positive consequences of smoking, if and when occasionally found, would be pointedly reported to the general public. Likewise, the diseases routinely screened and registered often include mainly illnesses related to 'immoral' lifestyles – sexually transmissible diseases and the like. And when it comes to the free distribution of items that prevent the spread of diseases, the health authorities have in some countries been forced to exclude, for instance, condoms and free syringes, because of strong medico-religious sentiments against extramarital sexual practices and intravenous drug abuse.

All these varieties of benevolent constraint – actual, potential and alleged – in medicine and health care bring to mind the words of a letter written by John Stuart Mill to Harriet Taylor on 15 January 1855, referring to the general state of society in those days:

On my stay here cogitating thereof I came back to an idea we have talked about and thought that the best thing to write and publish at present would be a volume on Liberty. So many things might be brought into it and nothing seems to be more needed – it is a growing need too, for opinion tends to encroach more and more on liberty, and almost all the projects of social reformers in these days are really *liberticide*.[32]

With the patriarchal structures and moralistic attitudes that prevail in Western health care systems, the adequate question now seems to be whether or not there is an act of *medical liberticide* in process behind silent hospital walls and closed cabinet doors.

To throw light on the situation, let me, at this point, turn to a historical and systematic analysis of the basic concepts in the issue. For the best part of the next five chapters, I shall be leaving the actual medical matters to one side, in order to concentrate on the theoretical lines of argument without interruption. Medicine and health care will again be the focus of my attention in chapter 7, where the most important instances of medical paternalism will be surveyed in the light of the principles which will emerge in what follows.

2

FREEDOM, CONSTRAINT AND THE VALUE OF LIBERTY AND AUTONOMY

The best place to start an analysis of the concepts involved in paternalism on a general level is undoubtedly John Stuart Mill's classic anti-paternalistic statement in *On Liberty*, first published in 1859. At the outset of the study he defined his position against any sort of 'liberticide' as follows:

> The object of this Essay is to assert one very simple principle, as entitled to govern absolutely the dealings of the society with the individual in the way of compulsion and control, whether the means used be physical force in the form of legal penalties, or the moral coercion of public opinion. That principle is, that the sole end for which mankind are warranted, individually or collectively, in interfering with the liberty of action of any of their number, is self-protection. That the only purpose for which power can be rightfully exercised over any member of a civilized community, against his will, is to prevent harm to others. His own good, either physical or moral, is not a sufficient warrant. He cannot rightfully be compelled to do or forbear because it will be better for him to do so, because it will make him happier, because, in the opinion of others, to do so would be wise, or even right. These are good reasons for remonstrating with him, or reasoning with him, or persuading him, or entreating him, but not for compelling him, or visiting him with any evil in case he do otherwise. To justify that, the conduct from which it is desired to deter him, must be calculated to produce evil to some one else. The only part of the conduct of any one, for which he is amenable to society, is that which concerns others. In the part which merely concerns himself, his independence is, of

right, absolute. Over himself, over his own body and mind, the individual is sovereign.[1]

In this oft-quoted passage Mill manages to introduce, in part explicitly and in part implicitly, most of the justificatory and conceptual problems of the issue at hand. A brief survey of these problems will facilitate the more thorough-going discussion later on.

HOW MANY PRINCIPLES?

First, it is a matter of some dispute whether the principle asserted by Mill is either 'one' or 'very simple'. Gerald Dworkin in his pioneering essay on paternalism pointed out that there are at least two principles involved: one which asserts that harm to others *is* a relevant ground for restricting individual or collective freedom, and another which asserts that harm to self *is not*.[2] And this is only the beginning: in fact, these claims further generate a whole set of principles which can be divided loosely into *other-regarding* (referring to harm inflicted on others) and *self-regarding* (referring mostly to harm inflicted on oneself).

The other-regarding principles of restricting individual liberty can be split into different categories according to three major criteria: first, the kind of unpleasantness inflicted on others; second, whether the unpleasantness is inflicted actively (by actually 'harming') or passively (by 'withdrawing or denying a benefit'); and third, whether the unpleasantness or embarrassment is faced by an individual or an institution.[3]

Employing the first criterion, at least four principles can be spelled out, stating, for instance, that a person's individual liberty may be curtailed

(1) to prevent *harm* to others;
(2) to prevent *hurt* to others;
(3) to prevent *offences* to others;
(4) to prevent *other kinds of unpleasantness* to others.

This division is introduced by Joel Feinberg, who in his own presentation quite sensibly stresses the primary importance of the major division into *harmful* unpleasantness on the one hand and *non-harmful* experiences on the other.[4] 'Harm' is defined by Feinberg as a frustration of a person's vital interests, and the definition conceptually implies that there is an interest, the interest not to be harmed, that all normal adult human (and possibly some non-human) beings share.[5] 'Hurts' and 'offences' in their turn can be defined, respectively, as non-harmful *physical* and *mental* pains or other discomforts. In addition to them, there are states such as anxiety and extreme boredom, which do not seem to fit readily into either of the categories, and must be labelled as 'other'. None of these non-harmful experiences is, according to Feinberg, unpleasant enough to amount to a genuine frustration of vital interests.[6] Of course, much depends here on the actual use one is going to make of the divisions. By placing, for instance, people's religious feelings in the centre of their personal integrity one may argue that offences directed against such feeling are truly harmful. By placing religious sentiments in a less focal area within the human constitution, however, an argument to the contrary could equally well be made, stating that no vital interests will be frustrated by blasphemous offences, and therefore no real harm will be done by committing them.

The question of activity and passivity in causing harm to others can be extended to cover the whole set of principles (1) – (4), but it makes best sense with regard to actual harm (1). Two principles can be formulated by applying the distinction, stating now that the individual liberty of one person may be curtailed either

(1.1) to *prevent harm* to others; or
(1.2) to *benefit* others.[7]

The latter principle makes it the proper business of the law and public opinion to sanction persons who do not voluntarily wish to further the vital interests of other people although they have the means and the opportunity of doing so. The validity of the principle may be a matter of dispute, but the interpretation at any rate is clear. This is not necessarily true regarding principles (2.2)–(4.2), whatever the correct formulation for them might be. Furthering a vital interest is an objective matter: a doctor, for instance, can save somebody's arm or leg, thereby benefiting the patient enormously. But what would a corresponding example in the field of, say, religious offences be? Creating an atmosphere where such offences would most probably not occur? Or, what might be much more efficient, accustoming people to blasphemy so that they will not be offended by it? Either way, the principles seem difficult to express.

The final dimension, that of causing injury to individuals versus impairing institutional practices that are in the public interest,[8] also seems to apply more readily to genuinely harmful injury than to the other categories. Strictly speaking, it is not possible to inflict physical or mental pain or discomfort on an institutional practice, and thus offences and hurts to institutions are conceptually out of the question. As regards harm, it *is* more comprehensible that an institution may have vital interests which are capable of being violated by individuals or groups. But, even so, the harmfulness of attacks against institutions must ultimately be measured in terms of individual injuries to individual persons caused by the weakening or abolition of beneficial institutionalized practices, since these practices are, after all, only an instrument to further the wellbeing of the people, not ends in themselves. Accordingly, the relevant division in this context is one between direct and indirect (individual) harm rather than one between individual and institutional harm. Principle (1.1) can now be formulated to state, for instance, that individual liberty may be curtailed either

(1.1.1) to prevent *direct* harm to others; or
(1.1.2) to prevent *indirect* harm to others.

Corresponding principles can be formulated with regard to benefit (1.2), and probably with regard to offences, hurts and other kinds of unpleasantness (2–4) as well.

Thus, the first part of Mill's 'one and very simple principle' alone divides, under scrutiny, into a variety of sub-principles. Furthermore, it is not at all clear from Mill's own writings which of these various reasons for curtailing individual freedom would have been acceptable to him. Other-regarding unpleasantness was, according to him, *sometimes* a good ground for constraining people's behaviour, but not always. The other half of Mill's view is more rigidly expressed: since self-protection is the 'sole end' and 'only purpose' for which the liberty of one person may be legitimately curtailed by others, self-regarding harm can *never* justify constraint. That there are, however, exceptions to this even in *On Liberty* will be discussed later. Let me first spell out the self-regarding candidates in favour of restrictions in Mill's statement quoted above.

In addition to the positive harm principles, Mill in fact presents three or four major negative principles. A person, in Mill's opinion, 'cannot rightfully be compelled to do or forbear'

(5) because it will be *better* for him to do so;

(6) because it will make him *happier*;

(7) because, in the opinion of others, to do so would be *wise*; or even

(8) because, in the opinion of others, to do so would be *right*.

The problem with the status of these sentences is that it is not clear whether Mill intended to interpret them cumulatively, as increasingly stronger expressions of one paternalistic rule, or distinctly, as formulations of four separate principles. As these matters will be dealt with in detail further on (chs 4–6), a few remarks will have to suffice for the time being.

First, at least two interpretations can be given to the separation of principles (5) and (6) – if Mill intended that such a distinction should be made. One possibility is to presume that a person's happiness is not necessarily good for her – that from a higher viewpoint her life would be better without excessive happiness. In this interpretation 'happiness' would most probably mean a maximum amount of pleasurable experiences (in the Benthamite manner),[9] and the underlying point would be that there are more important things in life than mere pleasure. Another possibility, however, would be to assume that the principles are presented in order from the concrete and personal to the abstract and impersonal, and take (5) to be the most immediately self-regarding statement. It would, in this case, refer to the here-and-now satisfaction of interests and desires, as opposed to the further-reaching possibility of aiming at a good and happy life as a whole (6).

Mill himself very probably did not mean to draw any sharp distinction between (5) and (6), but the latter interpretation concerning their difference, however, points to an interesting direction. It may be useful, at some point, to distinguish between cases where constraint or coercion is argued for in the name of the person's immediate or almost immediate good, and cases where the immediate good is sacrificed because even greater benefits are offered in the future. I shall coin these arguments, respectively, *short-term paternalistic* (5′) and *long-term paternalistic* (6′).

The number of self-regarding principles for curtailing individual freedom can be multiplied further by applying the direct–indirect and harm–non-benefit divisions. According to these principles, the liberty of a person may be restricted

(5′.1.1) to prevent the direct frustration of the immediate interests of that person;

(5'.1.2)   to prevent the indirect frustration of the immediate interests of that person;

(5'.2.1)   to directly further the immediate interests of that person;

(5'.2.2)   to indirectly further the immediate interests of that person;

(6'.1.1)   to prevent the direct frustration of the long-term wellbeing of that person;

(6'.1.2)   to prevent the indirect frustration of the long-term wellbeing of that person;

(6'.2.1)   to directly further the long-term wellbeing of that person; or

(6'.2.2)   to indirectly further the long-term wellbeing of that person.

However, a mere look at these principles makes it obvious that the boundaries, in practice, cannot be very distinct. Direct–indirect, harm–non-benefit and short-term–long-term are all matters of degree rather than matters of clear-cut classes. So although the variety of possible reasons for paternalistic intervention ought to be registered and recognized, it seems probable that the finer details of the divisions will not be able to carry much weight in justificatory considerations.

Working on the assumption that sentences (7) and (8) at least are intended to express ideas different from those presented in (5) and (6), the ideals of rationality and morality again emerge, as they did in chapter 1 when dealing with the medical examples. Put in these terms, the principles say that individual liberty may be curtailed

(7'.1)   to prevent irrational behaviour, or

(8'.1)   to prevent immoral behaviour

or, if the activity–passivity dimension is added,

(7'.2)   to further rationality and rational behaviour, or

(8'.2)   to further morality and moral behaviour.

In later chapters it will be discussed whether or not these principles can be meaningfully separated from the principle(s) of paternalism in practical discourse, and whether it was Mill's intention to do so. Systematically, at any rate, the division exists, and I shall call the doctrine expressed by principles (7') *prudentialism* and the one expressed by principles (8') *moralism*, to keep them apart from the *paternalism* expressed by principles (5') and (6').

If every distinction made here were to be taken equally seriously, the theory of legitimate restrictions of freedom would immediately lose the rare elegance of Mill's formulation. Fortunately, this is not necessary: given that all sorts of harms and offences, direct and indirect, active and passive, are implicitly included, *five* principles suffice to voice the major ideas involved. According to these principles, it is legitimate to curtail the individual liberty of a person

(I)   to prevent harm to others;
(II) to prevent offence to others;
(III) to prevent harm to the person herself;
(IV) to prevent irrational behaviour; or
(V)   to prevent immoral behaviour.

In the principles, 'harm' means frustration of vital interests, 'offence' refers to all non-harmful unpleasantness. Since immorality can offend and harming oneself can be considered irrational, and since irrationality and immorality may be intertwined in some theories, the offence principle (II) and the principles of paternalism (III), prudentialism (IV) and moralism (V) may sometimes be seen as complementary rather than competitive. With the harm principle (I), however, things are different: it is ordinarily assumed that the later principles refer to irrationality, immorality and self-inflicted harm which are *not* harmful to persons other than the agent.

The legitimacy of principles (I)–(V) is, naturally, of utmost importance in the present study. But before considering the legitimation matter at any depth, I must complete my brief survey of the conceptual foundations of the issue, as stated by Mill in his anti-paternalistic statement.

FREEDOM, CONSTRAINT AND COERCION

Moving on to the question of what exactly is forbidden on paternalistic grounds or permitted in spite of their presence, an array of expressions can be found in Mill's text. The passage quoted at the outset of this chapter alone embodies eight different formulations:

the dealings of society with the individual in the way of compulsion and control;
physical force in the form of legal penalties;
the moral coercion of public opinion;
interfering with the liberty of action of any person;
power exercised over a member of a civilized community against his will;

compelling to do or forbear;
visiting a person with an evil in case he do otherwise; and
to deter a person from certain conduct.

In the most recent discussion, two modes of interpersonal influence have been frequently chosen for closer examination: first, coercion; and second, interferences with an individual's liberty of action, or restrictions of individual freedom.[10] Furthermore, it has usually been assumed that Mill's view as well as more modern accounts can be encapsulated by these select terms. To clarify the matter, brief accounts of (i) *freedom*, (ii) *constraint* and (iii) *coercion* are therefore required at this point.

All three concepts are slightly difficult to analyse because there is a tension between two prominent elements in every one of them. Freedom, constraint and coercion can be understood both descriptively and normatively, and these interpretations constantly overlap each other in attempts to define the concepts. My strategy here is to start from the descriptive end, and keep the discussion as neutral as possible for as long as possible. There will, however, be a point beyond which any further clarification of the concepts will require attention given to the normative and axiological elements, and the required attention will then, of course, be duly given.

(i) Freedom

The basic nineteenth-century liberal interpretation equated freedom with *non-interference*, or as John Kleinig puts the matter, with 'absence of coercion or constraint on the implementation of desires'.[11] This definition is, at least initially, attractive for two reasons. First, the reference to desires seems appealing: is a person not free in an important sense when she gets all she wants, and unfree when she does not? Second, the elegance of the definition is obvious: once 'coercion' and 'constraint' are explicated, their presence will always indicate lack of freedom, their absence freedom.

But closer examination shows that there are difficulties even in these initially attractive features of the standard non-interference view. As regards the first point concerning desires, the problem is that traditional expectations, manipulation, persuasion and self-discipline, among other things, can be employed to suppress, eliminate and alter what people want. Thus, according to this view, a slave can be completely free if only he can be made to want exactly the things that he gets – say, hard work, minimally tolerable living conditions and a lifelong subordination to an autocratic slaveholder. To give another example, an imprisoned person would be free the minute she could persuade herself to wish to be imprisoned. Clearly there is something wrong with a definition of freedom which produces applications like these.

The solution to the problem has been to substitute 'options' for 'desires' in the definition. Freedom, according to this view, should be seen as the *non-restriction of options*, or if the more substantive form is preferred, as the absence of coercion or constraint on a person's action alternatives.[12] This approach has the obvious advantage over the desire-based one that it does not set slaves or prisoners free at will. On the other hand, its disadvantage seems to be a certain lack of content as a theory of human freedom. All the action alternatives open or closed to a given class of agents at a given point of time cannot be equally important and meaningful to them as determinants of their freedom. That I cannot, for example, swim across the English Channel, means that my action alternatives are limited by a mixture of natural and social hindrances, but this does not matter much, since I do not consider that particular athletic performance important anyway. Nor does it say much about my personal sphere of freedom that I could take a long walk at 5 o'clock every morning if I wanted to.

However, even though all options, or action alternatives, are not equally important, there is nothing paradoxical about saying that a person is unfree to swim the Channel if she cannot do it, or that she is free to walk on the streets early in the morning if the option is available to her. If a connection with desires is really needed, it can be established by referring to hypothetical or contrafactual states of affairs: *if* I had an urgent desire to swim the Channel, my desire would be frustrated either by lack of strength and exercise (natural inability) or by a husband who would probably prevent me from doing anything so risky (social constraint).

The second point in favour of the view of freedom as absence of coercion and constraint is its conceptual economy. This, however, is a double-edged sword, since the economy has been gained by including in the definition itself two unexplained terms. Of course, if coercion and constraint could be defined clearly and concisely, their absence would be a good determinant of freedom. But it is also possible that they cannot be defined at all without circular references to freedom. Therefore, it seems best to assume only the first half of the early liberal formulation and contend that in an important sense freedom equals the non-restriction of options or action alternatives.

Towards the end of the nineteenth century, however, some liberals began to wonder whether mere 'negative' liberty of action, or freedom from obstacles, comes to grips with the most meaningful dimensions of the concept at all.[13] For them, it was the 'positive' freedom, or *power to make things happen one's own way* that really counted. A person can, for instance, be free from all legal and social sanctions to retire from his work, buy a house in the countryside and live there happily ever after – but if he lacks the money to do so, what is all his negative freedom worth to him? Or the citizens of a state can be free from legal restraint to participate in political decision-making, yet because of poor education they may be unable to do so. In these cases, clearly, only half of the requirements of genuine freedom have been fulfilled by the absence of legal prohibitions or social pressures.

The distinction between positive and negative freedom can be made in at least two major ways, depending on what features of the original, negative freedom are stressed. Using Joel Feinberg's terms, liberty can be defined in a strict manner as the *absence of positive and external constraint*,[14] creating thus two opposites to this kind of freedom, namely absence of *negative* constraint and absence of *internal* constraint.

In Feinberg's vocabulary, positive constraints work by being present and negative constraints by being absent. The former include 'headaches, obsessive thoughts, and compulsive desires' as well as 'barred windows, locked doors and pointed bayonets'; the latter class consists of things such as 'ignorance, weakness, and deficiencies in talent or skill' along with 'lack of money, lack of transportation, and lack of weapons'.[15] If this division is considered relevant in the present context, a person can be understood to be 'positively' free if, and only if, in the absence of internal and external obstacles she is sufficiently equipped both materially and mentally to make things happen the way she wants them to happen. In the examples above, a person is free to retire only if he also has the financial means to do it, and people are politically free in the 'positive' sense only if they have the technical ability to use their negative civil liberties.

This interpretation, as Feinberg correctly observes, makes positive freedom reducible to the original idea of freedom as the non-restriction of options.[16] The only remaining difference between the 'positive' and 'negative' forms of freedom will within the view be found in the kinds of constraint that are required to be absent in either case. 'Negative' freedom will be an absence of obstacles which would work by being present, 'positive' freedom will be an absence of the lack of something which would be required to achieve the desired object. Thus it seems that there is no real need for an independent analysis of 'positive' freedom.

But this conclusion is exactly why Feinberg's account can be criticized: if those who raised the question concerning the positive aspects of freedom had any point at all in their queries, there must be a deeper, irreducible element to freedom which somehow escapes the non-restriction view. And, in fact, Feinberg's own division into internal and external constraints opens up possibilities in this direction.

Feinberg himself suggests that for *political* purposes at least the simplest and most convenient way to draw the line between the inner and the outer would be to employ a spatial criterion: external constraints come from outside a person's body–mind continuum, internal constraints are a part of it.[17] Whether or not there is an 'inner core' in human beings which can be contrasted with our 'empirical selves' is not important according to this view, and thus the deep values a person possesses have the same status in the analysis of freedom as, say, headaches and sore muscles. If my moral convictions warn me against killing innocent human beings, I am unfree to kill a person in the same sense as I am unfree to write letters in Swahili – in both cases there is an internal constraint rendering me unable to act efficiently.

However, those who criticized the non-restriction view of freedom and wanted to introduce more positive elements into it, most probably had different ideas about the importance of self-determined values and moral convictions. For them, empirical 'inner' events and experiences such as headaches, hungers and hangovers would no doubt have fallen within the domain of negative liberty – or rather, the lack of it. But things more focal to the human personality – for instance, one's values, character, morality or rational life-plans – would probably have a higher status in their book: these could very well be counted as true elements of the positive human freedom which does not always recognize the non-restriction of options either as its sufficient or its necessary condition.

At this point, the introduction of the axiological and normative aspects of freedom becomes inevitable. A prominent liberal inter-pretation along the lines sketched above is that the possibility of positive freedom should be seen as a justification of liberty as non-interference. According to the view, the development of human individuality, or *personal autonomy*, cannot occur in oppressive or coercive circumstances, and as autonomy is what makes individuals valuable both to themselves and to their fellow creatures, oppression and coercion which thwarts individuality must be condemned. This is more or less the view taken by, for instance, Mill in *On Liberty*.[18]

But there is a difficulty in the solution, namely that certain kinds of individuality and free self-expression are most often felt to fall outside the legitimate scope of defensible positive freedom. Even for Mill, at least three large groups of people – children, lunatics and barbarians – were such that their negative liberty of action can justifiably be restricted even when mainly self-regarding action is concerned. The relevant factor here seems to be that only a certain developed capacity for rational choice, or in Stanley Benn's terms, *autarchy*, gives a person a right to self-determination by guaranteeing that the autonomy of the person is of the valuable variety.[19] Autarchy, as described by Benn, 'is a condition of human normality, both in the statistical sense that the overwhelming majority of human beings satisfy it, and in the further sense that anyone who does not satisfy it falls short in some degree as a human being', and deficiencies which cause lack of autarchy include epistemic irrationality, impulsion, schizophrenia and incoherent sets of action commitments.[20]

It seems, then, that at least three concepts of freedom may be useful in discussions concerning liberal and anti-liberal principles. Freedom as the non-restriction of options, or negative *liberty* of action, derives its value from the value of personal *autonomy*, which is usually seen within the liberal tradition as individuality and which presupposes a certain degree of decision-related rationality, or *autarchy*, in the individual in question. The deep rationale of this kind of theory is, I presume, an urge to protect the individual against society and its demands: society and the individual are seen as antagonistic to each other, and the greater power of the larger unit is checked to prevent the emergence of political tyrannies.

But the status of autarchy and autonomy as prerequisites of negative liberties can be quite radically converted by abandoning the Anglo-American liberal viewpoint altogether, and assuming, instead, some continental notions on freedom. Jean-Jacques Rousseau[21] and Immanuel Kant[22] are perhaps the most relevant theorists in this respect: Rousseau's 'general will' and Kant's 'rational will' are concepts which imply very different views on freedom and autonomy from the liberal ideas. Basically, both postulate that genuine freedom and autonomy can only be achieved by accepting the necessary or rational or moral constraints imposed upon us by either life in human society (Rousseau) or the ideal nature of all human beings (Kant). Neither of these views emphasizes the negative liberty of individual citizens from state coercion or social pressure. In fact, Rousseau's view would not even define laws or social policies dictated by the general will as coercive, whatever their impact on 'abstract' (as opposed to the 'concrete' rational) freedom of individuals. People can only be genuinely free or autonomous, to quote from *The Social Contract*, when 'each of us puts his person and all his power in common under the supreme direction of the general will'.[23]

The communitarian and rationalist notions of freedom, distant though they may be from the individualist liberal view, are important for my present purposes, because many actual and potential critiques of liberal anti-paternalism come from other philosophical traditions, and hence tend to rely on ideas and ideals which may differ drastically from the Millian credos. Thus, freedom as the *acceptance of the inevitable*, be the form of inevitability in question 'natural', 'rational' or social, has to be taken into account in considering the legitimacy of paternalism. Such a concept may seem fatalistic to a liberal mind, but, on the other hand, it is probable that, in turn, any other view will appear unrealistic to the supporter of this approach.

(ii) Constraint

The second concept in need of explication in the present framework, constraint, can be interpreted in as many ways as the concept of freedom. Lexically, there are three principal meanings of the word, namely: (a) the act of constraining; (b) the state of being checked, restricted, or compelled to avoid or perform some action; and (c) a constraining condition, agency or force.[24] Since two of the definitions refer to the verb 'constrain', it is also elucidating to see which modes of action are thought to constitute instances of constraining. These include: (i) forcing; (ii) restricting; (iii) securing; (iv) clasping tightly; and (v) holding back.[25] By adding two terms from definition (b), constraint in sense (c) can be seen as a condition which restricts, checks, secures, compels, forces, clasps or holds. So the dictionary defines 'constraint' rather exclusively as something antagonistic to negative freedom.

Systematically, starting from the simplest interpretation, constraint can be seen, much in the lexical spirit, as the *restriction of options*, or action alternatives. According to this view, constraint is the contradictory opposite of freedom, and freedom equals liberty of action. Within this view, it is not necessary for the constrained person to notice the condition, nor is it necessary that he would obviously be worse off due to the constraint. These matters depend entirely on the status the restricted or eliminated action alternative happens to occupy in the person's preferential system. If somebody permanently locked the gates of the Taj Majal, it would take a very long time for many people even to hear about it, let alone to be disadvantaged by it – even though it would immediately deny every ordinary individual the freedom to enter the palace as she or he wishes. On the other hand, the constraint would at once be noticed and experienced as painful by, say, a group of art historians involved in a field research expedition within the confines of the monument.

Independently of the definitions of 'freedom', the domain of constraint could, however, be limited to those restrictions of freedom which cause inconvenience to the person subjected to them, or at least enter their awareness. A natural interpretation of the view would be that checks which do not frustrate people's actual desires ought to be excluded from the scope of genuine constraint, for a reason parallel to that presented in defining freedom as the non-frustration of desires. Not all options are so important as to warrant the use of the term 'constraint'.

The response, however, is also parallel to the one presented earlier, namely that it is not in any way paradoxical or ambiguous to state that restrictions of options which are minor or distant create minor constraints in the same manner as restrictions which are major and proximate create major ones. On the contrary, it might be paradoxical to claim that restrictions which go unnoticed or for other reasons do not arouse opposition would not be constraining.

Consider the classic example presented by John Locke in *An Essay Concerning Human Understanding*:

> Again, suppose a man be carried whilst fast asleep into a room where is a person he longs to see and speak with, and be there locked fast in, beyond his power to get out; he awakes and is glad to find himself in so desirable company, which he stays willingly in, i.e. prefers his stay to going away. I ask, is not this stay voluntary? I think nobody will doubt it; and yet being locked fast in, it is evident he is not at liberty not to stay, he has not freedom to be gone.[26]

By calling the situation constraining the simple idea can be expressed that *if* (hypothetically or contrafactually) the man carried into the room happened to want to go out, doing so would not be within his power as long as the door is locked, and this holds true whether the state of affairs actually bothers him or not.

This account of constraint is perfectly compatible with the theory of freedom as negative liberty, and even its potential shortcomings are similar. Constraints divide, as suggested by Feinberg, into 'positive' and 'negative', 'external' and 'internal', and by considering inner axiological and normative controls as a special class of freedom rather than constraint, the foundations of the view can be challenged.

There is, however, an additional complication in the restriction theory of constraint in that within the theory moral considerations can also be evoked with regard to external factors, not only with regard to internal ones as in the non-restriction theory of freedom. It is, in fact, possible to claim that only those obstacles – positive or negative, internal or external – for whose existence somebody is morally responsible, can be identified as constraints in a serious sense. David Miller for one has defended such a claim by referring to the problems that he sees facing any alternatives to the contrary.[27]

Miller begins his argument by calling attention to a distinction: some obstacles, or restrictions of options, are humanly caused, whereas others are 'natural'. Thus, for example, if a malevolent person has blown away the bridge so that people cannot cross the river within the next few days, the obstacle to their freedom of movement is humanly caused; however, if a sudden hurricane hits the bridge with the same result, the obstacle is 'natural'. Furthermore, there is a long tradition stating that 'the nature of things does not madden us, only ill will does'.[28] Combining these two points Miller concludes that 'the appropriate condition for regarding an obstacle as a constraint on freedom is that some other person or persons can be held morally responsible for its existence'.[29]

Note that Miller's view does not presuppose anybody *deliberately acting* to create the obstacle which makes a genuine constraint: unintentional action causing restrictions, as well as omissions failing to remove them can equally well belong to the sphere of 'morally responsible' behaviour.[30] Miller does not, however, accept the view that any obstacles for which human agents are *causally* responsible would be real constraints, since this would lead to an excessive impoverishment of the category of natural inability – as opposed to genuine unfreedom.[31]. For the same reason Miller rejects what he calls the 'strong doctrine of moral responsibility' invoked by utilitarian theorists, a doctrine which would make us morally responsible for everything we are causally responsible for.[32] Instead, Miller himself relies on 'an everyday understanding of obligations', which implies that we are only responsible for matters which fall within the scope of our conventional or legal duties.[33]

Miller could well be criticized for a number of obscurities in his argument. To begin with, even if it were a fact that it is only 'ill will' and never 'the nature of things' that maddens us, what relevance would this fact have in discussions concerning freedom and constraint? Have we not already seen, in considering the impact of desires on constraint, that what 'maddens us' has no necessary connection with our being unfree? And second, as Matti Häyry and Timo Airaksinen have pointed out,[34] it is conceptually rather unhelpful to introduce moral elements at the very beginning of a discussion about constraint. It seems to be Miller's view that all constraint is, by definition, prima facie morally blamable.[35] Consequently, the core of his problem is that if somebody asked him *the reason why* constraint is morally questionable he could not produce an answer save by appealing to definitions of terms and conceptual truth. Yet it would seem reasonable to expect a more substantive response.

However, my main objection to Miller's view has to do with the distinction between genuine constraint and natural inability, and with his exaggerated fear that the partition will be lost if the 'causal responsibility' approach is accepted. Miller argues that since the causal responsibility view would imply that 'any obstacle which it is possible for human beings to remove or fail to impose' is a constraint, within the view 'the scope of mere inability will shrink almost to vanishing point'.[36] His example is that if all human efforts were concentrated on sending to the moon everybody who wished to go there, the operation would perhaps be possible, and humankind would in that case be collectively responsible for not running such a space programme at the expense of all other goals. Accordingly, the collective omissions of humankind would create a social constraint preventing moon travel. Miller, however, thinks that if the distinction is to be defended at all, then 'natural inability' is the correct label to be used in the example.

But is Miller right? Does the scope of inability shrink to vanishing point if the causal responsibility approach is accepted? Both questions must be answered in the negative, since regardless of the lunar question there will always be, say, innumerable places in the universe where we cannot travel, joint effort or not. It may not be very important or interesting to state that people are unfree to travel to the moon due to everyone else's omissions, but it is not untrue either. The question falls, in fact, between natural inability and Miller's suggested morally blameworthy restrictions, for it is probably safe to say that humankind is not behaving immorally in not concentrating all its resources into this one project. Accordingly, it seems that constraint as restriction of options can be divided into *three* sub-categories, namely: (a) natural inability; (b) humanly caused or humanly removable obstacles; and (c) obstacles for whose existence a person or a group of persons are morally responsible – where 'moral responsibility' means something stronger than the mere causal responsibility referred to in alternative (b). Formulated like this (b) defines the whole scope of social constraint, and (c) defines the sub-category of social constraint in which obstacles both *can be* prevented or removed and prima facie *ought to be* prevented and removed.

So much for constraint as the restriction of negative liberty – what about the opposites of 'real' positive freedom? *Autonomy*, understood as individuality, will obviously be constrained if the individual in question does not or cannot herself make decisions concerning her own life. There are a variety of potential reasons for such a state of affairs: perhaps some individual or group imposes ready-made decisions upon her by force; maybe she enjoys doing things the way others want her to do without paying any attention to her own abilities of assessing alternatives for herself; or perhaps she has either lost or never even acquired the capacity for rational choice.

In the last case, freedom as personal *autarchy* is constrained, either by temporary loss of competence, or by permanent mental disorder. Small children can be put in the temporary loss of competence category, since they will normally develop their capacity for rational choice in due time.

These considerations lead us straight to the 'real' freedom discussed by Rousseau and Kant, and to its opposites. Freedom as the acceptance of the inevitable may well include constraining elements in the negative sense, that is, restrictions of action alternatives. Depending on the particular theory in question, the reason given for these restrictions may vary from the immorality or irrationality of the constrained action to the requirements of justice, equal freedom and democracy. Alternatively, or in addition, references can be made to the God-ordained social order, or to the system of natural human rights, or to the inevitable progression of history. Restrictions justified by these principles and theories do not count as elements of true constraint within the communitarian and rationalist models.

There are, however, at least three ways in which the 'real' Rousseauan freedom can be wrongfully constrained. First, every human being should, according to the theory, be left free to do what is right; thus restrictions in this area of human conduct are positive constraints in the proper sense. Second, no human being should, according to the theory, be allowed to do what is wrong, since such behaviour would not be an expression of a person's true autonomy. Accordingly, lack of restrictions in this area creates negative constraints on 'real' human freedom. Third, and finally, the theory postulates an interesting though slightly perplexing notion of internal constraint, namely *illusory freedom* or *alienation*.

The point of the concept of alienation is roughly that people sometimes – or often, or even always – possess an incorrect and perverted view of themselves, their nature and their possibilities. The distortion is in some theories attributable to the inner inadequacy of human beings, in others it is attributed to external factors such as social injustice or deliberate deception by others.

An early example of the former kind of thinking is Baruch Spinoza's theory, which states that our true freedom is blocked by our inclination towards passivity of mind and towards satisfaction of low desires. The correct alternative, in Spinoza's view, would be active self-awareness instead of murky desires.[37] More recently, there have been the existentialist theories of Martin Heidegger and

Jean-Paul Sartre, emphasizing the 'inauthenticity' of the human condition, or the *mauvaise foi* (bad faith), which stands between us and our true freedom.[38]

An example of the external factor view is to be found in the works of Karl Marx, who, in his turn, based his ideas concerning estrangement on the work of G.W.F. Hegel.[39] According to Marx, it is the entire economic system of the so-called free societies that alienates people from other people, from the means of their own productivity, and from the results of their work. In Marx's system, it is not until the working masses have fully grasped the situation and become conscious of themselves as a class struggling against other classes that true human freedom can be attained through revolutionary changes in the structure of society.

All in all, if constraint is understood widely as the contradictory opposite of freedom, there are different kinds of constraint corresponding to each separate interpretation of freedom. In the liberal framework, three types of unfreedom present themselves: (1) the restriction of action alternatives; (2) lack of autonomy; and (3) incapacity of even minimally rational choices. And in the communitarian–rationalist framework, three major categories emerge: (4) the restriction of correct behaviour; (5) the non-restriction of incorrect behaviour; and (6) alienation produced either by internal or external factors.

(iii) Coercion

The third and final concept abstracted for scrutiny from Mill's anti-paternalistic statement, coercion, is an exceedingly complex one, and has been discussed from many angles in the recent literature.[40] I shall not even try to cover all the aspects of the discussion – instead, I shall consider a few basic questions which are relevant in the present context. First, what is and what is not coercion? Among the modes of social interaction and the use of power there are, obviously, coercive and non-coercive ones, and separating them may be important in theorizing about paternalism. Second, is coercion constraining? And whatever the answer to this question, what about the other modes of influence and interaction – which of them are constraining and which are not? Third, is coercion immoral? Can 'non-coercion' be immoral? On what grounds?

As for defining coercion, a few elementary comments must suffice. I shall assume the view that coercion typically involves explicit or implicit *threats*, and is conditionally structured: if you do not agree to do something unpleasant, the coercer will see to it (or at least claims she will see to it) that something even more unpleasant will happen to you (or perhaps to somebody else).[41] A successful instance of coercion has occurred when the coercer has managed to get you to do what she wants as a result of a threat to interfere with your person or your interests, either by positively attacking you (or your interests), or by withholding a benefit.[42] In addition, it seems plausible to admit, as John Kleinig for one does, that withholding a benefit can become a part of a coercive threat only if there is a reasonable expectancy for that benefit – otherwise the result would be an offer rather than a threat.[43] But the same observation applies, although conversely, to positive interferences as well: withholding something undesirable cannot be a part of a genuine offer unless the disliked interferences are reasonably to be expected.

Robert Nozick's example of the slave who in a hypothetical slave society escapes his daily beating only by performing some special task for the slaveholder seems to shake the adequacy of the last remark: since regular beatings are to be expected in Nozick's society, the threat 'If you don't do *x*, you'll be beaten!' should be interpreted as an offer, namely, 'If you do *x*, you'll be spared from beating today!'[44] Nozick's own solution, when faced with the problem, is to distinguish between the 'normally expected' course of events and the 'morally expected' course of events, and to say that at least in this case the latter takes precedence. Accordingly, the slaveholder is, after all, threatening and coercing the slave, because it is surely not to be expected, in a moral sense, that people get beaten on a regular basis.[45]

As Nozick admits, however, there is a problem in the solution in that the 'morally expected course of events' is not always a natural basis for describing situations involving threats or offers. His example is that of a drug addict who will not get her normal supply of the drug she needs from her regular supplier unless she beats up a certain person.[46] Although it may be immoral to buy and sell drugs in the first place, the situation is obviously threatening to the addict, and she is therefore being coerced. Nozick concludes that if and when the 'normal' and 'moral' courses of events diverge in possibly coercive conditions, the description ought to be based on the alternative which the recipient of the action herself prefers.[47]

The remaining difficulty here is to determine how the normal and moral courses of events should be described and by whom. As Timo

Airaksinen has noted, something conceptually important may easily be lost if the recipient's viewpoint alone is taken into account. And besides, it is definitely a problem that the same situation can, by different recipients, be described both as an offer and as a threat.[48] At the same time, it is also true that if one assumes an 'external' moral starting point, one may paralyse the analysis: from the point of view of a slaveholding society a clearly coercive situation can sincerely appear to offer the slave a benefit for a reasonable cost.

Perhaps it should be inferred from these unclarities that coercion simply means slightly different things to different groups of people, depending on their views concerning the 'normal' and 'moral' courses of events, and their mutual priorities. Admitting this will introduce a certain amount of relativity into the concept of coercion, but that is not necessarily fatal, for at least two reasons. First, the core ideas presented before going into Nozick's queries can still be counted on, so that a notion of coercion as making a person do something unpleasant by threatening him with something even more unpleasant unless he complies has not lost its approximate validity. And second, even if the problems do retain some relevance in particular situations, the context will in most cases provide reasonable grounds for distinguishing between threats and offers, coercion and non-coercion.

It is more or less a matter of taste whether modes of influence such as *forcing, extreme intimidation, extreme temptation, extreme domination* and *extreme provocation* should be called coercive or not.[49] Reasons against such verbal practice might include the argument that these forms of action do not necessarily contain threats, and that they are usually not conditional in any way. What these points add up to is that coercion in a narrow sense works – or fails to work – through the voluntary choices of its victims, whereas it is generally assumed that forcing, both in its physical form and in its extreme psychological forms, does not leave room for any considered decision-making. Extreme forms of intimidation, temptation, domination and provocation are psychologically irresistible to everyone, or at least to any ordinary person, and the use of physical force against people is, of course, the most effective means to 'bypass their minds' – to prevent them from making any decisions at all.

On the other hand, there are theorists like J.P. Day who prefer to interpret the terms 'coercive' and 'coercion' broadly, so as to include the use of physical and psychological force as well as coercion in the narrow sense, or coercion through threatening.[50] The supporters of the broad definition seem to have the lexicographer at least on their side, since lexical definitions of coercion range from 'restraint or domination by force' to 'enforcement or bringing about by force or threat'.[51] Another point in their favour is that forcing and threatening do in a legal sense stand apart from 'softer' modes of influence such as *ordering, requesting, offering, persuading, advising, warning, praising, blaming, rewarding* and *punishing*.[52] The difference, as expressed by H.L.A. Hart and A.M. Honoré, is that force and threats, unlike these listed activities, *cause* or *make* the recipient do or forbear something.[53] In what follows I shall employ – whenever there are no specifications to the contrary – this latter, broader concept of coercion and coercive practices, and refer to the more restricted variety of coercion as 'coercion by threats' or as 'coercion in the narrow sense'.

Granted that coercion includes the use of force and threats, then, what about its relationship to freedom and constraint? Is coercion constraining?

Both physical and psychological *forcing* are unproblematic with respect to constraint on liberty of action: they are always, by definition, restrictive and prevent people from acting on their own discretion. The impact of force on autonomy, in turn, depends strongly on contingencies such as time, place, recipient, purpose, nature and frequency of forceful intervention. One's ability to make important decisions can doubtlessly be broken by constant (even minor) restrictions and intimidation, but it is also true that most of us lead by and large autonomous lives despite many major physical restrictions – positive and negative, internal and external – which limit the scope of our choices considerably. There is apparently a connection here between positive freedom as autonomy in the liberal sense and positive freedom as the acceptance of the inevitable in the communitarian and rationalist senses, since the restrictions which are felt not to be a risk to autonomy seem to be in many cases restrictions which are inevitable, either physically or morally. For example, although circumstances – and, by omissions, other people – can force large groups of people to spend their entire lives in the same geographic areas, this has seldom been thought to prevent them from being able to make their own decisions on most matters that they have considered important.

Coercion by *threatening* and its relationship with constraint is, however, more problematic on the level of liberty of action. Hillel

Steiner, for instance, has argued that both threats and offers differ from the straightforward use of force in that they do not restrict liberty at all.[54] To support the view he postulates a situation in which he himself receives an offer and a threat at the same time.[55] On the one hand, another university offers him a teaching post the duties and privileges of which are similar to those of his present position but the salary considerably higher. On the other hand, his own university threatens not to renew his contract of employment unless he undertakes in the next academic session to teach several additional courses in subjects unrelated to his own. Since even in the fresh situation it will still be possible for Steiner to choose his own university, he concludes that neither the threat nor the offer rendered him unfree to do so and from this he infers that threatening and offering cannot constrain one's liberty of action.

Steiner is obviously correct as far as his freedom to choose the teaching post is concerned. But if the idea of freedom as the non-restriction of options is to be taken seriously, there are more detailed action alternatives involved once the threat has been expressed.[56] If Steiner assumes, as he must, that in the normal and moral course of events his own university should renew his contract without additional demands, there is one option which was reasonably to be expected before the threat but was eliminated by it: unless the university authorities are playing a practical joke on him, or bluffing, he cannot, after the threat, *both* keep his job *and* teach the same amount as he has done before. And it is exactly this action alternative, or rather the elimination of it, that makes any serious coercion by threats constraining. Offers, in their turn, do not normally restrict options and do not therefore usually act as constraints on the recipient's liberty of action.[57]

There is, however, a potential exception to the latter rule. Matti Häyry and Timo Airaksinen have in a recent article introduced a class of offers which are supposed to restrict their recipients' freedom, a class labelled by them as 'hard offers'.[58] The point of these possibly constraining offers can be elucidated by an example.

Suppose that a thief sends his regular fence the following message: 'Wire me the agreed sum of money, and I'll see to it that you get the stuff, delivered to the usual place, tomorrow afternoon.' If this is a serious offer, 'hard' or 'soft', it implies basically two things: first, that if the fence wires the money, she will also receive the stolen goods; and second, that if she does not wire the money, she will not receive the goods either. Having the merchandise without adequate payment is absolutely against the logic of presenting, accepting and refusing offers and acting accordingly. Being left without the goods after providing the offerer with the payment, on the other hand, is not so much against logic as it is against the ethos of offering. In the example of the thief and the fence it will in any normal circumstances lead to retaliatory action against the thief on the grounds that he violates the implicit contract created by the presentation and acceptance of an offer.

Suppose, however, that the circumstances are not quite normal, and that, in fact, the fence's first preference would be to pay the agreed sum without receiving the goods. She would, for instance, like to see the thief happy and temporarily well-off as a reward for his hard work, although she would, at the moment, not wish to have anything hot delivered to her backyard where the local police officers' annual party will take place tomorrow afternoon. If the offer is normal, or 'soft', there should be no problem about this: the fence can contact the thief, inform him about the situation and wire the money without getting anything in return. But Häyry and Airaksinen state that the offer can also be 'hard', in which case its expression eliminates, once and for all, the fence's freedom to send the money and *not* receive the merchandise.[59] If this is possible, there are, after all, offers which act as constraints.

I can think of at least two ways in which an offer could turn out to be threatening to the recipient in the described manner. First, there may be no other means of communication between the parties than the money order: accordingly, unless the fence refrains from sending the money, she will receive the unwanted goods. Second, it may be only after the offer has been accepted that the fence finds out that she cannot receive the delivery, although she also knows – and knew from the beginning – that the thief, too, must rid himself of the stuff and will only be able to do so by following the original plan. In the latter case, the 'hardness' of the offer did not bother the recipient prior to its acceptance, but it nevertheless tacitly constrained her all along.

There are two principal objections to the view that constraining, or 'hard', offers exist. On the other hand, J.P. Day maintains that the mode of influence described by Häyry and Airaksinen, although real enough, is not a variation of offering at all, but something different.[60] This criticism is not entirely conclusive, for the simple reason that whatever the best name for the activity labelled here as 'hard offering' is, and however constraining the activity itself may be, it is on no account coercive. Given the ordinary preferences that people have under normal circumstances, the conditional suggestion voiced by the thief is clearly offering rather than threatening – even if it is known that once the offer is taken, the delivery cannot be prevented. Thus, what we have here is a verbally operated mode of influence which (arguably) restricts the recipient's liberty, but which is clearly non-coercive. Why not place it in the general category of 'offering'?

On the other hand, it could also be stated that it is not the offer in itself that causes constraint, but something else in the postulated situation. For instance, if the offer is formulated and presented in a manner that does not allow for informative verbal communication afterwards, it is, according to this view, the non-standard setting and not the offer that restricts the recipient's freedom. As regards the alternative where the constraint seems to appear later, it can be said that it is not the original offer – which could have been refused – but the implicit agreement created by accepting it that rendered the recipient unfree.

Whatever the ultimate status of hard offers theoretically turns out to be, I shall leave the door open for its reintroduction at later stages. What is apparent, however, is that there is a definite air of paternalism in these 'offers',[61] and in the remark concerning implicit agreements one can detect a parallel to the attitudes of heavily paternalistic medical practitioners. An innocent-looking offer, say, 'If you let me examine you, I may be able to help you!' may in some circumstances hide the more sinister thought, 'Just you let me examine you, and if there's anything at all wrong with you, you'll be in the straitjacket before you know what hit you.' But more about such medical attitudes and practices after the conceptual clarifications have been completed.

To return to the relationship between constraint in general and coercion by threatening, more positive interpretations of freedom bring out fresh aspects of the matter. Freedom as autonomy will obviously be curtailed by the form of coercion, which makes its victims choose as other people want them to choose instead of letting them make up their own minds. And the same point applies to freedom as accepting the inevitable: it somehow diminishes the value of apparently moral action, seen from inside the person, that the action is the result of explicit coercion. However, here as in the context of coercion by forcing, it also remains true that many implicit and generally accepted threats – such as those expressed in just laws – cannot be considered constraining within the theory of 'real' positive freedom.

After these considerations it is possible to give a conditional answer to the final question concerning coercion, namely, is it immoral? Since coercion, in all its forms and in the context of any theory of freedom, has proved to be constraining, the immorality of coercion is directly connected with the value of freedom. *If* liberty, autonomy and 'real' positive freedom are valuable, then coercion always destroys something good and can be deemed, at least prima facie, wrong. Depending on the precise value of freedom, both in general and in particular issues, the initial wrongness of coercion can be outweighed by even greater wrongs which would follow if coercion was not used. Mill's claim in the passage quoted (pp. 19–20) above was that only harm inflicted on other human beings can warrant the use of force and threats against 'members of a civilized community'. But other views can equally well be construed from the idea of balancing coercion with other prima-facie wrongs.

THE VALUE OF FREEDOM

Liberal theorists often say precious little about the basic axiological presumption of their views, that is, about the value of freedom. More precisely, they usually state that freedom is, in their opinion, valuable and therefore ought to be protected, but they do not often elaborate at any greater length *why* this should be so. As a popular method of acquitting themselves from laborious explanations, many theorists appeal to the *presumption of liberty* – an ethico-legal device which is supposed to settle the value of freedom without further argument.[62] Unfortunately, the 'presumption' seldom adds up to much more than an assertion of the author's feelings, intuitions and ideological preferences.

Joseph Raz has argued against the relevance of the presumption of liberty by showing what a 'presumption' in moral, political and legal contexts normally means.[63] There are two technical senses of the term, neither of which applies very well to the problem of freedom and its value, and, in addition, there is a commonsensical meaning which theoretically is poorly backed-up.

First, a presumption in favour of the defendant in a trial means that the prosecution has the initial burden of adducing evidence and marshalling arguments. Since courts are public official bodies and since it cannot be a person's duty to justify her conduct publicly except under very special circumstances, the claims against her must be adequately substantiated before she is obliged to answer to them.[64] The problem with this sense of a presumption, applied to the questions of freedom, is that not all restrictions of liberty are set by public official bodies. Although there might be a preference for liberty in the dealings of the individual with political institutions, this interpretation does not provide reasons for valuing freedom under less official circumstances.

Second, in a court of law, a presumption of death, for instance, means that in the presence of an urgent practical problem a person may be presumed dead on the grounds that nobody has heard of him in many years. That nobody has heard of a person for a while does not, of course, prove that he is dead; it just gives a minimal practical directive for an otherwise difficult decision-making situation.[65] But this sense of a presumption does not apply to freedom and its value any better than the burden-of-proof sense did. Academic studies concerning freedom and constraint can hardly be considered documents in which pressing practical reasons force the authors to base their cases on guesswork and only marginally supported hypotheses.

Third, a widespread understanding of a presumption is that there is a weak but so far unrefuted reason for believing that one state of affairs rather than another prevails. Raz sees this as a generalized form of the second interpretation, and the critique against it presented above also applies to this more general formulation. As Raz notes, a mere presumption concerning, say, somebody's whereabouts based on the hour when he was last seen should usually give rise to doubts expressed, for instance, by saying: 'Let's wait a little longer to be sure that he is really there.'[66] Unless an appeal to the presumption of liberty is the only argument in favour of the value of freedom, it does not seem wise to found a liberal theory on such uncertain grounds.

In fact, there are a variety of independent reasons for holding that freedom *is* valuable. The difficulty with many of these is, however, that they derive the value of freedom from instrumental considerations, thus rendering themselves inaccessible to rigidly non-consequentialist liberals. Such rigid liberals would like to see freedom defended for its own sake, or 'as an end in itself', on the ground that the pure contemplation of one's own freedom reveals to anybody how desirable liberty is.[67] As Joel Feinberg has put the matter, 'there is a kind of symbolic value in possessing a library with more books than one will ever read, or having access to a museum with more exhibits than one can ever see, or eating in a restaurant which offers more dishes than that which one wants most to choose.'[68] But even taking it for granted that freedom as the non-restriction of options is exhilarating and carries some symbolic value for the person with the options, this is obviously a relatively weak argument for freedom. Marijuana may be exhilarating and regimental standards symbolically valuable, but rigid liberals would hardly like to place as much weight on them as they would like to place on freedom. Rather far-fetched psychological assumptions would, however, be needed to prove that the desire for liberty is so deep and universal that it arises above all ordinary wishes, thereby justifying its worship over other good things in life.

The instrumental value of freedom is easier to detect on all interpretational levels. As regards liberty, or the non-restriction of options, there are two ways to proceed: either one can show how particular liberties are prerequisites for attaining certain good and desirable things, or one can lump all liberties together and look for a common axiological denominator to cover them all.

The first alternative calls for separate studies on a variety of freedoms or liberties such as the freedom of expression, liberty of movement and political freedom. Freedom of expression, for instance, has been defended by referring to the value embodied in truth, tolerance and genius which, according to the defence, flourish where expression of opinions is unrestricted.[69] Political liberties, in their turn, have been supported by reference to justice, equality, rationality and good government.[70] Liberty of movement, as well as freedom of expression and political participation, could probably be supported by claiming that there is an important causal connection between human welfare, or happiness, and the liberty in question.

The difficulty with this alternative is that the alleged causal connections are exceedingly difficult to confirm in each case. H.J. McCloskey, for example, has argued against Mill that unlimited freedom of expression empirically has very little to do with truth or the development of genius.[71] And there are conceptual problems as well: if one reads the idea of freedom into the notions of 'good government' and human 'welfare', a connection obviously exists, but in both cases an anti-liberal interpretation is also possible, and its employment would eliminate the link. One can hypothesize a

46

good government, in the anti-liberal sense, which would promote, say, material wellbeing and even an (illusory) impression of liberty without ever allowing free expression of dissent in any important matters.

The second alternative, the consideration of all modes of negative freedom under a common heading, seems more promising. Liberty of action in general is obviously one of the necessary conditions of human autonomy, and autonomy is arguably a good thing in and for human beings. One must not, of course, make too much of this connection: on the one hand, not all restrictions of action alternatives are likely to violate autonomy, and on the other, no amount of open options can in themselves make a person autonomous. But it is true that frequent restrictions, if they happen to accumulate on strategically important areas of an agent's personal life, do have a strong tendency to affect that agent's ability to make autonomous decisions concerning his own life. And since there is no way of knowing a priori which restrictions will have an evil effect, there is a prima-facie reason to suspect all of them of violating autonomy. Thus the (instrumental) value of liberty becomes conditional on the more basic value of autonomy.

Two arguments put forward by Feinberg for the instrumental value of liberty can be seen as explications of the view just introduced.[72] First, Feinberg notes that human beings need at least a minimum of available action alternatives just to keep physically and mentally sane: the mere sustenance of personal life dictates a *welfare interest* in the liberty of action. Second, even after a bare minimum of options has been secured, moderate expansion of liberty is important for personal development: the courage to improve oneself requires that a certain *security interest* in free choices is satisfied. Both remarks stress, from different angles, the fact that a person cannot be autonomous or develop her ability for self-determination unless she is given sufficient freedom to be and to do more or less what she wants.

On the level of autonomy, or self-determination, the question of intrinsic versus instrumental value arises again, only this time the more promising line of argument is based on intrinsic value. It could, naturally, be claimed that self-determination of one's actions, choices and life-plans is essential, say, to achieving happiness, but the validity of the claim would hang heavily upon the definitions chosen for the purpose. A common counterexample is based on the imaginary social order described by Aldous Huxley in his *Brave New World*.[73]

Huxley's New World is a peaceful and stable society from which all standard sources of conflict have been removed by eliminating family ties and other close human bonds, 'natural' reproduction, restrictions of sexual freedom, pain, anguish, suffering, illness, old age and the experience of death. Instead, human embryos and foetuses develop in a hatchery during their prenatal period, after which they are hypnopaedically programmed to the tasks, opinions and values of their caste. Adult inhabitants of the New World lead a 'happy' life in the sense that they are content, and there are always pleasures available to them when they want or need them. The main forms of recreation are sensual entertainment, games, promiscuous sex and the use of psychoactive drugs. Since the society has rather conclusively determined every decision an inhabitant is apt to make, the very idea of autonomy is alien to the new order. Accordingly, Huxley's world seems to be an instance of happiness achieved without autonomy.

The response to this is, obviously, that the 'happiness' enjoyed in the Brave New World is not the kind of happiness liberal ethicists have in mind when they make autonomy one of its prerequisites.[74] It is the dissatisfied Socrates rather than the satisfied pig they are referring to, and in these terms Huxley's society adds up to an enormous human piggery. But although the distinction can be made, it does not support arguments in favour of the instrumental value of autonomy. Rather, it seems more natural to postulate a conceptual rather than a causal connection between happiness and autonomy, and state the liberal view in terms of intrinsic value.

What would human happiness without autonomy be? The idea would imply a society or world filled with people who cannot decide for themselves what to do and what to think; people living together as parts of a machinery which reproduces itself and, meanwhile, keeps its human elements quiet and content so as to secure the smooth working of the system. This would be a world in which the only real value would be attached to the great plan regulating everything, and the designers of the plan. Pleasures, admittedly, could be experienced by individuals but not in a considered manner, not in a manner that would enable the individual to be proud of a good choice, thereby multiplying the value of the experience. It would be a grim world, and imagining what it would be like helps one to see that happiness without autonomy would indeed lack 'that little something' which gives human happiness its extra value over and above the purely hedonic pleasures enjoyed by all sentient beings. Happiness without autonomy would be inhuman.[75]

Granted that autonomy is intrinsically valuable, it is easy to see that autarchy, or the capacity of rational decision-making, as well as the nourishment and protection of that capacity by others, is instrumentally valuable as a necessary condition of determining the direction of one's own mind. Thus, within the liberal theory both liberty as the non-restriction of options and the basic ability to choose derive their value from the desirability of free self-determination.

In the quite antagonistic context of the Rousseauan–Kantian theories of positive freedom, the liberal presuppositions will, of course, be drastically challenged. Individual self-selection of values and norms, at least if it is not performed in a way that is prone to lead to moral diversification and social discord, cannot be desirable according to the communitarian and rationalist views. Rather, the Rousseauan idea would presumably be that the value of positive freedom, or freedom to live in an ideal society obeying its rational rules, is contingent on the value of the ideal society itself. Supposing that human beings can only be truly happy when everybody has submitted 'his person and his power under the supreme direction of the general will', the 'real' human freedom of accepting the inevitable coincides with 'real' happiness. Similarly, the Kantian point would most likely be that the value of positive freedom is closely linked with the ultimate value of rational morality. Instead of submitting one's decisions to the socially determined general will, however, the Kantian individual is bound to obey the transcendental 'real' will, which is to be found by a priori detection of one's own mind.

Whatever the mutual differences between the Anglo-American and Continental approaches may be, however, each seems to have its own way of placing high value on freedom in one of its forms. The opposition of the different views will need more scrutiny at later stages, where the justificatory questions will be discussed. But in a very general sense the liberal, communitarian and rationalist theories agree in that freedom is valuable.

3

PATERNALISM, COERCION AND CONSTRAINT

The value of freedom, considered together with the conceptual remarks made in the preceding chapter, combine to form a method of analysing and assessing the various forms of paternalism, medical and otherwise. Since freedom is valuable, and since coercion and constraint are antagonistic to freedom, there is something prima facie wrong with coercion and constraint. Accordingly, if paternalism – in one or other of its forms – is coercive or constraining, it is also prima facie condemnable. On the other hand, since the alleged evils of paternalism have generally been attached to its coercive or constraining effect, the converse inference seems to be valid as well. If paternalism – in one or other of its forms – proves to be totally non-coercive and absolutely non-constraining, there may be no general prima-facie reason to condemn it at all.

Consequently, for the purposes of analysis and evaluation, three sets of questions must be tackled. First, is paternalism entirely or in part coercive, and if so, in what sense? Second, is paternalism entirely or in part constraining, and if so, in what sense? Third, even if there were forms of paternalism that are coercive or constraining, it should be remembered that such interaction is only prima facie condemnable. Under which conditions, then, can paternalism be justified, all things being considered? Furthermore, under what conditions, if any, can it be said that paternalism is always wrong? In the present chapter I shall address these questions from a liberal – as opposed to a communitarian or rationalist – viewpoint. The other approaches will be discussed in the chapters immediately following where the justificatory aspects are more thoroughly examined.

DEFINING PATERNALISTIC INTERVENTIONS

A brief survey of the attempts towards defining 'paternalism' in recent decades shows what a variety of answers has been given to the questions.

One of the strictest definitions that can be found in the literature was presented in 1971 by Joel Feinberg, who in his article 'Legal paternalism' stated, very much in the classical liberal spirit, that

> [t]he liberty-limiting principle called legal paternalism justifies *state coercion* to protect individuals from self-inflicted harm, or, in its extreme version, to guide them, whether they like it or not, toward their own good.[1]

In the context of *legal* paternalism Feinberg's definition may, of course, have some validity – legislators represent the state and most legal directives can perhaps be counted as coercive – but there are at least two problems with these conceptual restrictions. On the one hand, since legislators and public authorities are not the only ones who want to protect people by interfering with their lives, all paternalism cannot involve *state* coercion; and, on the other hand, even within the authoritative action of the state it seems natural to think that at least *some* positive protective measures could be paternalistic but non-coercive.

Gerald Dworkin in his paper 'Paternalism' in 1972 set the tone for much of the contemporary discussion on the topic. Dworkin realized that the state is not the only source of benevolent control in society and, consequently, gave a slightly different characterization:

> By paternalism I understand roughly the *interference with a person's liberty of action* justified by reasons referring to the welfare, good, happiness, needs, interests or values of the person being *coerced*.[2]

But although no reference to the state is made in Dworkin's formula, coercion and constraint are both present as strongly as in Feinberg's version. Similar definitions often featured in discussions all through the 1970s. Here is how Jeffrie Murphy put the matter in 1974:

> Paternalism is the *coercing* of people primarily for what is believed to be their own good.[3]

And in 1980 Richard Arneson proposed the following extended but basically similar formulation:

> Paternalistic policies are *restrictions on a person's liberty* which are justified exclusively by consideration for that person's own good or welfare, and which are carried out either against his present will (when his present will is not explicitly overridden by his own prior commitment) or against his own prior commitments (when his present will is explicitly overridden by his own prior commitment).[4]

Although there are slight mutual differences in the definitions given by Feinberg, Dworkin, Murphy and Arneson, each and every one of them is based on the presumption that *coercion* or *constraint* or both are involved in paternalistic interventions.

The narrow notion of paternalism, however, has by no means reigned unchallenged: Bernard Gert and Charles Culver, for instance, explicitly attacked it in 1976 in their article 'Paternalistic behaviour'.[5] Gert and Culver stated that there are non-coercive and non-constraining modes of protective control, and held that the (mis)conception to the contrary probably had its roots in the fact that paternalism had mainly been discussed in a legal framework: coercion and restrictions on people's liberty of action are, according to their view, characteristic of law but not necessarily of paternalism. To prove their point, Gert and Culver gave the following example, also cited in chapter 1 above (p. 4) as the Case of the Dying Mother:

> Consider the case where a doctor lies to a mother on her deathbed when she asks about her son. The doctor tells her that her son is doing well, although he knows that the son has just been killed trying to escape from prison after having been indicted for multiple rape and murder. The doctor behaved paternalistically but did not attempt to control behaviour, to apply coercion, or to interfere with liberty of action.[6]

And indeed Gert and Culver seem to be right: especially when paternalistic action takes the form of deception and is intended to affect feelings rather than decisions, no coercion or constraint appear to be necessarily involved.

Gert and Culver suggest that what *is* involved in paternalistic behaviour instead of restrictions on liberty and compulsion is a 'violation of moral rules' or, in other words, 'something which needs moral justification'.[7] Taking into account all sides of the issue, Gert and Culver end up with the following definition:

A is acting paternalistically towards S if and only if A's behaviour (correctly) indicates that A *believes that*

(1) his action is for S's good;
(2) he is qualified to act on S's behalf;
(3) his action involves violating a moral rule (or will require him to do so) with regard to S;
(4) S's good justifies him in acting on S's behalf independently of S's past, present, or immediately forthcoming (free, informed) consent; and
(5) S believes (perhaps falsely) that he (S) generally knows what is for his own good.[8]

But although this view is original and perhaps even initially persuasive, closer scrutiny shows that the view involves severe problems.

Gert and Culver do not define what they mean by 'violations of a moral rule', but present instead a list of paradigmatic examples. They write:

It is not necessary that one explicitly hold some theory about what counts as a violation of a moral rule. All that is required is that one believes A is doing one of the following: killing; causing pain (physical or mental); disabling; depriving of freedom, opportunity, or pleasure; deceiving; breaking a promise; or cheating. All of these are universally regarded as requiring moral justification and hence are regarded by us as violations of moral rules.[9]

In the list, liberty-related evils are but a fraction of all the evils caused by paternalistic action, so that if the account can be defended, the more classical theory stating that all paternalism has something to do with restrictions of freedom is clearly false.

The problem with this view, however, is that paternalism does not in fact always require violations of intuitively felt moral rules. Gert and Culver themselves present the following example which proves this. A prospective mastectomy patient, in the judgement of her physician, does not show sufficient signs of concern and grief as regards the physical and cosmetic implications of the operation. Being afraid that such indifference might lead to severe problems afterwards, the doctor talks with the woman, against her will, about the effects of the operation in order to minimize the emerging difficulties.[10] The discussion following the example is illuminating. Gert and Culver suddenly realize that telling the truth – as such – is not usually considered to be a violation of a moral rule. *Ad hoc* explanations are acutely needed, and this is the first reaction they have:

> This last example goes against a common view of medical pater-
> nalism. If one is presented with the following question: Which
> doctor is acting paternalistically, one who confronts a patient
> with a painful truth, or one who withholds the truth in order
> to avoid the pain it will cause the patient? most will answer that
> it is the latter, not the former, who is acting paternalistically.
> But as the example . . . makes clear, this need not be the case.
> Which, if either, doctor is acting paternalistically depends upon
> whether he will proceed with what he thinks is best for the
> patient *regardless of the patient's wishes on the matter*.[11]

The analysis shows, contrary to the authors' formerly presented views, that what is primary in the two cases is not that one involves deception and the other truth-telling, but that *both* involve acting against the patients' wishes. Thus the violation of a moral rule prohibiting killing, deception or other sinful deeds does not in itself seem to be crucial after all.

In an attempt to save their definition Gert and Culver added to it the disjunctive parenthetical expression of the third feature:

> (3) his [the paternalist's] action involves violating a moral rule
> (*or will require him to do so*) with regard to S.[12]

However, the authors' own 'clarifying example' shows how strained the interpretations become if one actually applies the extension:

> Giving [a] blood transfusion to [an] unconscious member of [a]
> religious sect [which does not believe in blood transfusions] is a
> paternalistic action which does not itself constitute a violation
> of any moral rule, but which does involve doing that which
> will require one to violate a moral rule. For, if the person lives,
> the doctor must [afterwards] either deceive him regarding the
> blood transfusion or cause him painful feelings by informing
> him of the action taken.[13]

Admittedly, this solution does, in a formal sense, manage to safeguard Gert and Culver's view against many possible counter-examples. But what about the substance? Should the definition of paternalistic action really be based on something that may or may not happen long after the action itself has taken place? It appears far simpler to state that if there is a violation of a moral rule involved, it occurs at the minute the doctor performs the blood transfusions, not afterwards.

Steven Lee, in an article entitled 'On the justification of paternalism', offers some important hints towards solving the problem evoked by Gert and Culver. His solution is that while moral rules or principles are indeed involved in the issue of paternalism, the whole matter should be seen as a clash between *two moral principles* only. At the outset of his essay Lee gives the following definition:

> A paternalist action may be defined, roughly as an action that avoids another person's self-regarding harm in a way that interferes with his or her choices.[14]

From the starting point provided by the definition Lee moves on to claim that the only two moral considerations that arise with paternalism are, first, 'the avoidance of harm to a person', and second, 'interference with another person's choices'.[15] The acceptability or unacceptability of a given case of paternalism, according to this view, will be determined by weighing against each other the principles of (self-inflicted) *harm* on the one hand, and *liberty* on the other.

But adopting Lee's view as such would only bring one back to the position held by Feinberg, Dworkin, Murphy, and Arneson – the position which was quite plausibly challenged by Gert and Culver. There will not normally be any restrictions on the liberty of action, say, of the patients to whom the doctors lie about their sons, or on whom the doctors perform blood transfusions while they are unconscious.

However, the use of slightly different concepts might show a way out of the difficulty. *Coercion* and *constraint* as restrictions on a person's liberty of action may be absent in many instances of paternalistic influence, but even in those situations it is usually presumed that something is done *against the recipients' expressed or unexpressed wishes*. The dying mother wishes to hear about her son, and although she quite probably would like to hear reassuring things, it is not at all clear that she wants to hear lies, when reality does not conform with her hopes. And the aforementioned member of the religious sect would not express a wish to have a blood transfusion if she were conscious; on the contrary, if asked, she would most probably explicitly refuse the treatment.

Richard Lindley, in a paper called 'Paternalism and caring', suggests that *autonomy* instead of liberty of action is the key concept in the present issue.[16] In instances of paternalism one always finds, according to Lindley, 'a conflict between concern for a person's welfare, and the desire to protect her or his autonomy'. Consequently, he gives the following definition:

[A] paternalistic act is such that:
(1) The agent is motivated by respect for the person, who is the intended beneficiary of the act.
and
(2) The will of this person in regard to the agent's relevant conduct is either disregarded, or overridden by the agent.

The two elements referred to by Lee, welfare and freedom, are present in this formulation, albeit in an altered form, and the conflicting moral principles also lie in the background. Thus it seems that the autonomy-related account of paternalism can incorporate the core ideas of most other attempts at a definition.

SOME REMARKS ON THE NATURE OF AUTONOMY

Granted, for argument's sake, that autonomy rather than liberty of action is the relevant aspect of freedom in defining paternalism, the concept needs some clarification before it can be used in an intelligible manner. The vague hints normally given in the liberal literature to 'personal growth' and 'individuality' which are supposed to make autonomy valuable must be enriched by more systematic observations.

Joel Feinberg in his *Harm to Self* has explored the numerous aspects of the concept of *autonomy*. He discerns four closely related basic meanings of the word when applied to individuals:[17]

(i) 'the *capacity* to govern oneself';
(ii) 'the *actual condition* of self-government and its associated virtues';
(iii) 'an *ideal of character* derived from that conception' (i.e. from the actual condition of self-government); and
(iv) 'the *right* of self-determination', 'which is absolute within one's own moral boundaries'.

Feinberg notes that one may possess both the capacity and condition and yet not have the right, and that one may possess the right and the capacity without having the condition. However, he holds that capacity is a *sine qua non* of both the right and the condition: if we are not capable of self-government, or – to use Stanley Benn's term introduced in the preceding chapter – if we are not autarchic, autonomy cannot be imposed on us from the outside, and it would be futile to acknowledge a right to do something we simply cannot do. Small children and mentally disturbed persons may have the right to every help in developing their autarchy, but as long as they are not capable of making decisions for themselves, they have no right to make them.

Autonomy as the *actual condition* of self-government (ii) is very strongly a matter of degree. There are a number of virtues that people, according to Feinberg, attach to those persons who are regarded as autonomous, and each one of the virtues can be possessed to a greater or lesser degree. Feinberg lists the following manifestations of *de facto* autonomy:

> self-possession,
> distinct self-identity or individuality,
> authenticity or self-selection,
> self-creation,
> self-legislation,
> moral authenticity,
> moral independence,
> integrity or self-fidelity,
> self-control or self-discipline,
> self-reliance,
> initiative or self-generation, and
> responsibility for self.[18]

It can easily be seen by consulting the list that if one wants to claim that autonomy – rather than mere liberty – is valuable and worth pursuing, one must set limits to these alleged virtues. As Feinberg notes, for instance, self-reliance 'can become not only an unsocial virtue but an anti-social one, inhibiting cooperative participation in group projects'.[19] In the same way, self-control 'can be totalitarian repression, and self-discipline can become self-tyranny'.[20] Autonomy as an *ideal character* of a human being (iii), consequently, must be based on the idea that the development of self-regarding virtues will be checked so as to keep them compatible both with our own personal happiness and with our respect for the autonomy and happiness of other people.

Although the boundaries of desirable self-determination may

be vague, the value of autonomy as an actual condition and ideal character is often considered obvious, both in comparison to mere liberty of action, and to other things which might be considered prima facie desirable. Richard Arneson neatly elucidates the superiority of autonomy to *liberty* by presenting an example:

> Imagine that the development of technology permits society to equip each person with a mechanical robot capable of monitoring the individual's behavior and gently but coercively correcting it whenever it threatens to lessen the freedom [of the individual] over the long run. . . . The mechanical robot so described can increase a person's freedom, but it cannot increase a person's autonomy. (If it has any effect at all it must decrease autonomy.) Any reluctance we would feel to assign robots to people, against their will, if it lay in our power to do so, must rest on a value preference for autonomy over freedom.[21]

Granted that autonomy is preferable to liberty of action where they stand in conflict, there are other things in life apart from these essentially freedom-centred options which may be considered desirable. One of the most important rivals of autonomy in ethical theories is *pleasure*. But even a regular supply of pleasurable experiences, like the ones people are provided with in Huxley's *Brave New World*,[22] does not seem genuinely desirable if the price paid for them is a total lack of autonomy. Happiness, or human good, may be a complex of a variety of elements, but autonomy as a condition (ii) and as an ideal (iii) is surely one of the major factors both in defining it in theory and in pursuing it in practice.[23]

Autonomy as the *capacity* to govern oneself (i) is, in contrast to actual self-determination, an all-or-nothing matter: either one has it or one does not have it. As Feinberg notes,[24] people who are capable of self-government do not necessarily manage their affairs wisely or in a manner that merits sympathy or admiration. Their decisions may be foolish, unwise, reckless, even positively perverse. But self-government even in a foolish and perverse manner requires the *capacity* to govern oneself. Feinberg contrasts adult human beings with jellyfish, magnolia trees, rocks, newborn infants, lunatics and irrevocably comatose former persons, and comments that the members of such groups are not capable of making even stupid decisions. In a note he gives an example:

> The point applies to higher animals [than the jellyfish], too.

Could a cow, for example, if given the choice of living on a ranch in Texas or Nebraska, decide *at all*, much less 'wisely' or 'foolishly'? There is a kind of minimal compliment in being called 'foolish'.[25]

So even if actually being autonomous is a matter of degree, the capacity to be autonomous, or autarchy, is something one either does or does not possess.

Feinberg goes on to admit that some of us 'are no doubt more richly endowed with intelligence, judgment, and other relevant capabilities than others', but draws attention to the fact that it is the above conception, 'the threshold conception of natural competence' that is normally employed 'in stipulations of necessary and sufficient conditions for the sovereign *right* of self-government ascribed to individuals', or *de jure* autonomy (iv).[26] Regardless of our de facto skills to govern ourselves wisely or foolishly, it is the elementary ability to make decisions for ourselves that gives us the right to live our own lives according to our own values as we choose. Small children perhaps only possess the right to local autonomy in some matters, but every competent adult human being is a sovereign controller of her or his own life as a whole.[27]

After stating that everybody should have a right to personal autonomy, Feinberg tackles in his usual thorough style the problem of justifying the claim.[28] The reason why I find his suggestions less than conclusive is that while holding what is essentially the Millian liberal position, Feinberg nevertheless bases his argument on considerations of natural and inalienable human rights rather than on considerations of the instrumental value of autarchy. Taking into account the considerations of chapter 2, I see no compelling reasons to depart from Mill's decision, stated in *On Liberty*, to 'forgo any advantage which could be derived to [his] argument from the idea of abstract right, as a thing independent of utility'.[29]

An attempt towards explaining why people should, in the Millian framework, be let alone to make their own decisions when they want to is made by Richard Arneson in his article 'Mill versus paternalism'. Making the broad assumption that paternalistic behaviour is always autonomy-violating, Arneson writes:

> Perhaps we could summarize Mill so: given that autonomy is a great value, paternalistic restrictions will never (or hardly ever) advance the interests of the individuals they are intended to benefit. Moreover, the long-run indirect consequences of

paternalism are likely to be very bad – that is, inimical to social progress. . . . [This argument does] not contradict obvious facts such as that in specific circumstances coercing an individual may make him more unique, more rational, or even more self-cultured than would the alternative of letting him be.[30]

The 'long-run indirect consequences' of paternalism – the same is true, according to Arneson, of restrictions on the freedom of speech – are lack of intelligence and initiative in the management of private as well as public affairs, and a consequent repression in cultural and economic life.[31] In Mill's original words, 'a State which dwarfs its men, in order that they may be more docile instruments in its hands even for beneficial purposes – will find that with small men no great thing can really be accomplished'.[32]

In his essay 'Two concepts of liberty' Isaiah Berlin attacked the foregoing Millian justification of liberty or autonomy as a right by referring to historical facts. He wrote:

No one would argue that truth or freedom of self-expression could flourish where dogma crushes all thought. But the evidence of history tends to show . . . that integrity, love of truth, and fiery individualism grow at least as often in severely disciplined communities among, for example, the puritan Calvinists of Scotland or New England, or under military discipline, as in more tolerant or indifferent societies; and if this is so, Mill's argument for liberty as a necessary condition for the growth of human genius falls to the ground.[33]

This is indeed a persuasive counterargument, and if Berlin is right, the Millian view is apparently incorrect.

The argument contains, however, some points that can be disputed. First, if we take it that Mill defended autonomy as opposed to mere liberty of action, it is not absolutely clear that 'integrity', 'love of truth', and 'fiery individualism' even begin to exhaust the meaning of what Mill was arguing for. Second, if Britain had been tolerant or at least indifferent, it would have kept the Calvinists who, because of religious intolerance, emigrated to the New World instead of staying where they were and serving the nation in which they had originally lived. General tolerance includes the idea of mutually incompatible value systems and ways of life, and it is presumably not against the ethos of liberal thinking that autonomous persons are allowed to be, for example, Calvinists. Third, Berlin interprets Mill as holding the view that no matter what happens to individual human beings and to society, the greatest value will be derived from the development of human genius. To the degree that Mill does think along such lines, it is certainly not necessary for all liberals to follow him. And besides, whatever Mill may have thought about the matter, his own notion of instrumental value, or utility, as the ultimate ethical criterion for legal and social policies fills the gap perfectly: the greatest happiness of the greatest number is what societies and humankind should aim at by advocating the (instrumental) value of autonomy as a right to self-determination, not the emergence of extraordinary talent and genius for its own sake. And as the 'greatest happiness' in a pluralistic society means different things to different people, the realization of the maxim is most likely to be effected by respecting everybody's right to autonomy.[34]

PATERNALISM WITHOUT PRIMA-FACIE VIOLATIONS OF AUTONOMY?

It was concluded above (p. 53) from Bernard Gert and Charles Culver's counterexamples that paternalistic behaviour does not necessarily contain coercive or constraining elements with regard to the recipients' liberty of action. Gert and Culver's own proposal was then challenged on the grounds that violations of moral rules in general are not always present in paternalistic interventions either. It is now time to take still one step further and study the possibility that even violations of the recipient's autonomy may not be needed in acts of caring control.

An example will elucidate the point. Dr Smiley is a dentist, and in the waiting room of her office there are magazines for the patients. Now, if Dr Smiley decides to add to the reading selection some pamphlets propagating the importance of dental hygiene, her behaviour will hardly constitute violations of the patients' autonomy or other transgressions of major moral rules. Nevertheless, it makes perfect sense to say that at least her motivation is probably paternalistic, and it might well go against the common usage of language to say that her behaviour cannot be described as paternalistic unless there are violations of some sort present.

This issue is addressed by N. Fotion in an article entitled simply 'Paternalism'. At the very beginning of the essay the following comments of definition take the emphasis of the discussion away from coercion, constraint and immorality:

> The best way to understand 'paternalism' is to view it as a concept, based upon an analogy, in competition with other concepts, most of which are also based upon analogies. The analogy to which the concept of paternalism draws our attention is concerned, quite obviously, with the special family relationship of father to child. A state, organization, or even an individual is said to be acting paternalistically with respect to another state, organization, or individual when it is acting as a father acts with respect to his child or children.[35]

Making the assumption that the paternalism of a state or some other authority is fully analogous to that of a father, Fotion rejects the idea that paternalistic action need be coercive or constraining (or, it may be added, in any way opposed to any moral principle).[36]

To support the point, Fotion draws attention to the proper role of the father in a family:

> As a father, the father hovers over the child, as it were, anticipating those outside dangers which he has some control over, satisfying the child's needs whenever possible, and, if necessary, preventing the child from harming himself. In the latter case, should the child persist in engaging in activities which will harm him, the father may be forced to deter or even punish him. It would be a mistake, however, to see the father's role exclusively in terms of depriving the child of its freedom and administering punishment. Daddy's role is neither exclusively nor primarily that of a benevolent policeman or enforcer.[37]

Using the analogy between the father and the state, and assuming that it is complete, Fotion infers that coercive paternalism as discussed by liberal theorists since Mill's *On Liberty* is only a fraction of the whole of (potentially legitimate) state paternalism.

Fotion's model includes a number of points, some of which are obviously acceptable, others not. It is important to distinguish between Fotion's treatment of questions of justification and those of definition, since all that is valid in the view can be found within the latter category.

As regards justification, the rough outline of the theory is as follows. The paternalism of the father is always justifiable, presumably because 'daddy always knows best' and because his superior knowledge, according to Fotion, entitles him to use power. Coercion, deterrence and even punishment are appropriate features of a father's protection of his children, since from time to time daddy 'may be forced' to use the more unpleasant methods of education to prevent his children from harming themselves. By analogy, it must be inferred that the state is also justified in coercing its citizens for their own good.

There are at least three major difficulties with this line of argument.

The first one is Fotion's blind acceptance of the father's legitimate power over his children. In particular, punishing children for harming themselves does not, after consideration, seem as unproblematic as the theory boldly states. Should not the father be looking for reasons for the child's behaviour instead of using force? Does the punishment actually deter the child from harming herself, or does it end up with her hiding her unaccepted behaviour from the parents? Are punitive attitudes the best possible basis for healthy relationships within the family?

Second, even if these questions could be answered in a satisfactory manner, it is far from clear that the analogy model can sensibly be employed. Many people who take the father's role in the family for granted, still nurture doubts concerning benevolent state control over its citizens. Most of them presumably think that it is in fact the most humiliating aspect of paternalism that it lets adult human beings be protected and guided by a group of perfect strangers as if they were children.

And the third problem is closely connected with the second one: does the state possess the competence to guide its citizens in the first place? It may be that a father knows something about the needs of his children even without consulting them, but does the state know what individual citizens need? Is it possible to force people to be happy? There are so many unanswered questions here that it seems very difficult indeed to argue plausibly for Fotion's theory as far as justification is concerned.

In the field of definition, however, the situation is entirely different. Fotion's claim is that the paternalism of a father – etymologically the root reference of the concept – contains elements which do not include coercion, constraint, or violations of moral rules of any kind. This much seems to be obviously true. Furthermore, it is probable that the paternalism of other authorities, including the state, resembles the paternalism of the father closely enough to allow the inference that the observation applies to paternalism, or 'paternally protective action', in general. Consequently, it seems plausible to define the concept so that non-coercive, non-constraining and perfectly moral behaviour is not automatically excluded.

A PRELIMINARY DIVISION OF MODES OF PATERNALISM

It seems, then, that a broad definition of paternalism should be employed for two major reasons. First, there appear to be no good grounds for going against commonsense intuitions – referred to by Fotion – which indicate that fathers can act paternalistically towards their children even when they do not coerce them, or restrict their freedom, or violate other prima-facie moral rules. Second – and this is a forward-looking point – in systematically considering the issue of justification it will most probably be helpful by way of comparison to have access to a variety of activities which can be described as paternalistic.

Accordingly, I shall assume a working principle stating that the action or inaction of a person (or group of persons) towards or on behalf of another person (or group of persons) can be paternalistic even if the interaction between the parties does not contain coercive, liberty-restricting, autonomy-violating or otherwise prima-facie immoral elements. Since violations of autonomy seem to be the most basic category here, I shall use their presence and absence as the criteria for the first distinction between various modes of protective control. Thus, I stipulate that protective behaviour which does not even initially violate the recipients' autonomy can sometimes (i.e. when it is analogous to parental control) be labelled *soft paternalism*, whereas protective behaviour which does violate the recipients' autonomy always belongs to the class of *hard paternalism*. Assuming that respect or disrespect for the autonomy of others is generally the only morally relevant factor here, it follows that soft paternalism is generally not in need of justification, and that, in turn, hard paternalism invariably is.

PATERNALISTIC VIOLATIONS OF AUTONOMY

Now that the existence of soft paternalism has been recognized, and its nature defined, let me put it aside for a while and turn, instead, to the obviously more intriguing questions of hard, or prima-facie autonomy-violating, paternalism. First of all, how does one distinguish, in practical terms, between control which is autonomy-violating and control which is autonomy-respecting?

Gerald Dworkin in an essay entitled 'Autonomy and behavior control' gives a useful list of what may and what may not be done to influence persons, if respect for autonomy is taken seriously. Dworkin points out the following attitudes, norms and preferences:

(1) We have favourable attitudes towards those methods of influence which support the self-respect and dignity of those who are being influenced . . .
(2) Methods of influence which are destructive of the ability of individuals to reflect rationally on their interests should not be used . . .
(3) Methods should not be used which affect in fundamental ways the personal identity of individuals . . .
(4) Methods which rely essentially on deception, on keeping the agent in ignorance of relevant facts, are to be avoided . . .
(5) Modes of influence which are not physically intrusive are preferable to those which are . . .
(6) There will be some restrictions on the time in which the changes take place and the ability of the agent to resist the effects of various modes of influence . . .
(7) We prefer methods of influence which work through the cognitive and affective structure of the agent, which require the active participation of the agent in producing the change, to those which short-circuit the desires and beliefs of the agent and make him a passive recipient of the changes.[38]

The value of these points is twofold. First, assuming that the variety of factors employed by Dworkin is indispensable, it must be admitted that the list cannot be straightforwardly applied to everyday practical situations. Although there may be a few paradigmatic cases at both ends of the continuum, it is probably impossible to determine, once and for all, say, which methods of influence 'support the self-respect of those who are being influenced' and which do not. And to take another example, granted that short interventions are generally preferable to longer ones, for how long can the intervention be sustained before it does actually violate the recipient's autonomy? These and many other questions must be answered separately and in their proper context, starting from the beginning every time a new practical issue arises. Consequently, there is no clear-cut separation between cases of hard and soft paternalism.

Second, however, concrete rules of violating or respecting autonomy, such as those presented by Dworkin, are useful as points of comparison in attempts to calculate whether or not a presumably 'hard' act of paternalism can be justified. A prima-facie violation of autonomy does not necessarily imply that the action which would cause it must be illegitimate, or irrevocably immoral: minor violations can perhaps be tolerated if the positive value of their consequences can reasonably be expected to outweigh the initial evil. And, despite the obvious lack of precision on the general level, the acceptability of hard paternalism in particular classes of situations can probably best be assessed by reference to such factors as those listed by Dworkin.

But what is there to be said about the more general questions? Some information will be gained by studying an example Mill gave of a situation where, in his opinion, paternalistic interference is justifiable. This is how the oft-quoted passage of *On Liberty* goes:

> If either a public officer or any one else saw a person attempting to cross a bridge which had been ascertained to be unsafe, and there were no time to warn him of his danger, they might seize him and turn him back, without any real infringement of his liberty; for liberty consists in doing what one desires, and he does not desire to fall into the river.[39]

For Mill, then, paternalistic action after all seems to be justifiable, if no real infringement of the recipient's liberty occurs.

As Richard Lindley has noted, however, an infringement of liberty indeed does occur in the described situation. The person attempting to cross the bridge does not wish to fall into the river, but he *does* wish to walk over the bridge. So, for Mill, who himself in the cited paragraph defines liberty as 'doing what one desires', the person's liberty to walk on the bridge will be infringed if we 'seize him and turn him back'.[40]

Lindley's suggestion is that the situation should be described in terms of autonomy. The person approaching the bridge is about to do something which will, in the last analysis, be a greater threat to his autonomy than the liberty-restriction of forcibly stopping him in order to warn him of the danger. Lindley distinguishes two levels of autonomy,[41] the first of which is the condition of not being prevented from doing what one presently wishes to do, or bare autonomy; and the second is the possibility of determining one's own values and goals, or self-determination. Presuming, as Lindley does, that the latter kind of autonomy is more important than the former, the spirit of Mill's example can be restored by noting that while the 'bare' autonomy of the person crossing the bridge will be violated if he is stopped, this evil will be generously outweighed by the fact that unless he is stopped, he is bound to fall into the river, and if he should suffer severe injuries or die, his future ability to control the direction of his own life will be substantially diminished or even completely ineffectual.

Some theorists, including Lindley, tend to think that autonomy may legitimately be violated *only* for the sake of greater autonomy.[42] My own view, however, is that the self-inflicted harm prevented by violating a person's autonomy which may justify hard paternalism should also include death, injury, loss of money and other misfortunes which may or may not be directly and visibly connected with autonomy as the actual condition and ideal of self-determination. The weighing of various prospective evils cannot always be one-dimensional if justice is to be done to the facts in real-life situations. The appreciation of facts and the subsequent extension of concepts would no doubt complicate matters to an intolerable degree if the object were to lay down once and for all every possible scale for measuring and comparing different kinds of harm. But if the original Millian view is taken, that people should in most cases be free even to harm themselves if they wish to, such construction of scales is by and large futile. And if it is admitted that the forms both of autonomy violated and harm inflicted must be studied separately in each particular class of cases, constructing scales would, on the general level, be impossible as well.

If people ought to be free even to harm themselves, why is it that one sometimes feels that paternalistic interventions in many everyday situations are, after all, appropriate? It seems to be particularly obvious that children and the mentally defective cannot always be treated with the same *laissez-faire* attitude as normal adults. It would be immoral and negligent to let small children play with loaded guns, for example, even if they very much wanted to do so. And there are cases in which even adults seem to be legitimate targets for paternalistic action. The person nearing the bridge in Mill's example is a case in point. But what is it that in these cases justifies an intervention for the good of the person whose life or action or plans are interfered with?

THE ROLE OF VOLUNTARINESS

Voluntariness, or rather lack of voluntariness, as a quality of the agent's decisions is the usual liberal response to the question concerning the necessary conditions of justifiable hard paternalism. The discussion once again starts with Mill – more specifically, with one of his many formulations of the 'one and very simple principle':

> That principle is, that . . . the only purpose for which power can be rightfully exercised over any member of a civilized community, *against his will*, is to prevent harm to others.[43]

A close reading of the passage, and especially the italicized phrase, clearly seems to provide an explanation for the protection of children and the mentally defective, as well as for the bridge example. Even members of a civilized community may, after all, be compelled for their own good if only the compelling *does not occur against their will*. But there is an element of paradox in this interpretation. How can compelling a person fail to be against his will? Common sense seems to tell us that if I wish to do something – that is, I possess the relevant will – then there is, ordinarily, no need to compel me. If, on the other hand, it is necessary to compel me, then I obviously lack the relevant will, or, worse still, possess a contrary will.

It is easier to see the point of the Millian position if one focuses on will, or voluntariness, solely as a determinant or quality of a person's *decisions*. There are many ways in which even apparently autonomous decisions can fail to express what the agent genuinely wishes, and the view I am going to assume in this chapter is that if (and only if) they do, action flowing from these decisions may be a legitimate target for prima-facie autonomy-violating paternalistic interventions. C.L. Ten has presented four criteria for distinguishing decision-making which may justify restrictions for the recipient's own good. According to his account, one may be dealing with or detect

(a) special categories of persons;
(b) lack of knowledge;
(c) lack of control; or
(d) undue influence.[44]

If any one of these factors is present when an agent decides to undertake a course of action which to outside observers looks disproportionately dangerous, the observers are permitted and sometimes even obliged to intervene to some extent at least. But let me first say a few words about each criterion introduced, and then spell out some limiting considerations.

(a) Members of Ten's 'special categories' – children, the mentally subnormal and the mentally ill – are 'persons who do not have the same capacities as normal adults, and whose decisions are therefore generally subject to vitiating factors'.[45] The point here is that since the capability of autonomy of these persons has not yet been fully developed or will never be fully developed or has been permanently lost, prima-facie violations of their autonomy are not necessarily immoral in the last analysis, and can actually support their self-determination instead of suppressing it. Voluntary decision-making is not possible without autarchy, and involuntary choices are not entitled to the full respect of other agents.

(b) When lack of knowledge is involved in the decision-making, the agent 'may do something without being aware of the harmful consequences of his acts,' or 'be lacking in knowledge not with respect to the consequences of his act, but to the nature of the act'.[46] Ten gives as an example of the first category somebody who takes a medicine without knowing about its harmful side-effects. Mill's bridge-crosser would also fall under this description. The latter condition, in its turn, can, according to Ten, most likely be satisfied by a case where a female patient's 'modesty is outraged by a [male] doctor who pretends that he is giving her some special medical treatment'.[47] Lack of knowledge may, as in this case, be due to the deceptive influence of others; it may also be the result of negligence on somebody's part; or it may be simply accidental.

(c) By lack of control Ten means that an agent 'may be aware of the consequences of his act, but because of temporary emotional unbalance, may not be able to appreciate the full significance of these consequences, and to exercise rational judgement with respect to them'.[48] This emotional unbalance, or lack of control over one's decisions, 'may be caused by grief, distress, or severe strains'[49] and, as Ten notes, it has often been referred to as a potential justification for denying the possibility of voluntary euthanasia.

(d) Finally, decisions may be impaired because of undue influence on the agent from the outside. Undue influence takes many forms, most notably the explicit use of coercion, but 'there are also the pressures of economic inducements, and sometimes of customs and traditions'.[50] Duelling for reasons of honour is given by Ten as an example of 'the tyranny of custom', which could call for legitimate paternalistic interventions.[51]

But even if one of these vitiating factors is present in a decision-making situation, it is not necessarily right to violate the agent's autonomy in order to spare her from self-inflicted harm. At least three considerations are relevant here: first, the seriousness of the harm about to be caused; second, whether or not the harm is irreversible; and third, how long a time the agent is subjected to paternalistic interference. Since, obviously, there is a difference between what one minute alone in a locked room and several months in an asylum can do to a person's autonomy, the longer the intervention lasts, the more serious and final the harm justifying it must be. Two examples will illustrate the point.

If a person beside me is about to drink some deadly poison, and he has, as far as I know, expressed no intention of suicide, then I am *of course* justified in warning him about the danger. I am also justified in arresting his hand, despite the possibility that grabbing his arm might spill the liquid everywhere, and thus spoil his well-considered suicide attempt that I did not know of. And if I know him well enough and feel certain that he could not possibly want to die, even heavier measures would be justifiable. I could, for instance, if there was no other way of stopping him in time, quite legitimately shoot him in the arm to save his life.

If, however, the agent is merely going to drink something foul-tasting, thinking it is his favourite wine, what others are justified in doing is limited to warning him and perhaps grasping his arm. When the harm or offence inflicted on oneself is small and not irreversible, there are no grounds for disproportionately harmful interventions.

Although in the first example it may be legitimate to employ rather drastic measures to prevent an agent from harming himself, it must be kept in mind that the purpose of the intervention even by shooting is merely to make sure that the agent is adult, sane, aware of the risk, calm and under no pressure. As an illustration of the 'check-out nature' of justifiable paternalism, consider the following variation of Mill's bridge. The watchman on a bridge knows that the bridge is unsafe, and because of this knowledge she seizes a potential crosser, turns him back and warns him. But once she has finished explaining the situation, the crosser – who is clearly adult, sane, and so on – calmly reports that he does not mind taking the risk, and turns towards the bridge again. Faced with the situation in real life, the watchman may have *other* reasons for still preventing the stranger from crossing the bridge (e.g. the company who owns the bridge will have bad publicity and she will be sacked if someone is injured), but it is clear that *the best interest of the crosser himself* does not justify any more intervention. Even the irreversibility of the expected harm cannot change the fact that, within a Millian liberal framework, reasonably informed and relatively clear-headed persons ought to be free to take their own risks when no one else is substantially involved.[52]

It would be possible, at this point, to question the rationality of anybody who attempts to cross an unsafe bridge, but this would shift the focus of attention from the *technical* and *descriptive* criteria of reasonable decision-making to *normative* views concerning the legitimate *content* of rational and moral choices. These lines of thought were already introduced in chapter 1, where the medical examples of voluntary euthanasia and refusals to sterilize a healthy young person were discussed. The problem with prudential and moral considerations is that, if they are employed, it is not only the recipients' own best interest that the paternalist is supposed to know best, but also how the recipients ought to think and conduct their behaviour to reach the same knowledge. The violations of autonomy intrinsic to this kind of paternalism would be severe, since they would in many cases have to be designed to change the fundamental ways of thinking and feeling of individuals. Following Dworkin's list presented above, for instance, this would mean at least undermining the recipients' dignity as persons, affecting their personal identities in thoroughgoing ways, and rejecting any suggested limits to the temporal duration of the interventions.

To distinguish between the different kinds of caring control I shall call the legitimate, autonomy-respecting variety *weak paternalism*, and the illegitimate, autonomy-violating kind *strong paternalism*.[53] The difference is that in the former type control is based on the best interest of persons whose decisions are seriously viti-ated, whereas in the latter category restrictions are based on the content rather than formal voluntariness of the recipients' choices. Since attempts at justifying strongly paternalistic inter-ventions are mostly founded on prudential or moral arguments, the principles generating them could sometimes equally well be coined *prudentialism* and *moralism*. These maxims will be more extensively examined in studying the ethical acceptability of strong paternalism below (chs 4–6).

VOLUNTARINESS, RESPONSIBILITY AND PERFECTION

Before summing up the contents of this chapter, let me briefly describe, by way of an example, how theorists who allegedly accept the liberal position may try to smuggle 'strong' interventions into their systems by defining them as instances of weak paternalism.

C. Edwin Harris, Jr in an article entitled 'Paternalism and the enforcement of morality' argues that in between the extremes of fully voluntary and fully involuntary action there is a third category which takes some relevant features from both. Using as his examples laws forbidding people from swimming at public beaches when the lifeguards are not on duty, and obligatory payments for one's own social security later in life, Harris writes:

> There seems to be a middle way between [the] two extremes which I shall refer to as *irresponsible action*. Such action is neither the result of deliberate policies nor is it wholly beyond the individual's control, but it is the kind of thing all of us do from time to time. Take the example of laws which forbid swimming at a public beach when the lifeguard is not on duty. It is not that people are coerced into dangerous swimming, nor on the other hand, is it that they are unaware of the possible consequences. It is simply a case of not fully and responsibly considering the possible consequences, weighing these consequences against the immediate and temporary pleasures of a swim, and then having the self-discipline to follow through with what one knows he should do. Similar considerations apply to the laws requiring Social Security payments. One knows he should put aside a portion of his income for retirement, but he may fail to consider fully and responsibly the consequences of not doing so, or simply lack the discipline to do what he knows he ought to do.[54]

Harris goes on to state that 'irresponsible actions are close enough to nonresponsible or involuntary actions' to fall within the sphere of legitimate paternalistic intervention. According to his view these

72

actions are, in Joel Feinberg's authoritative words, 'substantially less than voluntary'.[55] The laws mentioned as examples, then, are in Harris's theory justifiable on 'weakly' paternalistic grounds.

It seems to me that Harris could not be more wrong either with his choice of examples or with his conclusions. There is no reason to apply the concepts of 'irresponsibility' or 'lack of discipline' to the cases he mentions, especially not in a sense that would imply legitimate paternalistic intervention. In the beach case, there are no a priori grounds whatsoever for the legal prohibition of competent adult human beings swimming when they choose to swim, whether or not there happen to be life-guards present. It would be quite correct, of course, for the authorities to warn people of the danger, but it is not at all clear why legal sanctions *on paternalistic grounds* should be assumed without argument, as Harris does. And as to the social security issue, the obligatory payments can equally well be argued for by appealing to the best interest of other people who are presently unemployed or elderly as by reference to the long-term self-interest of the paying persons themselves. By financing the social security functions of the state, those who are presently working and earning guarantee the security of those who are not, whether the reason is old age, disability preventing someone working, unemployment or something else. When the working people of today grow old, there will probably be others who will take care of them.

One possible source of criticism in Harris's view might be that he turns the assessment of (in)voluntariness into a very inexact matter by introducing the notion of irresponsibility. But this is not my complaint here. Joel Feinberg in his *Harm to Self* considers the issue of voluntariness in such detail that Michael D. Bayles noted in a review that 'the book might have been better had the concern with paternalism simply been dropped and the discussion focused on voluntariness in the criminal and civil law',[56] but even Feinberg could not on a general level go much further in assessing degrees of involuntariness than to pro-pose a few vague rules of thumb. So much depends on the particular circumstances and relationships between people that no precise and concise overall measuring methods can be spelled out anyway.

What *does* worry me in Harris's suggestion is the fact that his language is so obviously morality-laden. People in his examples are 'not fully responsible considering the possible consequences' of their actions; they are not seriously 'weighing these consequences against the immediate and temporary pleasures'; they lack 'the self-discipline to follow through with what they know they should do'. Consequently, it is the ideal character of an ideal human being rather than the autonomous person deciding for herself, right or wrong, that is taken up as the model of the kind of citizen legal and social institutions should aim to create and uphold.

There is a connection between Harris's view concerning irresponsibility and lack of self-discipline and the grand theories of Kantian rationalism and Rousseauan communitarianism in that they all take *perfection* to be a necessary condition of genuine human liberty, and tend to see violations of people's autonomy as justifiable by reference to their perfection or true freedom. Views like these are frequently used to back up strongly paternalistic and moralistic policies: political authorities can claim that the restrictions they impose on individuals and groups are justifiably paternalistic, since the plans they frustrate are not the products of sufficiently voluntary decisions. The imperfection of citizens places on the clergymen or the party leaders or members of the upper classes an obligation to thwart people's 'alleged' wishes.

The problem is that looking at alien cultures Westerners often tend to think that there is some truth in these views, especially when applied to 'undeveloped' or 'developing' countries. Within some non-Western cultures there are practices such as prearranged marriage, polygamy and self-mutilation for religious reasons, which to an outsider seem disgusting and irrational. Westerners may very easily catch themselves thinking that these practices cannot be based on 'really' autonomous decisions: once these primitive people have been taught what freedom really means, the Westerners may think, they will be more than happy to reject their old customs. Only then will they be actually free, and international laws and policies must assist them in reaching that goal.

At this point it must be remembered that cultural traditions, autonomy and views concerning voluntariness are closely linked. Comparing the ideas of epistemological and moral authority, Gerald Dworkin in his essay 'Moral autonomy' argues that even the most autonomous person or group makes a wise choice in recognizing, to some degree at least, the relevance of traditions in ethical issues.[57] He writes:

> There are various reasons why such a policy is rational. We lack time, knowledge, training, skill. In addition there is a necessary and useful division of labor. It is more efficient for each of us to specialize in a few areas of competence and be able to draw, when we need it, upon the resources and expertise of others.[58]

According to Dworkin, authorities or traditions should not be accepted blindly – our reliance on them is ideally based on the idea that somebody has checked either that the authority is likely to be correct and generally 'knows better' or that the same is true in the particular case at hand. But it is neither necessary nor rational that everybody at all times insists on checking every judgement made by the authority.

De jure autonomy, or the right to self-determination which should not be violated according to the morality I have been defending, could be interpreted here as an option to check the validity of one's authorities whenever one feels that it *is* necessary and rational. As long as this option is available, the influence of one's authorities on one's decisions is not 'undue', and does not justify allegedly protective violations of autonomy. So even if people in non-Western cultures seem to outside observers to harm themselves by consenting to physically or socially damaging practices, the outsiders have no right to interfere unless they can show that individuals are forced to participate in them by more explicit means than the power of tradition.

This same line of reasoning also applies to another sufficient condition of involuntariness, the condition of temporary emotional or mental disturbances. For instance, as long as the people of a given 'undeveloped' country hold on to the view that self-mutilation is not a symptom of mental imperfection, there is nothing much outsiders can do. If lack of knowledge is suspected, information can legitimately be spread, but that is all. Since autonomy does not exist in a vacuum, the ideological traditions within which it acquires shape in people's minds should be tolerated, however peculiar they may seem, unless they become totalitarian and deny people the option of changing their opinions and modes of behaviour through reflective thinking. Toleration of different views is a necessary condition of the large-scale realization of autonomy in the world.

Accordingly, theories that attempt to introduce paternalistic policies by reference to human irresponsibility, imperfection or alienation from our true nature, should not according to the liberal view be given normative power, at least not in the form of a *carte blanche*. There may be valid descriptive elements in these theories, and these, of course, ought to be given adequate weight in considering actual policies. But it would not be advisable to abolish entire ways of thinking or cultural traditions in the name of an abstract concept of 'true humanity' or 'genuine liberty'. The voluntariness of our decisions and choices of authority may be a matter of varying degrees, and sometimes even a matter of pure self-deception, but if the irresponsibility or self-deception is a reflection of our own minds and our own cultures, there are no morally justifiable grounds for autonomy-violating intervention.

THE LIBERAL VIEW ON PATERNALISM

The time has come to draw whatever conclusions can be drawn from the discussion of this chapter, and to state explicitly the liberal view on paternalism which has taken shape in the course of the discussion. The distinctions and arguments are summarized in a schematic form in Figure 1.

According to the liberal view, paternalism does not necessarily contain coercion, constraint, violations of autonomy or other prima-facie condemnable elements. Caring control may be autonomy-respecting, in which case it can be called *soft paternalism*, the relevant dividing line being respect towards autonomy rather than absence of coercion and constraint in other senses. The more ordinary type of paternalism, usually discussed in the literature, can be coined *hard paternalism* and defined as caring control which is

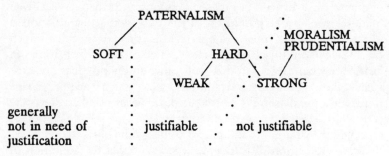

Figure 1 The liberal view on paternalism

at least prima-facie autonomy-violating. Because of its prima-facie autonomy-violating nature, this kind of paternalism is always in need of moral justification.

The way to justify 'hard' interventions is to show, first, that the recipient of the interventions is not at the time capable of reasonably voluntary decision-making, and second, that the recipient would without the intervention inflict relatively grave harm on her or himself. If these conditions are fulfilled, then the control in question is legitimate, and can be labelled *weak paternalism*. If either one of the conditions is not fulfilled, then attempts to control the recipient are illegitimate, and should be identified as *strong paternalism*. Since the best interest of the recipients cannot in the long run be served by 'strong' paternalistic measures, prudential and moral considerations are often evoked to support them. This is why 'strong' interventions can sometimes be equally well placed under the categories of *prudentialism* or *moralism*.

The liberal view sketched here is not directly applicable to real life situations, since the lines between soft and hard, weak and strong paternalism remain vague on a general level. The gravity of a given violation of autonomy, the seriousness of an instance of self-inflicted harm, and the degree of voluntariness of a decision are all factors that must be assessed and compared separately in each particular class of cases.

4

THE UTILITARIAN CASE FOR STRONG PATERNALISM

The liberal view on paternalism can be challenged from two diametrically opposed directions. On the one hand, an anarchist or libertarian case could be made stating that restrictions on an agent's freedom should not be allowed even if her decisions are impaired, and even if she will otherwise inflict harm on herself. All constraining control, the weak forms of paternalism included, should according to this view be condemned as indications of, or steps towards, oppressive totalitarianism. On the other hand, the contrary claim could be made stating that liberal policies are too permissive, and that utility, morality or rationality demand more active interference in the affairs of individual human beings. According to this latter view, references to oppression and totalitarianism simply disguise immoral and negligent attitudes towards one's fellow creatures.

I shall not go into the problems presented by the first challenge for two reasons. First, I tend to agree with the latter view – anarchism and libertarianism which are advanced enough to deny the legitimacy of all weak paternalism would indeed lead to unfounded egoism and negligence.[1] Second, since caring control is an essential element of health policies and medical practice, it is probably better to take one step at a time, and see if, provided that *some* instances of medical paternalism are legitimate, a line can still be drawn between these and other, illegitimately paternalistic, practices.

With the second challenge, however, the situation is entirely different. In this and chapters 5 and 6 I shall study three criticisms of the liberal view, based on utilitarian, moralistic and prudential considerations, respectively. If any of these criticisms proves to be valid, then the paternalistic attitudes and practices prevailing within the modern health care system may well be justifiable, after all. Only if all three can be rejected or shown to be irrelevant to the issue at hand, is it possible to attack the prevailing situation on liberal and anti-paternalistic grounds.

THE EARLY ANTAGONISTS: MILL *V.* STEPHEN

The utilitarian critique against liberal anti-paternalism was for the first time presented in full in 1873, when 'the great Victorian judge and historian of the Criminal Law',[2] James Fitzjames Stephen, attacked Mill and especially *On Liberty* in his book *Liberty, Equality, Fraternity*.[3] In what follows, I shall survey Stephen's arguments against Mill at some length. There are several reasons for choosing Stephen to represent the classical utilitarian case for strong paternalism, despite the fact that his theory is not exactly the last word in consequentialist thinking. First, after the contributions of Mill and Stephen, very few utilitarians have been interested in the problems of caring control. Notable philosophers like Henry Sidgwick,[4] G.E. Moore,[5] R.M. Hare[6] and R.B. Brandt[7] have endorsed the doctrine and developed it further, but they have mainly concentrated their efforts on the purely *ethical* aspects of utilitarianism, leaving the questions of law and social policy virtually untouched. Second, Stephen's criticism of liberal ideals is stated in clear and simple terms, which are readily intelligible also to those who do not accept his conclusions. More recent discussions on utilitarianism as a theory of social policy arrangements tend to be complicated by unnecessary formalism and decision-theoretical jargon.[8] And third, Stephen's arguments for paternalism have not been given the attention they deserve for their technical cogency as well as for their historical importance. Stephen's critique of Mill was lightly touched upon by H.L.A. Hart in his *Law, Liberty, and Morality*,[9] but Hart's main interest was elsewhere – in his opposition to Patrick Devlin's legal moralism.[10] For the rest, apart from such passing remarks as the ones made by Martin Golding in his *Philosophy of Law*,[11] Stephen's work has gone unnoticed by philosophers.

Stephen dedicated a good half of *Liberty, Equality, Fraternity* to the criticism of Mill's theories concerning liberty. As a utilitarian of a slightly different persuasion himself, Stephen was particularly worried about the change for the worse he saw in Mill's work in its development from such earlier works as *A System of Logic* (1843) and *Principles of Political Economy* (1848) to the later ones such as *On Liberty* (1859), *Utilitarianism* (1863), and *The Subjection of Women* (1869).[12] For Stephen, Mill's intellectual development from classical utilitarianism to anti-paternalistic liberalism was not a sign of growing independence from the theories of Jeremy Bentham and James Mill, but rather an incomprehensible conversion directed against some of the most fundamental values in human life.

According to Stephen's own view, as formulated in his article entitled 'Note on utilitarianism', human acts can be called 'right' if (and only if) they are likely to promote the general good of mankind.[13] As the proper task of legislation, too, is to promote general good, the concrete problem for legislators is, in Stephen's view, how to bring it about that people act in the right manner, or, in other words, virtuously. Stephen took it that Mill, being a fellow utilitarian, was claiming in *On Liberty* that the general happiness (or good) of mankind can never be furthered by coercing people to do or forbear doing something on the grounds that it would be for their own good, or prudential or ethical.[14] The only kind of common morality Stephen saw emerging from Mill's theory was, accordingly, summed up by him in the maxim: 'Let every man please himself without hurting his neighbour.'[15] And this seemed to him to be a strangely weak and modest sort of morality, and most unlikely to promote the general good of mankind.

A PRELIMINARY ATTACK

Before going any deeper into Stephen's own utilitarianism, let me introduce an independent counterargument he presented against the Millian theory. In reflecting on Mill's 'one very simple principle' Stephen drew attention to the fact that Mill himself only recognized the validity of the principle when 'members of a civilised community' were involved, not 'in dealing with barbarians, provided the end be their improvement, and the means justified by actually effecting that end'.[16] Stephen asked what should be inferred from this exception. His answer begins by pointing out that, according to Mill:

in all the countries which we are accustomed to call civilized the mass of adults are so well acquainted with their own interests and so much disposed to pursue them that no compulsion or restraint put upon any of them by any others for the purpose of promoting their interests can really promote them.[17]

Very well, then, says Stephen in the face of this assertion, its importance is obvious, 'but where is the proof of it?'[18] He continues:

> Before he affirmed that in Western Europe and America the compulsion of adults for their own good is unjustifiable, Mr Mill ought to have proved that there are among us no considerable differences in point of wisdom, or that if there are, the wiser part of the community does not wish for the welfare of the less wise.[19]

If equal wisdom or malevolence among the wise cannot be shown, why should the Europeans and the Americans be treated any differently from the barbarians of Asia and Africa?

The question was answered on Mill's account by his disciple John Morley, who reviewed Stephen's book immediately after its publication.[20] Morley attempted to refute Stephen's criticism by commenting on the above quoted passage concerning the proof which Mill allegedly should have produced:

> Why so? Mr Mill's very proposition is that though there is a wiser part, and though the wiser part may wish well to the less wise, *yet* even then the disadvantages of having a wiser course forced upon the members of civilised societies exceed the disadvantages of following an unwise course freely. Mr Stephen's allegation of the points which Mr Mill should have proved rests on the assumption of the very matter at issue – namely, whether freedom is not in itself so valuable an element in social life (in civilised communities), that for the sake of it we should be content to let the unwiser part have their own way in what concerns them only.[21]

Morley's point is the same as Mill's, that since even mistakes, if made freely, are more valuable than coerced 'right' decisions, it is not necessary for the Millian theory to produce proof concerning people's equal wisdom or the malevolence of the wise who are presently in power.

In trying to defend the Millian view in its entirety Morley clearly misses the point of Stephen's specific attack. The plain statement that freedom is valuable in Western countries, even if true, hardly helps in explaining the difference in this respect between Western countries and the rest of the world. If the difference is not the one Stephen proposed, then there is still no reason not to treat civilized people and barbarians alike.[22]

There seems to be no method of saving Mill's view as it stands. However, Stephen's challenge can none the less be countered by liberal considerations: as shown towards the end of chapter 3, it is in fact not necessary or even plausible to distinguish between the 'members of civilised communities' and 'barbarians' as regards respect for their autonomy. The way one's autonomy manifests itself depends strongly on the cultural context within which it is exercised, and it is therefore dangerous to develop culturally imperialistic attitudes towards 'other' peoples. A genuinely autonomy-respecting variety of liberal thinking can thus avoid the difficulties raised by Stephen's question.

'WHY SHOULD I DO WHAT IS RIGHT?'

Stephen's full-fledged criticism against Mill goes considerably deeper. He presents an entire theory of morality, society and human nature to show how coercion, legal as well as moral, is necessary even when agents do not visibly hurt anybody other than themselves. Since for Stephen individual morality is equivalent to prudence, and prudence to the consistent pursuit of self-interest, what he is trying to accomplish is, in fact, a joint justification of moralism, prudentialism and paternalism. And he seems to be well aware of the fact that to make the case he is forced to show how coercion really can benefit even the most autonomous persons.

In his 'Note on utilitarianism' Stephen lays down the semantics of utilitarian value theory as follows:

> The utilitarian says, I observe that, speaking broadly, men desire the same sorts of things, and I call the attainment of these objects of desire by the general name of happiness. I also observe that certain courses of conduct tend to promote,and that others tend to prevent or interfere with, the attainment of these objects of desire by mankind, and that the popular use of the words 'right' and 'wrong' has a marked general correspondence to these two classes of conduct. Speaking generally, the acts which are called right do promote or are supposed to promote general happiness, and the acts which are called wrong do diminish or are supposed to diminish it. I say, therefore, that this is what the words 'right' and 'wrong' mean. . . .[23]

Stephen himself expressly accepts the form of reasoning used by the supposed utilitarian of the passage. In *Liberty, Equality, Fraternity* he notes that he is 'in a certain sense ... a Utilitarian'[24] himself, although he prefers another interpretation or definition of the concept of *good*, which, according to him, denotes 'not the greatest happiness altogether, but the widest possible extension of the ideal of life formed by the person who sets up the standard'.[25] Nevertheless, he considers utility to be the ultimate ethical test of the value of acts and policies, as did Mill.

The next step Stephen takes in formulating the utilitarian theory is to take note of the epistemic question,

> How am I to know right from wrong?

In response to the question, he continues:

> The utilitarian answer is, that the knowledge of right and wrong does not differ from other branches of knowledge, and must be acquired in the same way.[26]

'The same way' of acquiring knowledge presumably means, taking into account Stephen's semantics of value statements, either sociological studies into the standards prevailing in the society, or psychological studies into the ideals of those who set up the standards. In any case, some of us are, according to the theory, capable of learning with perfect objectivity and relative accuracy which actions are right and which actions are wrong for all of us.

In his preface to the second edition of *Liberty, Equality, Fraternity* Stephen makes it clear how the superiority of some persons in moral matters should be regarded. He writes:

> The real difference between Mr Mill's doctrine and mine is this. We agree that the minority are wise and the majority foolish, but Mr Mill denies that the wise majority are ever justified in coercing the foolish majority for their own good, whereas I affirm that under circumstances they may be justified in doing so. [In] my opinion the wise minority are the rightful masters of the foolish majority. . . .[27]

Stephen here reflects the paternalistic attitudes and social ideals of the early Victorian England, according to which the ruling classes had justifiable privileges over the lower classes, but also obligations towards them. As David Roberts puts the matter in his book *Paternalism in Early Victorian England*, the 'paternalist mentality of the country squire' and other property owners 'was a curious mixture of prejudice, self-interest, local loyalties, and benevolence'.[28] The early Victorian property owners were opposed to change and social reform, partly out of naked self-interest, but partly because they genuinely wanted to protect their 'own' employees and tenants against what they regarded as wrongful and dangerous state paternalism. It was believed that to know and to be known by those one rules over is a necessary condition of good government, and it is obvious that the monarch cannot very well be familiar with every Smith and Jones of the country. The right to use coercive power, then, mostly derived from hereditary superiority, but was checked by the ability and obligation of the upper classes to use force in a way that was conducive to the happiness of the lower classes as well as to the maintenance of social order. The phrase 'property has its duties as well as its rights' which, according to Roberts, became 'in the 1840s the hallmark of the paternalist',[29] was probably in Stephen's mind when he contended that the wise are the rightful masters of the foolish.

In order to determine the circumstances in which coercion in general is justified Stephen presents the following straightforward rules:

> Compulsion is bad: (1) When the object aimed at is bad. (2) When the object aimed at is good, but the compulsion is not calculated to obtain it. (3) When the object aimed at is good, and the compulsion employed is calculated to obtain it, but at too great an expense.

> If, however, the object aimed at is good, if the compulsion employed such as to attain it, and if the good obtained over-balances the inconvenience of the compulsion itself I do not understand how, upon utilitarian principles, the compulsion can be bad.[30]

Thus, those who are more knowledgeable than others are entitled and even obliged to coerce the ignorant whenever conditions (1)–(3) above are absent.

To show that coercion is needed in actual social life, Stephen considers the relation between the individual and the community, between personal prudence and common morality, by introducing the third question he thinks an ethical theory should account for:

> [W]hy should we do what is right and avoid what is wrong?[31]

According to him,

> the utilitarian answer . . . the only one which can possibly be given . . . is, I ought to do right, because to do right will conduce to my greatest happiness.[32].

Conceptually this response is unproblematic. But empirically, in our actual world, this prudential interpretation of 'I should' or 'I ought to' at once gives rise to the more important question,

> Why [then] should [a person] do a specific right action when it happens to be opposed to his own interest?[33]

The standard utilitarian answer, that the general happiness of mankind is what should motivate our actions, not our own good, is not good enough to Stephen, because it merely leads to a further question,

> Why should a man consult the general happiness of mankind?[34]

Short of proving without a shadow of doubt that all people do, in fact, try to promote general happiness, there is no way of convincing Stephen that there is any other way except the use of coercion to ensure that people act virtuously, that is, do what is right and avoid what is wrong. In other words, in his theory coercion is a necessary element of social life because it is the only instrument efficient enough to motivate people to advance the good of mankind.

Accordingly, the solution to the difficulties utilitarianism seems to find itself in is as follows. The question 'Why should I?' translates, in prudential terms, into 'What motive do I have?' and the expression 'to consult the general happiness of mankind' translates into 'to do what is right and avoid what is wrong'. The only adequate answer to the question quoted above is, then, 'My motive for doing what is right and avoiding what is wrong is that unless I do so I will be punished by other people, either through legal procedures, or by the use of social and moral sanctions.'

Stephen's line of argument is clear, and it seems equally clear that the applications of his theory contradict Mill's results. Not all forms of self-regarding action which are foolish or immoral would be restricted or prevented by Stephen,[35] but he makes it quite clear that his theory certainly does not recognize 'the one principle' presented by Mill.

THE ULTIMATE JUSTIFICATION:
LIFE AFTER DEATH

There is, however, still one more question that must be put to Stephen to find out whether his theory holds water or not. It is, 'Why should a person choose his model rather than, say, Mill's, if the consequences of the choice happen to be opposed to her own interests?' The only way he can answer this is to state that since the choice is the best possible one for any given individual, the question never really arises. Any other way of responding would contradict his own semantic and psychological premises.

The conclusion Stephen is attempting to draw is that in Western countries at least, legislation is good only if it, at the same time, gives support to the Christian religion, enforces the prevailing morality, and promotes the general good.[36] What needs to be done to prove the case is to show, first, how the three tasks can be accomplished together, and second, and more importantly, how this triple accomplishment will promote the personal interests of any given individual.

There is a smack of conceptual trickery in Stephen's answer to the first of these questions. As already seen in the above, Stephen refuses to define 'good' either in terms of happiness as individual citizens experience it, or in terms of objective values, and refers instead to 'the widest possible extension of the ideal of life formed by the person who sets up the standard'.[37] The person who sets up the legal standard is, obviously, the legislator, and this is what Stephen has to say concerning priorities in his work:

> In a word, the happiness which the lawgiver regards as the test of his law is that which he, after attaching to their wishes whatever weight he thinks proper, wishes his subjects to have, not that which his subjects wish to have. . . .[38]

And in another statement concerning the work of legislators Stephen writes:

> Their object is to get people to accept their view of happiness, not to make people happy in their own way.[39]

Thus, already in defining the 'good' that the laws should promote, Stephen smuggles in his own anti-Millian presuppositions.

If, however, Stephen's definitions are accepted, then it is easy to equate the promotion of general good with the enforcement of prevailing morality on the one hand and with Christian ideals on the other. The prevailing morality in Stephen's day was, no doubt, essentially Christian, and the ideals of the legislators in England were those professed by the Christian religion. In enforcing their own ideals, then, the legislators simply could not help enforcing, at the same time, the prevailing Christian ideas of morality.

The second question, and to Stephen the more important one, is how the enforcement of morality and religion will promote the personal interests of any given individual. It should be kept in mind that Stephen's psychological theory forces him to account for the motivation of each individual. Accordingly, unless individuals can find a prudential justification for obeying moralistic laws which seem to conflict with their own interests, the rational motivation to respect the law is absent and the doctrine of legal moralism collapses. What is needed here is a paternalistic or prudential justification of moralism.

Stephen grounds his defence of the value of legal moralism on the postulate, or presupposition, that human life continues, in one form or another, after our bodies have ceased functioning and are 'dispersed to the elements'.[40] He holds the view, namely, that the character of our morality depends and must depend upon the conception which we may form as to the world in which we live; that upon the supposition of the existence of a God and a future state, one course of conduct will be prudent in the widest sense of the word, and if there is no God and no future state, a different course of conduct will be prudent in the widest sense of the word.[41] To put it more precisely, Stephen thinks that if there is no God, no heaven or hell then it is irrational to act virtuously, that is, to aim at promoting general happiness. In that case every human being has a prudential duty to maximize his or her own happiness, at the expense of other people and of morality, if necessary. On the other hand, if there is a God, and a heaven and a hell, then it could well be prudential to show respect to the moral law by acting virtuously.[42]

An early critic of Stephen's, Frederick Harrison, accused him of professing a 'religion of inhumanity' by 'preaching of hell' and by identifying the idea of a future life with the idea of moral reward and punishment.[43] And, indeed, had Stephen been discussing the standard 'place or state of infinite torture reserved for the wicked after death',[44] the accusation would have been both relevant and conclusive. But he was not:

As I have already said, [he writes,] the common doctrines about heaven and hell do not appear to me to be supported by adequate evidence.[45]

The belief in a 'future state' remains, however, although in an altered form, as he continues:

But the opinion that this present life is not our whole life, and that our personal consciousness in some shape survives death, appears to me highly probable.[46]

He then goes on to confess his ignorance as to the exact character of our lives after death, but continues again in terms of probabilities:

I think, however, that though we have no knowledge on the subject, we have some grounds for rational conjecture. If there is a future state, it is natural to suppose that that which survives death will be that which is most permanent in life, and which is least affected by the changes of life. That is to say, mind, self-consciousness, conscience or our opinion of ourselves, and generally those powers and feelings which, as far as we can judge, are independent of the constantly flowing stream of matter which makes up our bodies.[47]

This non-standard conception of life after death is not as readily open to the criticism presented by Harrison as would be any common doctrine concerning heaven and hell.

Stephen is at no point altogether clear regarding the link between morality and the future state as he understands it. But the general idea seems to be that as our minds somehow keep on living after our bodies have died, we shall spend the rest of eternity by ourselves, thinking about how we behaved during our temporal lives on earth. This is why it pays to be virtuous. As Stephen writes:

The immense importance which men attach to their character, to their honour, to the consciousness of having led an honourable, upright life, is based upon the belief that questions of right and wrong, good and evil, go down to the very man himself and concern him in all that is most intimately, most essentially himself. . . .[48]

Stephen goes on to say:

Would a wise man [accustom himself to practice vices, and to neglect a variety of duties] or not? If he regards himself as a spiritual creature, certainly not, because conscience is that which lies deepest in a man. It is the most important, or one of the most important, constituent elements of his permanence. . . . To tamper with it, therefore, to try to destroy it, is of all conceivable courses of conduct the most dangerous, and may prepare the way to a wakening, a self-assertion, of conscience fearful to think of.[49]

In plain words Stephen is saying that if we behave viciously during our stay here on Earth, we run a considerable risk of being tortured by our own consciences for the rest of our eternal lives. Thus the following conclusion becomes obvious:

Virtue, that is to say, the habit of acting upon principles fitted to promote the happiness of men in general, and especially those forms of happiness which have reference to the permanent element in men, is connected with, and will, in the long run, *contribute to the individual happiness of those who practice it*, and especially to that part of their happiness which is connected with the permanent elements of their nature. The converse is true of vice.[50]

And here we have a theory on which the required prudential and paternalistic justification of legal moralism can be based.

Stephen's theory can be formulated in a little less dramatic manner as follows. Individual human beings are weak, and often fail to act virtuously because of desire for immediate pleasure or fear of immediate pain. But by not acting virtuously they risk condemning themselves to a personal hell after the death of their bodies: their consciousnesses, which survive the bodily death, may start blaming them for their immorality. This is the worst possible fate a person can have, and should be avoided in the name of rationality and prudence.

Now, the only way to make sure that individuals will not be victimized by their natural weaknesses is by regulating immorality as such. In practice, this means attaching an adequate punitive price tag to each non-virtuous course of action which is likely to be chosen for the attainment of immediate pleasure or for the avoidance of immediate pain. A large part of this regulation has traditionally been specified and enforced by non-legal social processes and pressures. But 'the grosser forms of vice' should, according to Stephen, be persecuted by means of criminal law.[51]

In fact, taking into account the whole scheme, Stephen's utilitarian legislators not only have the permission they also have a duty to suppress immorality by law. Unless they do so, they most obviously fail to promote 'the happiness of men in general, and especially those forms of happiness which have reference to the permanent element in men'.[52] Moralistic laws do, in this view, fulfil the double requirement stated to them: they serve the long-term interests of every rational person individually, and they promote the general happiness of all people collectively.

DEFICIENCIES IN STEPHEN'S VIEW

Stephen's paternalism and prudentialism presuppose many elements that can be criticized. One major question mark is the presumption of the existence of a God and a life after death, or a 'future state'. As Stephen, following the tradition of Jeremy Bentham and James Mill, clearly attempts to build a scientific theory of ethics, the non-existent evidence on this point seriously injures the argument he puts forward. If the existence of a God and a future state are beyond empirical or theoretical proof, then what Stephen is trying to say will of necessity be reduced to the following.[53] Either a God and a future state exist or they do not. If they do, then every individual as well as every society as a whole has good grounds for being moral and enforcing morality in others, and the general happiness of humankind will be promoted. If they do not exist, then no individual has any motive to be moral, and unless society coerces its members to act virtuously, chaos and general unhappiness will follow. However, in either case the enforcement of morality brings about better results than its absence.

Unfortunately for Stephen, this twofold version of his argument does not fit in with his other views. Apart from the theological difficulties with regard to the first part of the argument, the second part fails to give individual human beings any sufficient prudential reasons for being moral, thus failing to support Stephen's prudential–paternalistic defence of legal moralism. The premises concerning life after death must be radically altered before the argument can be reconsidered.

There is, in fact, a way of revising Stephen's argument without completely losing its point. If conscience, or personal integrity in moral matters, is important, then why would it be necessary to refer to the time after one's death in order to show that virtue is individually prudential? Why not argue that, regardless of whether there is a future state of torment or not, deliberate immorality always carries with it the seeds of self-condemnation. Vicious conduct is dangerous, because one never knows when one's conscience starts to function, and when it does – today, tomorrow or even on one's deathbed – it creates something very much like the post-mortem personal hell Stephen referred to in his original theory. It is to protect people from this self-inflicted pain that moralistic laws should be introduced and enforced.

One source of criticism against Stephen's view becomes clearly visible when his argument is formulated in the above manner. How can it be proved that morality as dictated by a person's conscience has anything to do with morality in the wide utilitarian sense? Virtues and vices, as we understand them, are usually handed down to us by our parents, our teachers, and a variety of public authorities. Utilitarian virtues and vices, on the other hand, are characterized by Stephen himself as strong dispositions to act so as to promote the general happiness of humankind. The question quite naturally arises whether our teachers and guardians always know what is best for humankind, and how to achieve it. If they do not, then it is more than probable that laws designed to enforce the promotion of general good sometimes punish people for conduct they themselves regard as virtuous, and fail to punish them for conduct which they regard as unforgivably vicious. This, in turn, means that legislators cannot claim to be promoting the personal good of each citizen individually by enforcing utilitarian morality by law – or any one moral code, for that matter.

But let us presume that Stephen could somehow solve this difficulty, for instance, by demanding that every child within a given society should acquire the same moral education. The uniform morality could then be enforced by law, and everybody would once again have prudential grounds for genuinely respecting the existing law.

This is where, on a general level, the far edge of the controversy between Stephen and Mill is reached. The last question to be posed arises from within the utilitarian framework that the two thinkers share, but the answer goes even deeper, to different conceptions concerning human nature and historical progress. The ultimate question is: which one of the solutions for the problems of liberty and morality, that of Stephen or that of Mill, would be more effective in promoting the good of humankind? Should people be educated to have uniform moral codes, and then be legally punished if they fail to live up to its most important imperatives, as Stephen would have it? Or should diversity be respected in moral as well as religious matters, and the law be kept apart from immorality, imprudence and stupidity, whenever these do not cause serious harm to persons other than the agents themselves, as Mill suggested?

The answer to these questions depends largely on what the most reasonable notion of human nature is. If one thinks that the majority of people are weak and stupid and will always be that way, then it is natural that one chooses Stephen's view on legal paternalism, prudentialism and moralism. But if one thinks that people in general are physically and intellectually capable of conducting their lives well, or will be that way if their basic needs are met and they are given the opportunity to develop themselves, then Mill's suggestion will obviously be more attractive.

Another way of putting the question is to ask whether or not it is believed that people in general are competent to make their own decisions, at least in matters which mainly concern themselves, in a way that promotes, in the long run, the good of humankind. Mill's response is, of course, in the affirmative, Stephen's reaction in the negative.

Whichever way the question is put, it seems to me that Stephen's view cannot adequately be defended on a general level. His intention was to put forward a scientific argument for paternalism, prudentialism and moralism, but what he ended up with was a set of questions concerning philosophical anthropology and the philosophy of history. That the argument boils down to these controversial branches of philosophy by no means proves the correctness of Mill's liberal position. What it does prove, however, is that Stephen's line of argument falls short of achieving the objective he had himself set for his effort.

FUTURE REGRET AND HEALTH PROMOTION

Although Stephen's theory runs into difficulties as regards the enforcement of commonly accepted moral ideals, the situation may be different with matters related to health. The argument from future regret is obviously at its most powerful when one considers the possibility of coercing people into assuming healthy lifestyles. From the medical viewpoint, activities such as smoking and drinking are weaknesses which in the long run put those practising them in a high risk bracket with regard to many unpleasant diseases. On the other hand, self-denial and self-sacrifice in these matters as well as in matters related to diet and physical exercise are, medically speaking, virtues which tend to carry with them the reward of good bodily health.

Now, if a person is weak enough not to act according to the scientific advice available to almost anybody in the Western world, he will be likely to have an increased risk of acquiring burdensome diseases which may shorten his life expectancy. And if, subsequently, the person is actually stricken ill, he will most probably have regrets about the unhealthy life he has led, and he may even admit that it would have been in his own best interest if the authorities had coerced him into practising healthier habits. Based on this observation, it can be argued that strong medical paternalism is justifiable because, counterfactually, the recipients of the interventions would have come to regard them as necessary and good, had these not been effected. In a hypothetical sense, then, it would be individually prudential to submit oneself to medical prudentialism and moralism.

One possible problem with this argument in the context of Stephen's work is that it refers to *bodily* health, whereas Stephen's original line of thought was based on conscience, or the *spiritual* element of human life. This is not in any way fatal, however, since the theory in its 'spiritual' form was in the above found to be less than convincing, and a more mundane interpretation was substituted for it. Besides, it was Stephen's own idea that the aim of legislation and social policy is 'not the greatest happiness altogether, but the widest possible extension of the ideal of life formed by the person who sets up the standard'.[54] And as the person setting up the standard today is more often a physician than a priest, physical fitness will most probably be preferred to high morals in defining the goals of societal control.

But what is it exactly that can be said to follow from the fact that when people fall ill they may come to regret their previous unhealthy lifestyles? The argument from future regret can be interpreted in two ways, neither of which actually supports the legitimacy of strong paternalism in medical matters.

According to the first interpretation, it is truly and concretely the expected regret that is supposed to justify the medical interventions into people's personal affairs. Regret works as an indication to the effect that it is genuinely bad for individuals to be let alone to practise unhealthy habits if these habits lead to illness and premature death. This, of course, may be true as far as it goes, but the problem is that it does not go far enough. Not everybody with unhealthy habits falls ill, and thus the argument does not apply to all those failing to exercise moderation. Furthermore, illness is not the *only* evil in people's lives, and it is far from clear what its weight in an individual's personal considerations is or should be. Unhealthy practices may be necessary for one's livelihood, they can be socially useful, or they may give meaning to one's life. Consequently, even those who do fall ill and regret it feel bitterness against the unfairness of the world rather than any genuine remorse due to their own doings. Regret in itself, then, does not justify strong paternalism.

The second interpretation of the argument is more interesting, but it cannot be formulated adequately in the context of Stephen's theory. The hypothetical regret that people are supposed to feel if they are not medically coerced, can perhaps be translated into a *hypothetical consent* which people give to the authorities – or would give, if they only understood their situation as they may come to understand it in the future. The regret would in this case show that it is not against an individual's own will that she be forced to lead a healthy life. Since Stephen did not hold respect for people's own wishes valuable, this point is not important for his defence of paternalism. But I shall return to the question of hypothetical or future consent in the chapter dealing with prudentialistic arguments for strong paternalism below.

5

MORALS AND SOCIETY

The utilitarian argument for strong paternalism, in the form presented by J.F. Stephen above, is an argument in favour of very strong and extensive paternalism indeed. In matters related to health it would enable the authorities legitimately to coerce people into giving up habits that are usually regarded as mere trivial *weaknesses*, such as eating unhealthy food, smoking and drinking moderately. By saying that these practices are 'mere weaknesses' I mean that they are neither positively virtuous nor positively vicious – at the most, they reflect failures to live up to certain rather high behavioural standards. It is not ordinarily considered immoral or seriously wrong to eat too much fat and salt, or to smoke a cigar every once and a while, or to drink an occasional glass of wine. Nevertheless, if these habits have even the slightest tendency to adversely affect people's health, they are in principle at least legitimate objects of control within Stephen's model.

Another approach to justifying control over primarily self-regarding behaviour is to refer directly to morality, and focus on activities which are, according to some commonsense ethical system, clearly wrong. Tendencies towards drug abuse, unlawful sex, excessive drinking and taking one's own life, for instance, are not always seen as mere weaknesses but as genuine *vices* or *sins* – which often draw upon those practising them the moral condemnation of their fellow human beings. Attitudes towards alcoholism and drug-related problems provoke medical moralism on all levels of societal control, and even universal prohibitions have sometimes been considered a solution. Similarly, sexual codes and taboos influence both general legislation and everyday medical practice: contraception, sex education, abortion, artificial reproduction, venereal diseases and deviations from the monogamous heterosexual intramarital sex ideal persist as problems for many physicians as well as for many political decision-makers. And in the voluntary euthanasia debate, the perennial moral problems of suicide have entered the medical field.

In the present chapter I shall deal with the nature and grounds of legal *moralism*, as introduced by another critic of the Millian principles, Patrick Devlin. Devlin became famous towards the end of the 1950s, when he furiously attacked the liberal *Report of the Committee on Homosexual Offences and Prostitution*, also known as the Wolfenden Committee Report. The attack was shortly afterwards followed by a critique of its moralistic credos by H.L.A. Hart, and the discussion was later on continued by Ronald Dworkin, among others. The presentation of Devlin's views will be followed by the comments of Richard Wollheim, Hart and Dworkin.

After outlining the Hart–Devlin debate and its repercussions, I shall go on to introduce two recently evoked, independent lines of argument which, if successful, may abolish or weaken the Millian liberal position. The first is Simon Lee's indirect defence of moralism, and the second is Joel Feinberg's idea concerning participation as a necessary condition of preserving society.

THE WOLFENDEN REPORT AND DEVLIN'S POSITION

The Wolfenden Committee was appointed in 1954 to consider the state of the English laws concerning prostitution and homosexuality, and its report, with recommendations to change the regulations in both cases, was published three years later.[1] The practical conclusions of the report were, first, that homosexual practices between consenting adults should be decriminalized, and, second, that prostitution, even though it should not be criminalized as such, should be driven off the streets where it causes offence and nuisance to people who are neither buying nor selling the service. New legislation concerning prostitution was indeed introduced in England in 1959, but it took ten years before the Committee's recommendations concerning homosexuality were even partially adopted in the law.[2]

However, the ethos of the report is far more important for my present purposes than the fate of the Committee's recommendations. Private morality and the law were the two matters whose mutual relationship the Committee found of decisive interest for the inquiry. The authors of the report strongly emphasized the 'importance which society and the law ought to give to individual freedom of choice and action in matters of private morality'.[3] They continued:

> Unless a deliberate attempt is to be made by society, acting through the agency of the law, to equate the sphere of crime with that of sin, there must remain a realm of private morality and immorality which is, in brief and crude terms, not the law's business.[4]

And since the Committee obviously did not regard the equation of crime and sin as a rational or advisable solution, they concluded, in a Millian spirit, that privacy should be respected even if that meant nurturing immorality.

To be sure, the authors of the report were aware of the fact that immorality (as they understood it and as they seemed to think a majority of people understood it) in public places can be harmful or at least offensive. But, as a matter of principle, they distinguished between the two different spheres of immoral conduct by stating that in the field of their inquiry

> the function of the criminal law ... is to preserve public order and decency, to protect the citizen from what is offensive or injurious, and to provide sufficient safeguards against exploitation and corruption of others, particularly those who are specially vulnerable because they are young, weak in body or mind, inexperienced, or in a state of special physical, official or economic dependence.[5]

Thus public immorality, such as soliciting – as opposed to other aspects of prostitution – can be legally regulated while 'private immorality should not be the concern of the criminal law except in the special circumstances ... mentioned [above]'.[6] Or, in more general terms, it is not, according to the members of the Committee,

> the function of the law to intervene in the private lives of citizens, or to seek to enforce any particular pattern of behaviour, further than is necessary to carry out the purposes we have outlined.[7]

To summarize once more: the members of the Wolfenden Committee agreed that private immorality, or immorality as such, without offence or injury to others, should not be regulated by the criminal law.

Devlin first gave his counterargument to the report in the Maccabean lecture on jurisprudence entitled 'The enforcement of morals', presented to the British Academy in 1959.[8] The argument, according to his own statement, is motivated by his feeling as a judge who has to pass sentences in a criminal court that crime should be somehow connected with sin, that is, with 'transgression against divine law or the principles of morality'.[9] He states:

> I should feel handicapped in my task if I thought that I was addressing an audience which had no sense of sin or which thought of crime as something quite different.[10]

He goes on to record the fact that English criminal law as it exists parallels his own thoughts by quite obviously recognizing at least some basic moral principles. As examples he presents the laws forbidding voluntary euthanasia, suicide, attempted suicide, suicide pacts and duelling.[11] If criminal legislation were solely aimed at the protection of individuals, or some similar amoral goal, Devlin concedes, then these laws would not exist. The only way to justify them is by reference to a moral principle, in this particular case the principle of the sanctity of human life.[12]

But how to justify the prevailing legal enforcement of moral rules? Devlin considers two alternatives, the first of which he finds presently unacceptable, the second acceptable.

The first possibility is to state that since morals and religion are 'inextricably joined' – since no moral code 'can claim any validity except by virtue of the religion on which it is based' – it is only logical that a state which values its own religion should enforce the morality that goes with it. Thus a Western state could understandably protect its Christian religion by making it a crime to transgress against any important rules of Christian morality. But the factual problem here is that many Western states, England among others, have ceased to enforce Christian beliefs, showing a lack of appreciation towards the religious basis of their cultures and societies. These states do not, according to Devlin, possess the right to enforce Christian morals any more.[13]

The second argument for legal moralism seems to Devlin to be more prominent. It is based on the premise that a society can exist only if there is a public morality within it – morality being a part of the very structure of the society. Because of this tight connection it is impossible to offend public morality without hurting, at the same time, the society.[14] The enforcement of morals, accordingly, is a necessary means of protecting the fabric of society, and should be recognized as such.

Devlin takes the institution of marriage as his example:

> Whether a man should be allowed to take more than one wife is something about which every society has to make up its mind one way or the other. In England we believe in the Christian idea of marriage and therefore adopt monogamy as a moral principle. Consequently the Christian institution of marriage has become the basis of family life and so part of the structure of our society. It is there not because it is Christian. It has got there because it is Christian, but it remains there *because it is built into the house in which we live and could not be removed without bringing it down.* . . . It would be useless for [a non-Christian] to stage a debate designed to prove that polygamy was theologically more correct and socially preferable; if he wants to live in the house, he must accept it as built in the way in which it is.[15]

This way of thinking presents Devlin with an argument to refute the conclusions of the Wolfenden Report: homosexual practices and prostitution should be condemned and prohibited by criminal law, because they threaten the Christian idea of marriage, which, in its turn, is one of the basic elements of social life in Western countries.[16] By challenging the prevailing ideals of sexual morality, homosexuals and prostitutes not only call forth the 'intolerance, indignation, and disgust'[17] of 'every right-minded person', or 'the man in the jury box', or 'the man in the Clapham omnibus'; they also present a threat to the existence of the prevailing mode of society.[18]

The applicability of Devlin's observations concerning law and morality is not restricted to the original target cases, namely prostitution and homosexuality. In the mid-1980s, for example, there was a medico-legal debate in England about whether or not physicians should be allowed to give contraceptive advice and treatment to children under the age of sixteen without parental consent.[19] This debate was started by Victoria Gillick, a Roman Catholic mother of ten, who took the Department of Health and Social Security to court for one of their memorandums which stated that in 'exceptional cases' consultations without parental consent can be necessary and acceptable. Gillick argued that the licence given by the circular was *immoral*, and demanded *legal* guarantees to the effect that her own daughters would not be given either advice or treatment without her consent.[20] She first lost the case, then won in the Court of Appeal and ultimately lost 3–2 in the House of Lords. However, it is not the result of the legal battle so much as the ideas behind it that interest me here. The important thing is that the Gillick type of argument for legal moralism in medical matters is not intelligible without the mediating premise stating that common morality should dictate what can and what cannot be permitted by law: if something is strongly against the moral convictions of a Roman Catholic mother, it should be forbidden by law. Devlin's argument, if valid, would aptly fill the gap in Gillick's inference.

DEVLIN'S CRITICS: WOLLHEIM, HART, DWORKIN

There are several points on which Devlin's view can be criticized. Richard Wollheim was one of the first to point out the flaws in the argument in his review of 'The enforcement of morals', entitled 'Crime, sin, and Mr. Justice Devlin'.[21] Wollheim argues, first, that Devlin's conception of the moral nature of society is incompatible with the ideals of Western liberalism.[22] According to Devlin's theory, Wollheim says, 'the identity, and the continuity, of a society resides . . . in the common possession of a single morality', whereas according to liberalism it 'resides . . . in the mutual toleration of different moralities'.[23] And since 'toleration cannot be seen as a morality conformity to which issues in uniform behaviour', it is clear to Wollheim that 'those who find Liberalism . . . acceptable must reject the conception of society on which the whole of Devlin's argument depends'.[24]

Another argument Wollheim presents against Devlin's view is that the model of morality it implies is most peculiar. On the one hand, Devlin seems to say that moral judgements depend entirely on the subjective feelings of 'the man in the street' or 'the man in the Clapham omnibus', on the other hand, he seems to be claiming a wide objective validity for these judgements. That extreme objectivism and extreme subjectivism 'share in the desire to place morality outside the forum of discussion, to make its distinctions not the fit subject for reasoning and its verdicts something that cannot be overturned in argument'[25] is for Wollheim an additional reason to refute Devlin's considerations.

Wollheim's third and final criticism is directed to the inference in Devlin's view that from society's right to self-preservation it follows that society has the right to enforce moral judgements by law. For one thing, he questions Devlin's way of equating society's justifiable self-preservation with absolute, unqualified resistance to any sort of change. 'If we argue with Devlin', Wollheim says, 'we must concede that . . . the moral right of society to suppress those who would "subvert" it enjoys the same standing' regardless of whether we are talking about 'a democratic society . . . threatened by storm-troopers' or about 'a cannibal society . . . threatened by missionaries'.[26] A society, according to Wollheim's own view, only enjoys the right to protect itself as far as fighting against destruction and decay, corruption and amelioration are concerned. If this is a superior interpretation, then Devlin is obviously wrong in presuming that every society is justified in protecting its own morality or moral identity, whatever its nature and character.

Wollheim goes on to state that even if Devlin were right in his interpretation, his argument would still not justify the conclusion that legal enforcement of morals is within the rights of a self-preserving society. A society might be justified in preserving its morality, Wollheim admits, but this does not necessarily imply introducing legislation to enforce it. As a matter of fact, Wollheim considers it to be 'arguable that a morality, if enforced, ceases to be respected, and once it loses respect its existence is in danger'.[27] He presents the poor correlation between Prohibition and the virtue of temperance as an example of this danger, and concludes that, in sum, Devlin has failed to show that crime and sin should or even could be linked together for the true conservation of society.

Unfortunately for the cause of anti-moralism, however, Wollheim's counterarguments are less than conclusive. First, it may be perfectly true that 'those who find Liberalism acceptable' must reject Devlin's theories, but this is in no way a universal refutation of what Devlin states. Why should he be a liberal? Why should anybody who favours legal moralism be a liberal? Second, that valid moral judgements are to be attained from what the man in the street says, without further qualifications or discussion, might seem rather unsophisticated to a moral philosopher, but why should we seek to please moral philosophers? Is it impossible for a theory to be valid without being accepted by academic lovers of wisdom? And, third, why should we adopt such ethno-centric views about the moral goodness of society as Wollheim presents? If a democratic society has the right to protect itself against storm-troopers, why should we deny the cannibals the right to protect their culture and society against Christian missionaries?

In his final point Wollheim is partly right and partly wrong. Preserving a morality does not, of course, necessarily imply enforcing it by the law. But this is not in fact Devlin's claim. From 'The enforcement of morals' as well as from a footnote added to its later edition[28] it can be seen that Devlin does not imply that *every* moral rule should be transformed into law. To refute the premises of the Wolfenden Report or to discredit the Millian position in general he does not need such results. He only needs to show that from valid principles of legislative work – and with these he includes the principle of society's self-protection – it can be inferred that it is *sometimes* the law's business to enforce common morality without any further reasons.

But even if this is what Devlin attempts to state, his position is untenable. On the one hand, a practical counterargument emerges, hinted at in Wollheim's second point above, and developed more fully by H.L.A. Hart in his review 'Immorality and treason'[29] and by Ronald Dworkin in an essay called 'Liberty and moralism'.[30] And on the other hand, if the practical challenge is to be overcome, Devlin finds himself defending a view which no longer contradicts the positions held by Mill and the Wolfenden Committee.

The allegation made by Devlin to the effect that it is sometimes the law's business to enforce morality as such raises the question of the proper limits of such legislation. Under exactly which conditions is society allowed to employ its right to protect its popular morality? Mill's answer to this question refers to the harm-inflicted-on-others principle, and if Devlin wishes to be able to replace the Millian view, he must himself have a superior response available.

It is quite possible to read Devlin's line of argument in the following way, as Hart and Dworkin in fact do.[31] First, it is not advisable that society should prohibit all practices that are considered immoral and disliked by the majority. Practices that meet these criteria may still 'not lie beyond the limits of tolerance', which is a strong reason for not regulating them in law. But second, if a certain practice evokes, in the reasonable man (or 'the man in the Clapham omnibus'), 'a real feeling of reprobation' or of 'intolerance, indignation, and disgust', then it is more than probable 'that the bounds of toleration are being reached'. In these cases society is justified in regulating even private immorality as such.[32]

102

On this interpretation, Devlin's view is, of course, rather shaky, both practically and theoretically. Hart points out the practical risks of the view by the following remark concerning its evident democratic appeal:

> [I]t is fatally easy to confuse the democratic principle that power should be in the hands of the majority with the utterly different claim that the majority with power in their hands need respect no limits. Certainly there is a special risk in a democracy that the majority may dictate how all should live. . . . But loyalty to democratic principles does not require us to maximize this risk: yet this is what we shall do if we mount the man in the street on the top of the Clapham omnibus and tell him that if only he feels sick enough about what other people do in private to demand its suppression by law no theoretical criticism can be made of his demand.[33]

Dworkin, in turn, draws attention to a serious theoretical deficiency in the interpretation by noting how Devlin,

> without offering evidence that homosexuality presents any danger at all to society's existence, . . . concludes that if our society hates homosexuality enough it is justified in outlawing it, . . . because of the danger the practice presents to society's existence.[34]

If this is what Devlin really attempts to put forward, then he is obviously faced with a dilemma. One possibility is that there is no evidence to back up the claim that homosexual practices threaten society: in that case his position remains unsupported. The other possibility is that the mere hate and disgust of the majority show that society is endangered by the object of hatred or otherwise in a state that entitles it to suppress what it hates: in this case the problem of democratic tyranny presented by Hart arises.

But at this point another interpretation of Devlin's argument, presented by Hart in his *Law, Liberty, and Morality*, begins to acquire shape. Perhaps Devlin is not holding the extreme thesis described above, after all, but rather a more moderate one, according to which there must indeed be an observable threat to society in addition to the disgust and hate before given practices may be legally prohibited.[35] What Devlin actually says in the 'Enforcement of morals' readily allows this interpretation. About the unfavourable feelings of society and their relation to legislative reflections he writes:

> I do not think that one can ignore disgust if it is deeply felt and not manufactured. Its presence is a good *indication* that the bounds of toleration are being reached. . . . But before a society can put a practice beyond the limits of tolerance there must be a *deliberate judgement* that the practice is *injurious to society*.[36]

After noting that some practices are less injurious than others, and require more limited constraints, he goes on to state:

> It becomes then a question of balance, the danger of society in one scale and the extent of the restriction in the other. On this sort of point the value of an investigation by such a body as the Wolfenden Committee and of its conclusions is manifest.[37]

The point of the moderate thesis is, then, that practices which evoke strong unfavourable feelings in a given society should be thoroughly investigated to find out whether or not they are injurious enough to have to be regulated by law.

Since Devlin insists upon discussing morality 'as such', it can safely be presumed that by injuries to society he does not mean harm inflicted on individuals directly. But as Hart notes, it is also possible to cause harm to individuals indirectly, by attacking the basic moral principles prevailing in society, and thereby weakening it.[38] If protecting society by law against such attacks is what Devlin means by the enforcement of morality, then the criticisms directed towards the extreme thesis are irrelevant to the present issue.

However, the moderate interpretation is, by its own merits, just as problematic as the extreme one. If Devlin's claim is that morality as such should be enforced because immorality as such causes harm to society, he is stating a contradiction in terms. The expression 'as such' is, after all, supposed to mean that morality and immorality are seen independently of their consequences in terms of harm. On the other hand, if the claim is that morality (no qualification) should be enforced in certain situations because immorality in these situations causes harm to society, then Devlin finds himself holding what is, essentially, the original Millian position.

If this is the case, then one must conclude that Devlin did not succeed in his attempt to replace the general principle underlying the report of the Wolfenden Committee, the harm principle. Thus he also failed to justify legal moralism.

LIBERALISM – A FORM OF MORALISM?

A recent critic of the Millian principles, Simon Lee, has in his book *Law and Morals* focused his attention on the fact that liberalism itself can be regarded as a morality among other moralities.[39] After explaining how every society according to Hart[40] needs laws against violence, theft and deception, Lee in his book goes on to state that even these supposedly amoral evils in fact presuppose a definite moral stand for or against certain social institutions. He writes:

> If we are both selfish and yet social animals, if we want to survive and if we live amidst only limited resources then we must band together under the protection of rules against murder and other violence and against theft. But just because we all agree on these values it should not be thought that they are somehow morally neutral, or amoral. A law on theft presupposes a system of property, for example, but the capitalist value of private property might be considered immoral by those who see the force of Proudhon's aphorism that 'all property is theft'.[41]

By relying on the amorality of some basic collection of values, then, legislators are, according to Lee's interpretation, in fact enforcing the morality reflected by those values.

With these premises, it is easy to argue that liberalism, instead of being a genuinely anti-moralistic doctrine, is behind its mask just another form of moralism. As Lee puts it:

> The essential point to remember about liberal attitudes to law reform is that liberals, like everyone else, want the law to enforce morality – *their* morality of liberalism. To say that the law should not condemn homosexuality, for example, is perhaps to say that the law should respect citizens' autonomy over their own sexuality. But autonomy is a moral value just as much as the belief that homosexuality is unnatural is a moral value. Of course it is a more attractive value to liberals, otherwise they would not count as liberals, but there is no cause to regard liberalism as necessarily a superior creed solely because it is sometimes represented as being morally neutral. It is not neutral. It is partisan, affirming the value of freedom or of autonomy or liberty. That is one vision of morality and one which many of us find attractive, but it needs to be judged on its merits.[42]

This, in essence, is Lee's argument against accepting without further argument the Millian position.

Lee is quite right in claiming that liberalism is a moral doctrine much in the same way as Catholicism and Islamic fundamentalism are. But there is also a marked difference between these doctrines: belief in the value of liberty or autonomy is the only *public* morality which explicitly rejects the possibility of forcing its way into the citizens' *private* lives by legal sanctions. In an Islamic state, the citizens are free to act according to the religious regulations of the country; they are not, however, at liberty to omit acting according to them. Likewise, in a Catholic country citizens are largely – if not completely – in the same position: they are both allowed and obliged to be Catholics. But in a Liberal state the situation is different: for as long as the citizens abstain from harming each other, they may in their private lives be Islamic, Catholic, Liberal or whatever they wish to be.[43] Liberalism only aims at regulating public, or other-regarding activities, whereas all other moralities, or ideologies, seek to control the field of private, or self-regarding behaviour, too.

What surprises me in Lee's deduction is the emphasis he puts on the alleged moral neutrality of liberalism. From the fact that we all agree on certain values it should not be inferred that these values lack moral content: this much in what Lee states is true. But what can be inferred is that if indeed there are values agreed on by *everybody*, then those values are not morally problematic. This, in turn, means that they form the basis of legitimately regulating human action. Lee seems to believe that this conclusion can only be accepted by anti-liberals, not by liberals who according to his theory stand or fall with the neutrality of their fundamental values.

At this point the question arises as to which values are fundamental, and agreed on by everybody. Lee himself mentions attitudes towards homosexuality: some think it is unnatural to engage oneself in homosexual practices, others think it is not. Obviously, the belief that homosexuality is unnatural is not one of the values everybody would accept. But Lee hastens to add that the same applies to the adverse belief, according to which homosexuality is *not* unnatural, and moves on to conclude that a liberal non-interventionistic policy on this issue is just as moralistic as absolute legal prohibition of homosexual relationships would be.

What Lee fails to see is that the (Catholic) belief that homosexuality is unnatural is not confronted by proponents of liberalism with a statement to the contrary, but with a more general claim defending autonomy, that is, everybody's right to decide for him or herself what the best choice concerning one's own sexual behaviour would be. And what Catholics often fail to see is that autonomy is a fundamental value on which they, like their opponents, have to base their particular moral position. Unless autonomy prevails, Catholicism could very well be legally prohibited alongside of homosexuality.

Ultimately, the morality that should be compared with liberalism is not Catholicism, Islam or any particular ethical or religious doctrine, but the general morality of totalitarianism, that is, the absolute submission of individual interests and liberties to the authority of the Church, the State, or the Party. I do not suppose that anybody would voluntarily choose totalitarianism rather than liberalism, if the particular content of the totalitarian policy were different from one's own preferred ideology. But the problem is that with regard to their own ideologies people tend to think differently.

This is where liberalism shows its strength. Although there may be few persons who would consider the creed of autonomy to be the *best* policy, it is more than probable that the vast majority would agree that it is the *second best* alternative, preferable to the supremacy of any other ideology except one's own. Unless one particular ideology reigns in the minds of a people, then the nation would be wise to choose liberalism. And this is the situation at least in most Western countries.

The last resort of the anti-liberal is to remind people that legal moralism does not necessarily imply that everything which does not fit into the ideals of legislators would be automatically regulated by the law. But the fact remains that *some* solely self-regarding activities will be prohibited in each anti-liberal system – otherwise such systems would not count as anti-liberal. Thus, for as long as individual citizens do not know the exact scope of the moralistic legislation, they will have to live with the possibility that what will eventually be prohibited will be just the one thing they would have liked to do.

On the other hand, even if the particular individuals in question know that the system will one day be their own, and nothing that they consider important will be banned, the points made above concerning absolute totalitarianism would hold. Liberalism is still the all-round winner on account of its being the second best option for everybody. In the pluralistic societies found today in the West this means that the only way to challenge anti-moralism would be to reject the principle of democracy, which holds that people's opinions count in the choice of a legislative and political system. But I shall take the acceptance of this principle for granted.

'GARRISON THRESHOLDS' AND THE PRESERVATION OF SOCIETY

It seems to be very difficult to justify moralism and strong paternalism: every attempt to defend them appears to contain serious flaws, and the liberal position remains practically untouched. But there is still one possible way to defend the legal regulation of actions which are usually considered self-regarding, or private. This possibility has recently been introduced, though presumably not intentionally, by Joel Feinberg, and it was immediately pointed out and heavily criticized by Jonathan Schonsheck.

Feinberg in his book *Harm to Self* draws attention to the fact that legislation often has a double justification.[44] It is designed both to prevent harm which individuals might inflict on themselves, and to protect the public interests of society:

> Indeed, the public interest is always involved, at least to some small extent, when persons harm themselves. Society is deprived of the services of the injured party, and must also bear the more direct social costs of cleaning up, rescuing, retrieving, or repairing. If fifty thousand persons kill themselves every year by their own choice or through reckless disregard of their own safety, then millions of dollars of tax money are not paid to the treasury, millions of dollars are paid out in social security and death benefits, millions more are spent on police teams, ambulances, and hospitals. Even the sanitation workers who sweep the debris and wash the blood off the roads are paid from public funds. Self-caused deaths and injuries, in the aggregate, are a considerable public inconvenience, at the very least.[45]

Feinberg goes on to note that in Western societies such as the Victorian England of Mill's time – and presumably in present-day Western societies – a distinction can be made between other-regarding and at least primarily self-regarding behaviour. The distinction seems to be that behaviour is self-regarding if either the harm inflicted on others is indirect and unpredictable, or the harm predictably or even necessarily inflicted on others is 'altogether too trivial to justify, by itself, imposing burdensome constraints'.[46] Suicide in modern Western societies, for instance, is included by Feinberg in the realm of self-regarding activities, and is thereby excluded from the field of behaviour which can morally be regulated by criminal law because it involves harm inflicted on others.

But then Feinberg goes on to state something which is, from the liberal point of view, potentially alarming:

> One can imagine societies, however, in which our presupposition [concerning the division into self-regarding and other-regarding behaviour] would not hold. To take a simple example, imagine a beleaguered garrison of settlers under attack from warlike Indians. Everyone is working furiously to repel the assault. The men are all firing at the mounted marauders while the women load the muskets, and children pour water on fires started by flaming arrows.[47]

This miniature society, according to Feinberg, would be one in which the Millian division could not be made. To elucidate the point he continues the story as follows:

> At the peak of the excitement, John Wayne becomes so bored and depressed, that he withdraws with the announced intention of killing himself. 'After all,' he says, 'my life is my own and what I do with it is my own business'.[48]

But despite his previous classification of suicide in Western societies as each person's personal matter, Feinberg disagrees with the hero at this point, stating:

> Of course, he could not be more wrong. What he [John Wayne] does is *everybody* else's business since the issue is so close that the withdrawal of one party threatens to tip the balance. There is no distinction in these circumstances between self-regarding and other-regarding, or between not helping and positively harming. Anyone who does not help inflicts serious harm on all the others. Insofar as any larger, more complex, society resembles the garrison situation, the debate over legal paternalism is otiose.[49]

It is the last sentence, concerning the application of the garrison morality to normal societal life, that worries Schonsheck, who sees it as a threat to the liberal position Feinberg and Schonsheck are professing.

It should be noted, in passing, that in Feinberg's description the fact that John Wayne is contemplating suicide is, in the last analysis, quite irrelevant. After all, it could not matter less to the rest of the settlers what John Wayne does or does not do once he has left his post: it is the (apparently self-regarding) *withdrawal* that makes the difference to their position, not the (similarly self-regarding) suicide. Fortunately, even Feinberg himself does not, in what follows, build his case on the intended suicide.

Feinberg gives only one real-life example of how society can drift closer to a 'garrison threshold', as he calls the state in which the Millian division of activities does not hold any more:

> One way in which a society can approach the garrison model is through a steady accumulation of individual with-drawals, though each may seem in its own terms primarily self-regarding. A nonproductive life devoted entirely to lotus-eating, opium smoking, or heroin shooting, in which all one's waking moments are spent cultivating or enjoying dreamy euphoric states, may be 'no one else's business' when one, or a hundred, or ten thousand self-supporting persons do it of their own free choice. But when ten percent of the whole population choose to live that way, they become parasitical, and the situation approaches the threshold of serious public harm. When fifty percent choose to live that way it may become impossible for the remainder to maintain any society at all. The closer any society is to what we might call 'the garrison threshold,' the more the harm principle comes into play, until at a given point, any further withdrawals pose a clear and present danger, and can be emphatically prohibited by the harm principle without any help from the principle of legal paternalism.[50]

If all the remarks made by Feinberg are valid, then it seems that self-regarding – or, to be more precise, apparently self-regarding – behaviour cannot always be considered immune to legal regulation, as Mill would have had it. Even if legal paternalism and moralism are rejected, the possibility of public authorities quite legitimately controlling our private affairs remains.

The application of Feinberg's model to matters related to medicine and health care is obvious. If people assume indifferent attitudes toward their own health, their behaviour is initially self-regarding, and therefore outside the scope of legitimate regulation. When, however, the effects of unhealthy lifestyles start to accumulate, they may easily lead the society to a threshold situation. If a lot of people must give up working due to illnesses, society may well collapse as a result of these withdrawals from productive life. And what is more, the problem is further intensified by the issue of allocating scarce medical resources. Suppose, for instance, that a given nation could cure all the diseases and run substantive health care and social security programs, if only people with 'self-inflicted' diseases such as cirrhosis, lung cancer and venereal diseases would keep away and not burden the health care system. With regard to providing health care for all those who need and 'deserve' it, the society could under these circumstances be seen as being in a threshold situation, and if Feinberg is correct, the authorities should perhaps see to it, in one way or another, that smokers, alcoholics and the sexually active are not given any chance to ruin the fabric of society.

However, Jonathan Schonsheck has neatly summed up some of the difficulties one must face in applying the morality of the garrison situation to legislation in more peaceful times.[51] There are three aspects in Feinberg's example which render it unsuitable for comparisons with normal societal life.

First, much of the plausibility of the example derives from the fact that, in the garrison, efforts made by every individual for the common good are temporary, related to an emergency which will last only for a relatively short time. Laws, on the other hand, are a permanent part of societal life, and evoking them probably implies that the threat facing society is also permanent. But even if it sounds plausible that John Wayne should defend us to the best of his abilities against an attack which will presumably be over in a few hours, it does not sound equally plausible that he should spend the rest of his life trying to rescue us. And as Schonsheck notes, it does not sound in any way reasonable that legislators could place children under an obligation to put out fires until they are old enough to join the adult effort of firing and loading guns.

Second, what makes John Wayne's withdrawal in the garrison situation 'everybody else's business' is that he is a member of such a small community that everyone's contribution is essential to the achievement of the common goal. This is not true with regard to an ordinary citizen in an ordinary society. If one Englishman, American or Chinese withdraws from society, this will not cause public harm intensive enough to drive society towards chaos and confusion.

Third, the common goal of the efforts of the garrison community is clear, and so is the nature of a harmful withdrawal in that context. The success of the military defence in Feinberg's example requires that nobody ceases firing or loading the muskets, or putting out fires until the victory is won. In ordinary circumstances it is more difficult to see what will constitute a withdrawal in the proper sense. It is obvious that our common goals include survival and welfare, and that non-productiveness as described by Feinberg with reference to lotus-eating, opium smoking, and heroin shooting does in principle constitute a withdrawal which is a potential threat to society. But the problem is, as Schonsheck points out, that the activities Feinberg explicitly mentions are not in themselves instances of withdrawing from society. Opium smoking during one's holidays, for instance, need not in any way decrease one's efficiency while working. It seems that withdrawals in general cannot be connected to other classes of acts tightly enough to justify the legal regulation of withdrawing from society in any way.

Schonsheck's conclusion is that it is as difficult to prove that society has reached the garrison threshold as it would be to defend effectively legal moralism and legal paternalism. Thus, for the anti-liberal, the garrison model does not offer a shortcut to justifying the legal regulation of self-regarding behaviour. And, as far as modern Western societies are concerned, Feinberg seems to accept this result.

Granted that the garrison model cannot be used to back up criminal laws in our present societies under ordinary circumstances, the question remains whether or not there could be situations or trends of development which would force us to reconsider the matter. Perhaps the example stated by Feinberg is not an entirely happy one with its implicitly moralistic references to the use of opium and heroin. But suppose, for instance, that a country is at war: if one is to accept the original garrison model, there seems to be no reason not to criminalize withdrawals in the form of conscientious objection. Or, again, suppose that just when the hurricane of the century is about to hit the capital of the country, all the firemen suddenly decide to strike: unless the salaries of the firemen are well below a decent level of subsistence, would it not appear natural to hold them legally liable for the damage they could reasonably have prevented?

'Garrison laws' should not, of course, be enforced unless they fulfil two conditions stated by Schonsheck.[52] The first one is that the laws must be predictable and effective, that is, they must prevent just exactly what they are designed to prevent – the sudden decay of society or some specific part of it. The second condition is that the hardships inflicted by the legislation should be equally distributed among the population. In addition, Schonsheck's three earlier remarks must be taken into account: the threat must be identifiable and temporary, and if the whole of society is not mobilized to fight against it, there should at least be a specific group of people who clearly carry the responsibility.

By these remarks I am not saying that the garrison threshold model would make things any easier for the legal paternalist and the legal moralist. I agree with Schonsheck in that specific justifiable 'garrison laws' will be very difficult to establish. But the theoretical validity of Feinberg's view also has to be recognized. In principle, there may be situations in which apparently self-regarding actions turn out to be other-regarding and, potentially, legitimate targets for legal restrictions. The important point here is, as Feinberg notes,[53] that the regulation even in these cases can be justified by employing the harm principle, that is, by referring to harm inflicted on other human beings, instead of having to admit that protecting the agent's own good, or morality as such, could ever justify criminal legislation.

It is no doubt possible to find situations where the health care system is at the garrison threshold stage, and the medical authorities see semi-moralistic restrictions as a solution. It is, however, seldom the case that either the results of regulation are clearly predictable, or the burdens equitably distributed. Consider the experiments of Prohibition in the 1920s and 1930s in countries such as the United States and Finland. Obviously, there were alcohol-related social and medical problems before the enforcement of the legislation, especially among the working classes. Equally obviously, it may have been the primary purpose of the Prohibitions to abolish these problems. But the laws soon proved to be intolerably repressive, and their enforcement increasingly difficult. People kept on drinking, and, in addition to the initial problems, authorities soon had on their hands the problems of indifference towards law in general, organized crime, and poisonings due to illegally

– and unprofessionally – produced liquor. And to top it all, the rich were not much influenced by the laws, whereas the poor had to carry the main burden. Thus, in particular cases it may be that the applicability of Feinberg's model is, after all, limited.

6

APPEALS TO RATIONALITY: THE VARIETIES OF PRUDENTIALISM

The 'weaknesses' and 'vices' that human beings possess are sometimes looked upon neither with benevolent pity nor moral condemnation, but with intellectual suspicion or contempt. This kind of attitude, based on the belief that the object of observation does not behave in a rational or prudent manner, has already been coined in the above as *prudentialistic*. Caring control over individuals on the grounds that they are irrational can in principle be extended to anybody, but in medicine and health care at least it is perhaps more often applied to the young and the old than to the middle-aged, to women rather than men and to political dissenters rather than those who keep to the political mainstream. Even the extreme form of prudentialism, the hospitalization of radicals, has been prevalent in most corners of the world since the invention of modern psychiatry. Less far-reaching but equally dramatic appeals to (ir)rationality are made daily in courtrooms, hospitals and clinics when individuals are put under the protective custody of others, or denied voluntarily induced euthanasia or, as in one of the examples stated in chapter 1 above, denied sterilization.

Although appeals to rationality have not been discussed explicitly under the heading of 'prudentialism' (but rather under the headings of 'paternalism' and 'strong paternalism'), several approaches towards its justification can be distinguished in the literature. In this chapter the most important of these are discussed, along with various definitions of the concept of 'rationality' and the normative entailments of these definitions.

THE CIRCULARITY OF STANDARD APPROACHES

The history of prudentialism as a distinct principle can perhaps be seen to begin with the publication of Gerald Dworkin's essay 'Paternalism' in 1972.[1] Dworkin sets out by focusing on the notion of *consent*, which according to him seems 'the only acceptable way to delimit an area of justified paternalism'.[2] He first considers the force of *explicit* consent in well-defined circumstances:

> Under certain conditions it is rational for an individual to agree that others should force him to act in ways which, at the time of action, the individual may not see as desirable. If, for example, a man knows that he is subject to breaking his resolves when temptation is present, he may ask a friend to refuse to entertain his requests at some later stage.[3]

After giving Odysseus and the Sirens as a classic example of rational self-restriction, Dworkin moves on to discuss consent of a more political nature. In the political field, he notes, the measures to be used against those who have given their consent are not necessarily as well defined as in the personal field. He writes:

> What must be involved here is not consent to specific measures but rather consent to a system of government, run by elected representatives, with an understanding that they may act to safeguard our interests in certain limited ways.[4]

Dworkin then proceeds to define a kind of *implicit* consent for restrictions on a larger scale:

> I suggest that since we are all aware of our irrational propensities, deficiencies in cognitive and emotional capacities and avoidable and unavoidable ignorance it is rational and prudent for us to in effect take out 'social insurance policies'. We may argue for and against proposed paternalistic measures in terms of *what fully rational individuals would accept* as forms of protection.[5]

By using his own criteria Dworkin ends up trying to strike a balance between '"goods" such as health which any person would want to have in order to pursue his own good',[6] and the rational suspicion that people might have concerning paternalistic policies, 'knowing something about the resources of ignorance, ill-will and stupidity available to the law-makers of a society'.[7] The ultimate conclusion of Dworkin's essay seems to be rather strongly anti-paternalistic, partly due to his suspicion of authority, partly due to his liberal credo which he summarizes in the slogan 'better 10 men ruin themselves than one man be unjustly deprived of liberty'.[8]

The importance of Dworkin's essay in examining prudentialism is not, however, in his intuitive conclusions, but in the possibilities his attempt towards justifying (strong) paternalistic measures opens up. It is clear that the acceptance, or consent, of 'fully rational individuals' can be employed in a markedly less liberal manner than he himself chooses to use. Depending on the exact definition of 'rational' in this context, it is possible to argue for a variety of strongly paternalistic measures in the name of rationality and prudence. Since, for instance, health is one of Dworkin's own candidates for a good which may legitimate coercion and restrictions of liberty in the individual's own best interest, his views could no doubt, given a suitable interpretation, be used to support legislation regulating, say, unhealthy lifestyles.

The threat against the standard liberal position, emerging from Dworkin's theory, was well described by John Hodson in 1977 in an article entitled 'The principle of paternalism'.[9] In his article, Hodson notes that the decisions described by ethical theories can be divided into two categories: they can be either *empirical* or *rational*. He defines these categories as follows:

> The choice, decision or will that a person actually expresses at any given time I shall call his *empirical* choice, decision, or will.

> By the 'rational will' is meant the will which would be expressed by any fully rational being, as determined in abstraction from the individual characteristics of any such being.[10]

Now, in all paternalistic interventions, legitimate and illegitimate alike, the actual empirical decision of the recipient is overridden in favour of a decision or will of another kind. The important question, then, is exactly what kind of decision it is that is allowed to override the recipient's present choice.

There is a sharp division here between the measures of weak and strong paternalism. As long as weakly paternalistic interventions are concerned, it is only the *hypothetical empirical* decision of the agent herself that can override the actual choice, and this only in case the actual choice is somehow encumbered.[11] The legitimate business of the paternalistic authority is restricted to finding out what the protected person *herself would have chosen if her will had not been encumbered*, and to acting accordingly.[12]

The answer implicitly given by Dworkin, on the contrary, is that it is the *rational* will or decision that should take precedence over the actual choice made by the recipient of the paternalistic intervention. But if this solution is preferred, then it is impossible to keep within the limits of justifiable, autonomy-respecting paternalism. As Hodson writes:

> Since a correctly determined hypothetical unencumbered will is an unencumbered will, this would be to give greater weight to the rational will than to a person's unencumbered empirical will. But if the rational will can outweigh a person's unencumbered will, there is no restriction of intervention to cases in which the will of the person coerced is encumbered, for the greater weight of the rational will means that it should be followed. Thus, if the rational will were used, even someone whose decisions were not encumbered in any way could be coerced, so long as the coercion were in the direction indicated by the rational will.[13]

It is, of course, possible that the conclusion drawn by Hodson is what Dworkin wanted to accomplish, but it must be noted that if that is the case, he diverts clearly from the Millian tradition.[14] The justification of his view will then have to be found from independent considerations. At any rate, a mere general reference to what fully rational individuals would do is unhelpful if no explanation is added to clarify the principles on which these hypothetical individuals accept what the 'strong' paternalist alleges them to accept.

Theoretically, one way of determining the decisions of a fully rational person is to refer to what is called in the literature the *future-oriented* or *subsequent consent* of those whose choices are interfered with.[15] Especially as regards parental paternalism, it is easy to think that many restrictions which seem unattractive to the child will eventually be justified by his own future gratitude. As years go by, the child will realize that going to school, visiting the dentist regularly and doing one's homework before going out to play were all necessary inconveniences, as they proved beneficial in the end. There are, of course, some initially embarrassing counterexamples to this view.[16] Consider, for instance, the case of little Johnny who is made to do all the aforementioned things and who is then fatally hit by a car when he is only eight years old. If the lack of actual subsequent consent in this case entails that Johnny's parents acted wrongly, then the argument from future consent seems to run counter to our common intuitions.

Fortunately for the argument, however, it can be stated that the reasonably *expected* outcome of the parents' behaviour, not the actual contingent result, is what counts in the ethical evaluation.

The same answer can be given to Donald VanDeVeer, who in his book *Paternalistic Intervention* points out that in addition to accidents which cancel the subsequent consent, there may also be unexpected occurrences which create it. His example is that of a man who is knocked unconscious by a gang of hoodlums, and who later on feels gratitude towards them, as the plane he misses due to the attack crashes, killing all the passengers on board.[17] Here again the expected rather than actual result determines the moral status of the action.

But there is one difficulty with the doctrine of future consent which is serious enough to refute it altogether.[18] This is the possibility of manipulating the recipient of the paternalistic intervention in a manner that automatically leads to consent and gratitude later. Given a simple interpretation of the doctrine, it would be permissible for the public authorities to imprison people and turn them into religious or political fanatics, provided only that the manipulative programme in question includes a section which teaches the brainwashed people themselves to appreciate the treatment when it is over. Rosemary Carter, a proponent of the idea of subsequent consent, has argued that although these cases are real enough, they are nevertheless exceptional, and can be refuted without throwing overboard the whole theory.[19] But it is in fact hard to see how this could be accomplished, as the boundaries between brainwashing, manipulation and other kinds of legitimate and illegitimate modes of influence are far too vague to be used in drawing unambiguous distinctions between manufactured and spontaneous consent in practical situations.

Granted that the subsequent consent model does not work, another possible way of estimating what a fully rational person would do and accept is to evoke wholesale moral theories and see what ideal agents postulated by them would decide. The most popular approach has been an appeal to John Rawls' theory of 'justice as fairness', where rational persons make decisions concerning social and moral principles in a hypothetical 'original position' with only limited knowledge of themselves and their actual qualities and positions in the real world.

As Rawls himself claims in discussing the problem of justifiable (strong) paternalism in *A Theory of Justice*, the principles of paternalism are those that the parties would acknowledge in the original position to protect themselves against the weaknesses and infirmities of their reason and will in society.[20]

More precisely, according to Rawls, people

want to insure themselves against the possibility that their powers are undeveloped and they cannot rationally advance their interests, as in the case of children; or that through some misfortune or accident they are unable to make decisions for their good, as in the case of those seriously injured or mentally disturbed. It is also rational for them to protect themselves against their own irrational inclinations by consenting to a scheme of penalties that may give them a sufficient motive to avoid foolish actions and by accepting certain impositions designed to undo the unfortunate consequences of their imprudent behavior.[21]

As to the justifiable grounds for acting on somebody's behalf, Rawls states:

Paternalistic decisions are to be guided by the individual's own settled preferences and interests *insofar they are not irrational*, or failing a knowledge of these, by the theory of primary goods.[22]

It is important to note that what Rawls means by 'primary goods' is also connected to rationality:

The main idea [of the theory of the good adopted to account for primary goods] is that a person's good is determined by what is for him *the most rational* long-term plan of life given reasonably favorable circumstances. A man is happy when he is more or less successfully in the way of carrying out this plan. To put it briefly, *the good is the satisfaction of rational desire*.[23]

Interferences in people's lives in order to protect their own good should, all in all, according to Rawls be regulated and restricted by three considerations. First, it must be evident that the paternalist acts for the good of those whose lives are interfered with. Second, the 'intervention must be justified by the evident failure or absence of reason and will'.[24] And third, the intervention 'must be guided by the principles of justice'.[25]

Despite these guidelines, the message of Rawls' theory concerning paternalism and prudentialism remains unclear. It is possible to interpret the second condition above, the reference to the 'failure or absence of reason and will', in a manner that would allow only weak paternalism: if the failures and absences mentioned have to do with the *empirical* rather than *rational* will, then prudential justifications are automatically excluded. But it is also possible to read Rawls as saying that only rational desires, rational life-plans and rational decisions must be respected in legislation and social policy. In this case his theory permits coercion and constraint on prudentialistic grounds, but this conclusion still remains without independent support. To the question 'What is it that a fully rational individual consents to?' Rawls' theory responds: 'A fully rational individual consents only to restrictions which infringe the satisfaction or realization of her irrational desires and life-plans.' So, unless one wants to keep running in circles, it is time to examine what can be meant by 'rational' and 'rationality'.

RATIONALITY AND IRRATIONALITY

When people accuse each other of being 'irrational' or 'imprudential', they can mean a variety of things, ranging from genuine mental incompetence or disorder to mild differences of opinion. This variety can, however, be encapsulated by a set of definitions that give the necessary and sufficient conditions of a person's rationality in several different senses.

The most elementary form of rationality is the one already introduced (see p. 30) as a necessary condition of autonomy:

(1) A person is *minimally rational* (autarchic), if, and only if,
  (i) her beliefs form a coherent whole;
  (ii) her preferences form a coherent whole; and
  (iii) her decisions and choices are consistent with these beliefs and preferences.

Unless an individual fulfils these conditions to a reasonable degree, she is not capable of making choices and decisions in the sense that is standardly required in moral and legal theories. An individual lacking minimal rationality is usually not held morally responsible for her actions (if her reflexes can be called 'actions' at all), and is thought to be in need of education or therapy rather than deserving punishment if she breaks the law.

It should not, of course, be presumed that the 'coherence' referred to in conditions (i) and (ii) meant perfect non-contradictoriness or compatibility as regards the person's beliefs and preferences: there may well be areas of experience which seldom come into contact with each other, and which contain mutually contradictory elements. Locally – i.e. within one particular area of experience – this does not prevent an agent from being minimally rational. As for global, all-round consistency, another definition clarifies the picture:

(2) A person is *fully consistent* if, and only if,
    (i–iii) she is autarchic; and
    (iv)   her beliefs among themselves and her preferences among themselves are perfectly non-contradictory.

No actual person is, I believe, fully consistent in the way required by the definition, although people (and higher animals) can be *more* or *less* consistent. However, the important thing to notice here is that autarchy, as an all-or-nothing threshold capacity, can prevail in many areas of personal experience, while the person herself is less than fully consistent overall. Moreover, it is also worth noticing that when someone is accused of being irrational in the sense of being inconsistent, what is usually meant is that the accused is contradicting herself in an area which is considered by the critic to be central to human thinking in general, or to the issue at hand in particular. Appeals to full consistency are seldom made, and this is just as well, since they would lack applicability in the real world anyway.

One further division arises from the formulation of condition (iii) of definition (1) above. Even if a person's decisions and choices are 'consistent with her beliefs and preferences', this does not guarantee that the person *knows* this or is capable of *expressing* it. Let us stipulate that:

(3) A person is *explicitly rational* if, and only if,
    (i–iii) she is autarchic; and
    (v)   she can give a clear account of how she reaches particular decisions and choices by collecting evidence and basing her conclusions on it.

It has sometimes been alleged, first by male scientists and philo-sophers, later on also by some feminist theorists, that explicit rationality is a sex-related matter, and that it is more characteristic of men than it is of women.[26] The opposite of this kind of rationality has often been called *intuitiveness*, and this allegedly female capacity has been supposed to be an alternative way of reaching conclusions and making choices, by leaps of imagination instead of by taking the necessary steps starting from elementary evidence and working through logical inference to firm conclusions. In reality, there is no reason to doubt that members of both sexes are physiologically and psychologically capable of explicit rationality, although the rules of acceptable reasoning may sometimes favour men in such a way that it makes women reluctant to spell out their grounds for beliefs or action. But even this reluctance is not necessarily sex-specific: the same observation probably applies to any group whose members suffer from systematic social injustice because of their membership in that group.

Being sufficiently consistent overall and expressing one's reasons explicitly are both important additions to simply being autar-chic, but neither of them marks such a qualitative axiological difference in comparison to minimal rationality as autonomy, or self-determination. The cornerstone of liberal theory can be defined in the following manner:

(4) A person is *autonomous* if, and only if,
   (i–iii) she is autarchic; *and*
   (vi)   her decisions and choices are, to a reasonable degree at least, her own, i.e. they are not primarily the product of coercion, pressure or manipulation by others.

The addition 'to a reasonable degree' in condition (vi) is particularly significant, since individuals who make their choices completely on their own are not autonomous but psychopathic. Autonomy in the liberal sense is only possible within a community that shares a certain degree of values and ideas: to be autonomous is to be capable of genuine human happiness, whereas the self-made 'happiness' of psychopaths will eventually be infringed by their collision with the values of others. Axiologically, the instrumental values of autarchy and freedom rest on the intrinsic happiness-related value of autonomy.

Autarchy and autonomy define, from the liberal viewpoint sketched in the preceding chapters, the most important senses in which it is good for individuals to be 'rational'. But if the external aspects of rational behaviour are taken into account as well, then many other characterizations are also relevant. Consider, for instance, the following definitions of freedom:

(5) A person is *free in a technical sense* if, and only if,
   (i–iii)   she is autarchic; and
   (vii)   she can act according to her own decisions and choices without explicit internal or external constraints.
(6) A person is *free in a moral sense* if, and only if,
   (i–iv)   she is autonomous; and
   (viii)   free in the technical sense.

If a person is only free in the technical sense, her actions may well be decided upon by other people – by parents, guardians or other authorities. This entails that there is no intrinsic personal value in these actions, and that the parents, guardians or other authorities are to a large extent responsible for the consequences of the actions. If, however, a person is free in the more demanding, moral sense, she will normally be expected to assume full responsibility for her behaviour, both ethically and legally. This kind of freedom guarantees that action generated by the decisions and choices is valuable in itself, but it does not in any way guarantee that the actions were prudentially or morally acceptable.

An interesting addition, and a connection to virtue ethics, is provided by a definition which makes a reference to the person's inner life:

(7) A person *possesses personal integrity* if, and only if,
   (i–iv)   she is autonomous; and
   (ix)   she can herself concretely accept the totality of her own decisions and choices, i.e. she can commit herself to them in her intended conduct.

According to a standard Aristotelian interpretation of ethics, an agent can be called *virtuous* if her personal integrity is consistent with her position and role in a just society, and if it is combined with spontaneity in the sense that she can herself accept her own initial preferences as well as the actual choices based upon them. An individual who has to fight her spontaneous preferences to act morally is, in the framework of Aristotelian virtue ethics, *strong-minded* but not virtuous, and a person who makes the right decisions but is incapable of living by them suffers from *akrasia*, weakness of the will. All three forms of being or failing to be virtuous can be interpreted both as signs of rationality and as indications of irrationality.

Moving on to more demanding forms of 'rationality', self-interest is sometimes included in the definition:

> (8) A person is *prudential in the narrow sense* if, and only if,
> (i–iv) she is autonomous; and
> (x) (the most important of) her decisions and choices are designed, and can be expected, to further her own interests.

There are two points about condition (x) which need special attention.

First, the condition includes, in fact, the germs of two definitions which are different in spirit, depending on whether the parenthetical qualification is taken fully into account or not. According to one interpretation, each and every choice a person makes must be made after serious thought as to its influence upon her self-interest; according to the other, the more trivial decisions may be made in a more relaxed manner. However, there are good grounds for judging the former – i.e. the unqualified – definition unacceptable. If an individual can only be prudential by making every one of her decisions fit into a master scheme concerning her own interests (in the long run as well as in the short run), then the prudential individual must be an angel rather than a human being. It is characteristic of and perhaps essential to human life that we only stop to think when truly important matters are to be decided upon – in everyday life, actions must, for economy's sake, be based on reflexes and habits rather than on careful intellectual consideration.

The second point about condition (x) is that it leaves room for two ways of being imprudential: one can either fail to design one's decisions with one's own best interest in mind, or one can fail to see what the best way of furthering one's interest is. In the former case, the form of irrationality in question can sometimes be called *altruism*; in the latter case, ignorance and stupidity are the key words.

A category partially overlapping the scope of prudence is that of morality:

> (9) A person is *moral* if, and only if,
> (i–iv) she is autonomous; and

(xi) typically makes (the most important of) her decisions and choices on the grounds of what (she thinks) is moral.

In the case where it is a part of the individual's plan of life to be moral, morality can be seen as entirely subordinate to prudence. On the other hand, if the individual sees her personal plan of life as a part of a greater design – as in many religious doctrines – it is also possible to regard prudence as subordinate to the morality intrinsic in the greater scheme. However, whatever the mutual order of reason and ethics is, there are an infinite variety of interpretations of what is moral, and to a person defending any one of them, its opponents will always appear more or less irrational.

The definitions presented so far have all been more or less individualistic, and therefore automatically compatible with an anti-paternalistic view. But if the rationalist–communitarian theories of freedom are taken into account, the following definition must also be included:

(10) A person is a *concrete historical person* (a citizen) if, and only if,
   (i–iv) she is autonomous; and
   (xii) she is willing to live according to the rules of a given just society.

In a Rousseauan 'general will' model, it is only by submitting to the rules of a just society that an individual can be rationally free, and rational freedom is the state everyone should aim at. By being a citizen the individual can, according to the theory, be simultaneously prudential, moral and at least politically virtuous. And when all these good things flow from one's citizenship, it would be irrational to rebel against the arrangement by attempting to form one's own way of seeking happiness.

The last sub-category of rationality to be introduced here diverts from the 'spiritual' tone of the definitions given thus far. As regards the relationship between the agent's decisions and the facts on which they are based, it can be stipulated that:

(11) A person is an *ideal decision-maker* (in a technical sense) if, and only if,
   (i–iv) she is autonomous; and
   (xiii) she has good reasons to believe that the majority of her beliefs are essentially correct.

A person can be virtuous and moral, even prudential in the narrow sense, without being completely aware of the foundations of her choices, but it is, none the less, obviously a positive quality in a decision-maker to base her decisions on well-grounded beliefs. In matters of fact, it is usual in our scientific age to regard scientific knowledge as the ultimate foundation for considered choices. In matters related to value and justification, the situation is more complex, since it is not entirely clear what the criteria to be employed in assessments at a general level should be. However, even in axiological and normative issues a local consensus often prevails, making it possible for attitudes and moral feelings to be 'essentially correct' within a given culture, community or situation.

To conclude this series of forms of rationality, a definition of its opposite is required:

(12) A person is *imprudential in the wide sense* if, and only if, she lacks autarchy, autonomy, personal integrity, prudence in the narrow sense, morality, historical rationality, or one of the qualities of the ideal decision-maker.

It does not seem fair to state that those who are not fully consistent or not explicitly rational or lacking in freedom were imprudent, although such accusations may sometimes be heard. To be fully consistent is probably impossible, and explicit rationality as well as freedom are matters largely beyond the reach of the individual herself. But if an agent is missing any one of the genuinely essential and intrinsic characteristics of rationality, as given in definition (12), then it is possible to bring the charge of imprudence against her. And the charge of imprudence brings along with it the possibility of coercion and constraint on prudentialistic grounds.

FORCED RATIONALITY?

Strong paternalism backed up with prudential reasons means violations of an individual's autonomy, allegedly for his own best interest, when his behaviour is – or threatens to be – irrational in some sense which is considered important. The problem with this attempted justification is, however, that regardless of the definition of 'rationality' chosen for the purpose, it is either the case that violations of autonomy which are supposed to further rationality are conceptually or empirically impossible, or that the value of the form of rationality in question can be challenged. This can easily be seen by considering one by one the kinds of irrationality to be defined by negating definitions (1) to (11) above, and reflecting on their axiological status, as compared to that of autonomy.

To start with, *autarchy* (1) and *autonomy* (4) as forms of rationality are without doubt valuable qualities for an individual to possess, but it is difficult to see how they could be furthered by autonomy-violating interventions. If an individual cannot make rational decisions because he lacks the relevant capacity, he can perhaps be *helped* towards rational decision-making through therapy or education, but it would be a contradiction in terms to maintain that his current (rational) decisions could be suppressed in order to help him – as there are no rational decisions, there is nothing to be suppressed, either. And if the decisions made by an individual are not to a sufficient degree his own, the removal of intrinsic or extrinsic constraints may move him towards autonomy, but since there are no truly self-determined choices to be tampered with, paternalistic interventions are conceptually impossible. Largely the same considerations apply to *full consistency* (3) and *explicit rationality* (4): human beings cannot be forced into a state of having completely non-contradictory preferences, since such a state would be superhuman, and they cannot be coerced into giving clear accounts of how they reach decisions if they are physically or verbally unable to accomplish that in the first place. Besides, it is not entirely clear that there is any particular value in being able to express with accuracy the premises and inferences which lead to one's decisions, or in being extraordinarily consistent even regarding one's most trivial choices.

With *freedom*, in its technical (5) as well as in its moral (6) sense, things are different in that violations of autonomy can easily be employed for furthering an individual's liberty of action in the long run. There is no logical difficulty in the idea of strong paternalism practised for the sake of rationality in the sense of freedom. The problem is, however, that internal and external constraints on a person's freedom are seldom within his own control, and it is therefore patently dubious to consider the state of being unfree as a form of irrationality. Surely it cannot be considered irrational that a person does not leave a room through a locked door? And even if one lets that pass, the question of the comparative values of liberty and autonomy remains. It has been argued in the preceding chapters that only freedom which serves people's self-chosen decisions and values is really worth protecting, while a mechanical kind of liberty which is not connected with self-determination cannot override immediate autonomy as far as their comparative values are concerned. There seems to be no reason to depart from that earlier conclusion at this point, and appeals to freedom, therefore, provide no new justification for strong paternalism.

Irrationality as lack of *personal integrity* (7) takes two main forms: viciousness in the Aristotelian sense, and weakness of the will. Here again, the value of being rational – i.e. virtuous, strong-minded or strong-willed – may seem obvious, but as in the above with freedom, it is hard to see how a person could be coerced into being any better than he is. It is an integral part of being virtuous that one holds a position in life which corresponds with one's childhood moral education, and it is also necessary that one lives in a just and stable society. But how is an individual to be coerced into living in a just society? If he is not lucky enough to live in one, is it fair to subject him to violations of autonomy which are designed to put right the deficiencies of an unjust social structure? As regards the weakness of the will, if one is not capable of resisting one's inferior inclinations, or of transforming one's good intentions into action, how is one to be coerced into doing so? An individual can, of course, within certain limits be forced or coerced to abstain from criminal or immoral activities, but this does not make him rational in the sense that he would achieve personal integrity as a result of the use of force. And, contrary to one's first intuitions, a strong will is not necessarily a good quality in a person – a strong will, as such, can intensify the evils of a bad character as well as multiply the positive aspects of a good one.

Imprudence in the narrow sense (8) can, as noted above, result either from conscious or from accidental disregard of one's own best interest. If the former is the case, then it is not at all clear where the normative value of prudence lies; that is, if an individual deliberately chooses to favour other people over himself, most moral theories would find it difficult to condemn such a choice as unethical or irrational. If, on the other hand, the agent is too ignorant or too stupid to know what his own best interest is or how it can be furthered, then helping him would not be wrongfully paternalistic in the first place: lack of knowledge is a sufficient reason for weakly paternalistic interventions, and educating people so that they learn to recognize their own best interest is an instance of soft rather than hard paternalism. The only dispute here is over the definition of 'learning to know one's own best interest'. Frequently, of course, an authority claims to have superior knowledge concerning what is ultimately good for people, and claims that all those trying to make up their own minds are, according to the authority in question, wrong. Within the liberal framework coercion would on these premises be unethical, since the theory states that people's lives must only be interfered with in order to help them to make up their own minds. But even if the liberal view is not assumed, narrow prudentialism cannot be defended as such – it will require the support of morality, social unity or knowledge. If such support were not available, it would be hard to see why people would be obliged to further their own interests – in the sense the authorities maintain they would – when they do not spontaneously like to do so themselves.

Morality (9) and *good citizenship* (10) are obviously aspects of rationality that can and must be required of people, and some-times must be enforced on them by coercion and force. Constant immorality and rebellion against society on the part of one group of people would clearly be intolerable for the rest, as such conduct would mean undermining the foundations of regulated human life in the given community. However, the difficulty here is that if the rules broken and structures challenged are such that other people will be seriously involved, it is the harm inflicted on other people rather than imprudence as such that will be suppressed. In turn, if an individual practises private, self-regarding immorality (whatever *that* might be) or decides to turn into a hermit, the case for restricting his activities is at once considerably weaker. Thus, prudentialism which links rationality with the maintenance of morality and society turns out to be either a variation of the harm-to-others principle, or, alternatively, a doctrine that cannot be defended at all.

The last form of irrationality to be considered, the state of not being an *ideal decision-maker* (11), is particularly interesting in the context of medicine and health care. It is typically the *epistemic authority* of medical personnel that provides them with reasons to interfere paternalistically with other people's affairs. In most medical situations it holds true that as far as the professional aspect of the matter is concerned, the physician is a more ideal decision-maker than the patient. The mistake proponents of medical paternalism make, at this point, is that they straightforwardly equate professional competence and the capacity to decide what is best for a person. Yet, in matters related to the patient's plan of life, he himself is arguably the best judge, even though he does not necessarily know everything about his own physical condition.

But by focusing only on the conflict of authorities in medical decision-making, one may miss another – and in all probability a more important – ethical point. Granted that an autonomous individual is the ultimate judge of his own life, it is nevertheless quite possible that the decisions he makes, owing to lack of knowledge, run counter to his own plans. Accordingly, it would in many cases amount to no more than weak paternalism to inform the patient about his condition. In such cases it is in fact more in the nature of a duty than a right for the physician to inform her patient, since witholding information could only be interpreted as harm inflicted on a non-consenting person. The situation may, of course, be different if the patient has explicitly expressed a wish not to be told about specific conditions he may have, on the ground that knowing about them would not improve his life in any way. Here, as frequently in the above, the individual's own sufficiently well-informed decision should be rated above rationality which is defined by an external authority.

NO DIFFERENCE BETWEEN SELF-REGARDING AND OTHER-REGARDING?

Many of the refutations of strong paternalism presented in this chapter have rested on the tacit assumption that there is a distinction – perhaps not a very clear one, but in any case noticeable and tenable – between self-regarding and other-regarding activities. And although the clarity of the distinction has frequently been criticized,[27] it is, in principle at least, valid as long as one human self can in the ethical discourse be kept apart from all other human selves. But the problem is that this assumption concerning the separateness of human selves can be, and in fact has been, challenged. The most thoroughgoing recent work in this direction has been done by Derek Parfit in his book *Reasons and Persons*.[28] It is impossible to do justice to the richness of Parfit's arguments in the limited space that can be given to them here, but a rough sketch of some of his main points is needed in order to defend the anti-prudentialist view against his attack.

In considering the relationship between personal identity and morals, Parfit holds the view that what we do to ourselves can often be regarded, in the ethical sense, as equivalent to what we do to others.[29] Personal identity, according to his theory, cannot consist of an irreducible and permanent experience of being 'me' or 'I', as our everyday intuitions normally indicate, since such a view is in the last analysis too paradoxical to be intellectually accepted. Instead, Parfit maintains that the identity of any given person can be reduced to an impersonal description of some physical and mental events which are psychologically interconnected, or form a psychological continuum. The renewed (in Parfit's terms, *reductionist*) theory implies that a person may be as remotely connected with her future self which will be in existence in a few decades' time as she is to other people with whom she is living at the moment. Conversely, of course, it can also be said that one's connection with others who are living now is as close as one's connection with oneself in the future. This conceptual framework enables Parfit to infer that, assuming it is wrong to inflict serious harm on others, it must be equally wrong to inflict serious harm on one's future self.

Parfit presents the following example to illustrate the view he is professing:

> [Consider] a boy who starts to smoke, knowing and hardly caring that this may cause him to suffer greatly fifty years later. This boy does not identify with his future self. His attitude towards the future self is in some ways like his attitude to other people, such as the aged parents of his friends. This analogy makes it easier to believe that his act is morally wrong. He runs the risk of imposing on himself a premature and painful death. We should claim that it is wrong to impose on *anyone*, including such a future self, the risk of such a death. More generally, we should claim that great imprudence is morally wrong. We ought not to do to our future selves what it would be wrong to do to other people.[30]

After this example Parfit goes on to argue that the irrationality, and subsequent immorality, of harming one's future self in fact justifies coercive paternalistic measures. To be sure, he recognizes that there is something to be said in favour of not interfering in people's self-regarding affairs in the name of reason alone. He writes:

The person we coerce might say: 'I may be acting irrationally.

But even if I am, that is my affair. If I am only harming myself, I have the right to act irrationally, and you have no right to stop me.' This reply has some force. We do not believe that we have a general right to prevent people from acting *irrationally*.[31]

Parfit continues, however, in more prudentialist tones:

But we do believe that we have a general right to prevent people from acting *wrongly*. This claim may not apply to minor wrong-doing. But we believe that it cannot be wrong, and would often be our duty, to prevent others from doing what is seriously wrong. Since we ought to believe that great imprudence is seriously wrong, we ought to believe that we should prevent such imprudence, even if this involves coercion.[32]

And he concludes his case by stating:

Autonomy does not include the right to impose upon oneself, for no good reason, great harm. We ought to prevent anyone from doing to his future self what it would be wrong to do to other people.[33]

In sum, basing his argument on the reductionist view concerning personal identity, Parfit ends up equating three things: acting against one's own good (when no one else is afflicted), irrationality or imprudence and immorality. And since it is, according to his theory, immoral to act imprudently against one's own good, he thinks that coercive restriction of irrational self-regarding actions is justified.

The apparent superiority of Parfit's version of prudentialism over, say, the standard types of moralism professed by Patrick Devlin and Simon Lee,[34] is that *reason* has a far greater appeal to critical thinking than the popular morality of a given community. One is more apt to think that something dictated by rationality is good and valuable than one is to believe that the norms of an unenlightened population should be followed. But the problem with Parfit's view, in fact, lies elsewhere. It has not been seriously questioned in the liberal theory that there may be legislators or other authorities who know exactly what is good for certain people in certain situations. So there is no real need to evoke rationality just to prove that somebody sometimes – or perhaps everybody always – knows what is best for other people. The real problem is to prove that the others should not be allowed to make their own informed mistakes, if mistakes they be, without interference.

Parfit does not develop his points on paternalism any further, and in fact he deliberately weakens the strength of his own case by referring, after the defence of coercive measures, to the difficulties just mentioned. But the fact remains that his view of personal identity seems to have some striking repercussions on the coercive control of what liberal theorists would like to call self-regarding behaviour. If our connection with our future selves is approximately as strong or as weak as our connection with other people, paternalistic measures do not fundamentally differ from control which is based on harm inflicted on others. And in that case anti-paternalism is a doomed cause right from the start.

Everything, therefore, depends on whether or not there are compelling reasons for thinking that Parfit's 'reductionist' view of personal identity is correct. This is what I am prepared to deny. There may be good reasons for thinking that Parfit's view is correct, and there may be even better reasons for thinking that the view he opposes is incorrect. What I believe, however, is that one is not, emotionally or intellectually, bound to accept Parfit's contentions. My main reason for believing this is that the reductionist view of personal identity is in some cases at least as paradoxical as its traditional competitors, and there seem to be no overriding practical or emotional grounds for preferring Parfit's solution to the traditional one, if their intellectual statuses do not differ more drastically than they in fact do.

Parfit himself illustrates the paradoxical nature of the reductionist view by presenting the following example.[35] Suppose that one day engineers invent a device called the Teletransporter, which enables us to travel to Mars without considerable time delay. The crude versions of the machine destroy the brain and the body of the traveller while recording the exact state of each and every cell. The information is then transmitted by radio to Mars, and a new body is built out of new matter in an hour. A moment's unconsciousness is all the traveller experiences. Later on a more interesting, revised version of the machine is developed. The revised machine records the blueprint without destroying the body, and enables the customer *both* to stay at home *and* to travel to Mars simultaneously. Once the new body has materialized in Mars, furthermore, the customer who stayed on earth can communicate with him or herself on Mars.

The first time Parfit himself uses the revised version of the Teletransporter, however, a complication appears:

> Someone politely coughs, a white-coated man who asks to speak to me in private. We go to his office, where he tells me to sit down, and pauses. Then he says: 'I am afraid we are having problems with the New Scanner. It records your blueprint just as accurately, as you will see when you talk to yourself on Mars. But it seems to be damaging the cardiac systems which it scans. Judging from the results so far, though you will be quite healthy on Mars, here on Earth you must expect cardiac failure within the next few days'.[36]

As Parfit goes on to note, most of us undoubtedly tend to think that the traveller's prospect in the example 'is almost as bad as ordinary death'.[37] But in Parfit's own view this is not so: rationally thinking, he says, we 'ought to regard having a Replica as being about as good as ordinary survival'.[38] Assuming that the reductionist view of personal identity is correct, one should achieve great consolation from the fact that one's replicated 'person', as it was a few minutes ago, will continue its existence even though, subjectively, one will shortly have to die.

I do not have to argue for the contention that examples like this make the reductionist view paradoxical and difficult to accept – Parfit admits as much himself.[39] He is willing to admit that *what we believe* about our personal identities is what the 'non-reductionist' view states. But he claims that what we believe is incorrect, and that, on intellectual grounds, we *ought to assume* the reductionist theory because it tells the truth about us. Only emotional and irrational factors, such as the possible fear one may have of Teletransportation after reading Parfit's account of its hazards, prevent one from being convinced by the reductionist view, whereas there 'are sufficient reasons to reject' the non-reductionist view on intellectual grounds.[40]

It is difficult – for me at least – to see Parfit's exact point when he divides reasons for and against different theories into intellectual and emotional categories. I would have liked to say that the reductionist view is *intellectually* unsatisfactory because its application leads to totally unacceptable results. If I cannot say that, I cannot in any strict sense *refute* Parfit's view. But if the same criteria are applied to his points against the non-reductionist view, mainly dealing with imaginary split-brain examples, I do not think that he can produce a genuine refutation, either. For one thing, there is the problem that the complicated science fiction examples Parfit employs cannot be grasped clearly enough to be used as parts of an 'intellectual' argument. For another, however unintelligible the results of a split-brain experiment may be in the light of the non-reductionist theory, one can always state that the difficulties here are emotional, not intellectual in the proper sense. These considerations lead me to think that the reductionist view is not necessarily so superior that it would have to be accepted by every reasonable person.

Parfit could still defend the further view that ethical theories ought to be built on reductionist thinking, however, on the grounds that the resulting morality is preferable to any morality based on non-reductionism. The world would presumably be a better place if people avoided inflicting harm on others in the same way as they usually avoid inflicting harm on themselves. And it would certainly not be a bad thing if people also avoided transitory pleasures which tend to inflict serious harm on their future selves. In this sense, it might be desirable that people voluntarily assumed the reductionist view of personal identity.

As far as theories concerning the ethical outlook of an individual are concerned, I find no fault in this line of argument. Humankind could obviously do with an increase in altruism and prudence. But it is an entirely different matter whether these considerations can be applied to social, political or legal thought. It is not clear that altruism and prudence can be produced by constraint and coercion in the first place, and even if they can, the arrangement may easily cease to be desirable because of the implicit and explicit violence needed to maintain the status quo. According to the liberal principles that I have been defending in the above, it is normally acceptable to prevent people from inflicting harm on each other, directly or indirectly. But as I argued in the preceding section, it is extremely difficult to force people into being rational and prudent. Therefore, even though Parfit's arguments concerning personal identity may be persuasive, his remarks do not necessarily justify strong paternalism in practice.

Another way of formulating this point is as follows. Regardless of the possible theoretical flaws in the non-reductionist view, most competent adult human beings believe that they are irreducible individuals whose personal self-determination has considerable value. If the reductionist view is correct, the proper description here is that the majority of people tend to place epistemic and normative value on a mistaken belief in their individuality and autonomy. But even if the beliefs may be in some sense mistaken, they are also deeply rooted, and likely to counteract any legislative and socio-political attempts towards regulating behaviour which people see as self-regarding. Strong paternalism based on prudentialist considerations remains unprofitable in a world in which people are brought up to think of themselves as individuals who are, to a certain extent at least, separate from all other individuals.

7

THE LIMITS OF
MEDICAL PATERNALISM

It is now time to summarize what has been discussed in the preceding chapters, and to transform the conclusions into concise principles for application to issues within medicine and health care. The liberal view on paternalism, stated at the end of chapter 3 above, was challenged in chapters 4, 5 and 6 by arguments in favour of strong paternalism. These arguments, with their appeals to *utility*, *common morality* and *rationality*, all failed to establish their critical point, however, and the liberal theory – which only recognizes the legitimacy of soft and weak forms of paternalism – remained virtually intact. No sufficient grounds were given to the claim that overall autonomy-violating interventions would ever be justifiable in the recipient's 'own best interest' – either such interventions cannot be accepted at all, or their acceptability is in the last analysis based on other-regarding rather than self-regarding considerations. What *was* shown, especially in chapter 5, however, was that indirect or otherwise unremarkable harm should not be ignored in harm calculations, and that offended feelings may sometimes indicate the presence of a subtle form of injury inflicted or about to be inflicted on others. But this, of course, falls notoriously short of making out a good case for the 'strong' paternalist.

One point of clarification that was gained in chapter 6 is that the rationalist and communitarian views of 'positive' freedom, introduced and flirted with in chapter 2, provide no help when the legitimacy of paternalism is debated. It may be a deep moral or social duty that everyone should obey the rules of a just society, and perhaps the 'real' freedom of human beings can only be discussed in an intelligible manner by employing such a view. But whatever the merits of this approach, the fact remains that a just society may well wish to be blissfully ignorant about the self-regarding activities of its citizens: the force of justice, or rationality, is morally binding only where the conflicting interests of individuals and groups are involved, not where individuals make autonomous decisions which concern solely or primarily their own lives. Here again, of course, allegations of a lack of 'positive' freedom may lead to the detection of an otherwise inconspicuous kind of other-regarding harm, but this does not in any way further the cause of strong paternalism.

Subsequently, as I return to the problems of paternalism, prudentialism and moralism in modern medicine and health care, introduced in chapter 1, two simple points define the evaluative framework, namely:

(I) Interventions into the patients' affairs in their own best interest are justifiable only if these interventions do not lead to overall violations of the patients' autonomy.

(II) If additional appeals are made to utility, morality or rationality, an investigation into the other-regarding aspects of the behaviour which will be intervened with is called for.

Since these maxims embody a number of arguments and conclusions dealt with in more detail in the preceding chapters, it is perhaps appropriate to add a few clarifying remarks.

The concept of an *intervention* must, according to the liberal view sketched mainly in chapters 2 and 3 above, be given a rather wide interpretation. To start with, all kinds of coercion and constraint, whether produced by forcing, threatening or otherwise, are to be counted as interventions in the relevant sense. In addition, if a person's action alternatives (options) are restricted, her desires frustrated, her decisions influenced or her autonomy in any (other) way violated, her affairs are intervened with. Even if none of these is the case, the person's affairs are intervened with if her interests are either furthered or somehow negatively affected by others. Interventions, within this wide interpretation, can take place according to a person's wishes as well as against them.

The requirement spelled out in the first maxim, the generic condition of legitimate paternalistic interferences, can be fulfilled in either of two ways. First, it is possible that the intervention in itself is not even prima facie autonomy-violating, and that the paternalism in question belongs to the *soft* variety, as is often the case with the parental care mothers and fathers extend over their children. Second, even if a prima-facie violation of autonomy does occur, the evil inflicted can sometimes be overridden by other considerations. These 'other considerations' concern the welfare of the recipient on the one hand, and his ability to make autonomous decisions on the other. If without the intervention serious harm would befall him because he is not capable of sufficiently autonomous decision-making, then *weak* paternalism is what others should (try to) exercise over him.

Theoretically, the second point above is not directly related to paternalism at all – rather, its purpose is to stress the many disguises other-regarding evils may assume. From the practical viewpoint, however, there is an obvious connection: the argument for 'paternalistic measures' in real life is seldom confined solely or even primarily to self-regarding matters. What is called paternalism, say, in medicine and health care, often proves to be a set of restrictions on an activity which, despite the apparent absence of serious harm to others, somehow seems condemnable to the authorities in charge of the situation. When this is the case, one way of defending the restrictions is to state that the activity in question *offends* some individual or group either morally, ideologically or otherwise. But the difficulty with this approach is that regardless of the type of offensiveness appealed to, there are no tenable grounds for constraining some people in order to alleviate or prevent offence that others may feel. If moral or ideological matters are at stake, the critiques presented against Devlin and Lee in chapter 5 can be reintroduced: opinions, however deeply rooted, do not provide adequate grounds for moralistic dictatorship. On the other hand, if the behaviour about to be checked merely annoys people or 'hurts their feelings', it is hard to see why a serious stand should be taken in the matter in the first place – unless, of course, the irritation happens to indicate real harm to others. Surely it cannot be accepted that people are licensed without limitation to butt into each other's affairs whenever they see behaviour which they consider unusual or offensive.

Another way of defending allegedly paternalistic intervention is by an appeal to indirect and inconspicuous types of harm inflicted on others. Feinberg's garrison example, presented in chapter 5, draws attention to the *cumulative effects* of human actions: although it is generally true that society can survive without the individual contribution of any one of its members, it is also true that a sufficient number of individual withdrawals will eventually undermine the very continuity of social life. The same observation applies to positive evils, too: the transgressive behaviour of one individual may in itself be relatively harmless, but added to the similar behaviour of others it can, nevertheless, be socially quite destructive. Moreover, cumulative harm can befall individuals as well as communities – thus, say, a negligible and only slightly annoying injustice towards a person can, if repeated often enough, develop into a major harm. And the silent accumulation of modest injuries is only one way in which harm can be brought about in an inconspicuous manner. There are at least three criticisms that can be raised against permissiveness towards practices related to health, even if these seem to be primarily self-regarding. First, the rash and negligent lifestyle of one person may indeed directly harm only herself, but if she becomes hospitalized at some point, her treatment will, perhaps unfairly, drain *scarce resources* away from the treatment of people whose illnesses are not in the same sense 'self-inflicted'. Second, if complete freedom of choice were guaranteed for all those who are capable of autonomous decision-making, this would in many cases mean putting some less fortunate individuals in a high risk bracket with regard to undue influences, as it would be *impossible to discriminate* between those who can and those who cannot reasonably be expected to make optimal choices for themselves. Third, there is always the possibility of so-called *slippery slopes* – meaning that although a given kind of activity is not in itself harmful, its acceptance may lead to the legitimation of other, superficially similar but overtly harmful kinds of activity, through changing people's attitudes towards practices that they have traditionally considered immoral.

In what follows I shall apply these observations to the cases, prohibitions and policies introduced in chapter 1 above. At the level of individual doctor–patient relationships, the issues to be examined include lying, withholding information, revealing truths that the patients do not wish to learn, refusing to treat patients in the way they want to be treated, and compulsorily submitting them to treatments they do not want. At the societal level, these small-scale questions are supplemented by issues such as laws designed to save lives and preserve health, the incarceration of innocent people to halt the spreading of contagious diseases, prevention of illness by medical and social policy, health education aimed at altering people's lifestyles and the allocation of scarce medical resources.

Before going into any of these concrete questions in detail, however, I shall have to introduce a very basic principle in contemporary medical ethics, namely the principle of *informed consent*.

AUTONOMY, CONSENT AND PROFESSIONAL MEDICAL ETHICS

The requirement of the patients' consent to invasive medical procedures was originally expressed in a legal context in England in 1767, when in the case of *Slater* v. *Baker & Stapleton* it was ruled that in order to prepare themselves for the hardships of surgical operations without anaesthesia, patients ought to know what is happening and assent to the procedures ahead of them. This is how the matter was formulated:

> It is reasonable that a patient should be told what is about to be done to him, that he may take courage and put himself in such a situation as to enable him to undergo the operation.[1]

The purpose of the consent being primarily to gain the compliance and cooperation of patients, physicians in fact historically disclosed little or no information before proceeding to obtain the assent; even the distortion of facts was often considered appropriate, 'in the patient's best interest'.[2]

During the twentieth century, however, the principle of informed consent has in the Anglo-American common law systems been provided with a firm, twofold ethico-legal foundation.[3] First, since 'the unprivileged, unauthorized, intentional touching of a person by another' constitutes, in common law, the crime of *battery*,[4] physicians as well as other people must obtain the consent of the person they are going to touch in a suspect manner unless they want to be charged with physical assault. In the case in America of *Schloendorff* v. *Society of New York Hospital* (1914), for instance, it was stated that:

> Every human being of adult years and sound mind has a right to determine what shall be done with his own body; and a surgeon who performs an operation without his patient's consent commits an assault.[5]

Second, as consent without adequate knowledge and awareness of the situation is apt to undermine the patients' right to autonomy and self-determination, the physicians' failure to disclose all relevant and material facts can also be considered *negligence*. This implies, as stated in another American ruling, in the case of *Natanson* v. *Kline* (1960), that the physician has a legal obligation:

> to disclose and explain to the patient in language as simple as necessary the nature of the ailment, the nature of the proposed treatment, the probability of success or of alternatives, and perhaps the risk of unfortunate results and unforeseen conditions within the body.[6]

The difficulty with these two arguments for the necessity of informed consent is, however, that there is a tension between them, as the 'battery' approach emphasizes the removal of the *physicians'* liability for criminal charges, whereas the 'negligence', or autonomy approach is primarily designed for establishing the *patients'* positive right to informed personal decision-making and individual self-determination.

The tension between the two approaches reflects a division of medical ethics into two distinct branches. On the one hand, the term 'medical ethics' can refer to the professional mores and codes of physicians (or nurses and other health care workers).[7] Medical ethics in this sense is meant to define the boundaries within which the health care personnel can enact their professional duties without fear of moral blame or legal liability as regards prevailing laws and opinions. On the other hand, 'medical ethics' in a philosophical sense can equally well mean the critical study of the existing professional codes, as well as a scrutiny of the prevailing laws and opinions behind them. The main task of this latter kind of study is to examine the requirements and limitations that society at large, after careful consideration, ought to put upon those working within the health care system. For instance, in most countries the physicians' attitudes toward *active euthanasia* are negative, largely – if not entirely – owing to the laws against the intentional killing of fully developed and innocent human beings. The critical medical ethicists, not being restricted to obeying existing legislation in their work, can challenge these attitudes and laws, raising the question of justification at a more general level: granted that euthanasia is not legitimate, is its illegitimacy legitimate? In other words, is it beneficial to individual human beings, or to society as a whole, that doctors are allowed, even forced, to treat requests for voluntary euthanasia as invitations to murder? The answer to this question, and to many others like it, belongs to the sphere of philosophical medical ethics, as opposed to the uncritical, practical application of professional codes. And a similar distinction can – and should – be recognized in discussing the doctrine of informed consent.

As far as the professional self-defence aspects of informed consent are concerned, the principle bears no direct relevance to the study of paternalism in health care: as the physicians' first consideration probably is to protect themselves against liability, it would be somewhat hypocritical to maintain that what they really have in mind is the patients' best interest. This does not, of course, mean that the privacy and physical immunity of the patients have nothing to do with autonomy – naturally, a violation of privacy in the form of physical assault is, at the same time, an indirect violation of autonomy. Consequently, a strong professional feeling against battery will, in the long run, no doubt further the patients' ability and right to self-determination. However, what the physicians' understandable urge for self-protection can easily lead to is an over-emphasis of a simple unqualified type of consent which does not guarantee sufficient respect towards the patients' autonomy in direct day-to-day medical work. It is the disclosure preceding the actual assent that supports and even increases the patients' powers of self-determination, and, it is to be hoped, encourages their autonomous decision-making. Thus it is the disclosure, originally designed to protect doctors from charges of negligence before courts of law, that also saves them from accusations of wrongful paternalism at the level of critical morality.

The principle of informed consent, as defined by George Annas in his *Rights of Hospital Patients*, lays down the many qualifications that simple assent requires in order to become valid in a considered ethical sense. This is how Annas formulates the principle, or doctrine:

> A physician may not treat a patient until he has explained to the patient the risk and material facts concerning the treatment and its alternatives, including nontreatment, and has secured the patient's *competent*, *voluntary*, and *understanding* consent to proceed.[8]

The addition that the principle provides to the discussions concerning paternalism and autonomy in the foregoing chapters is, obviously, the requirement of 'understanding'. Competence and voluntariness are important conditions in their own right as well, but they are more or less accounted for by the general conditions that rule out illegitimate forms of paternalism. Sane, adult human beings who are autonomous, calm and emotionally undisturbed, and who are not being influenced in an undue manner, are no doubt in a position to consent 'competently' and 'voluntarily' to medical procedures – it is the question of disclosure and understanding that remains unclear, even when agents are apparently capable of free and autonomous decision-making.

To ensure that the consent given by the patient is 'informed', or 'understanding', in the spirit of Annas' definition, the physician should disclose at least four elements, namely:

(i)   the nature and purpose of the proposed procedures;
(ii)   the likelihood of success;
(iii) the hazards of the procedure; and
(iv)   alternative treatments, including nontreatment.[9]

A. Edward Doudera, who in his article 'Informed consent: how much should the patient know?' presented this particular list, interpreted it narrowly, as excluding certain more specific pieces of information. In a footnote referring to the list, he went on to mention that, to his apparent dismay, there are:

some writers [who] want even more disclosed: diagnosis, choice of treatment, alternative treatments including no treatment at all; specific methods to be used in the course of treatment; potential risks; side-effects and benefits of treatment; future risks; expected pain and discomfort; and prognosis.[10]

But the categorical exclusion of all these matters is not, in fact, all that simple. How is one to disclose, for instance, the 'purpose of the procedure' without uttering a word about the diagnosis? And how is one to make the distinction between 'the hazards of the procedure' on the one hand, and 'potential and future risks' on the other? Due to problems of this kind, a broader interpretation seems preferable, stating that all the items spelled out in the latter citation are already implicitly included in the more concise formulation.

That one assumes the broader reading concerning the appropriate content of the disclosure, removes one set of problems, but also immediately evokes another set. The benefit of the narrow interpretation would be that the scope of the physicians' duty to inform would be distinctly defined. As this alternative has to be rejected as unrealistic, the scope of disclosure is left without clear boundaries, and it becomes all the more important to determine, with some accuracy at least, how thoroughly matters should be explained and how firmly one ought to ensure that the patient has actually understood the explanations.

Three alternative approaches have been employed by American courts in determining the legal adequacy of the disclosure.[11] First, reference has been made to professional standards by maintaining that it is not the physicians' duty to tell their patients anything that their colleagues would not normally disclose. Since one can imagine an infinite variety of possible worlds where all doctors consistently disclose only a few irrelevant details of the treatment, this possibility does not seem very appealing as far as critical morality is concerned. As a protective shield for the profession, though, such a defence would presumably be ideal from the viewpoint of physicians themselves. Second, however, a diametrically opposite position can be taken by maintaining that patients, not doctors, are the primary measure for the sufficiency of the disclosure: if the patient did not understand the actual risk of the procedure, then no valid consent was given. The obvious problem with this suggestion is that if it were actually enforced by law, there would be very little that physicians would dare to do owing to the constant fear of malpractice suits. Presumably this is the reason why this course has not often been taken. Third, what Doudera calls the 'future trend' in American law concerning informed consent, was introduced in 1972 in the cases of *Canterbury* v. *Spence* and *Cobbs* v. *Grant*.[12] The point of this approach is that doctors should disclose no more and no less information than the patients can reasonably be expected to find material to their decision-making concerning the proposed treatment. It remains, of course, largely unclear what exactly should be considered 'material',[13] or what a patient 'can reasonably be expected' to think about the matter, but from a philosophical viewpoint this approach seems the most promising. Doctors can indeed quite legitimately hold back information if the patient would very probably ignore it anyway, since the autonomy of the patients' decision-making will not be violated by the non-disclosure. On the other hand, it is the doctors' duty to tell everything that their patients will be likely to find relevant, as otherwise the unbiased self-determination of the patients' choices will be negligently undermined.

One of the merits of the third view above is that it nicely

evades three general criticisms that medical professionals sometimes put forward against the whole notion of 'informed consent'.
These are:

(a) that there are in all medical decision-making situations an infinite
    number of potential risks;
(b) that the patients are usually incapable of grasping the medical
    information relayed by the physician; and
(c) that the medical situation in itself is most often emotionally
    charged.[14]

As for the first point, it does not matter whether the number of
potential risks is finite or not: the important thing is that most
probably the risks the patients can be expected to find material form
a substantially more limited set. As for the second point, patients
may well be unable to grasp the full scientific implications of, say,
a prognosis in Latin, but this, far from releasing the doctors from
informing their patients, further intensifies the need of an adequate
disclosure in terms of what the patients *can* grasp and are apt to find
relevant. And, finally, medical situations may well be emotionally
charged, but it does not in any way follow from this fact that
patients cannot receive and process such pieces of information that
they find material, and make reasonably free and informed use of
them in their decision-making.

However, regardless of the way the doctrine of informed consent
is defined, there are always situations in which other considerations
should possibly outweigh the duty to disclose. Michael D. Kirby in
his article 'Informed consent – what does it mean?' gives a useful
account by reviewing seven suggested exceptions to the requirement
of informed consent. These include

(1) acute medical emergencies;
(2) patients who already have full knowledge of their situation;
(3) confinement to general terms;
(4) the non-availability of alternative treatments;
(5) the non-harmfulness of the treatment;
(6) the best interest of the patient; and
(7) patients who do not wish to be informed.[15]

Employing patient autonomy as his primary ethical criterion,
Kirby finds exceptions (1) – (3) largely acceptable, points (4)
and (5) misguided, and appeals to (6) and (7) either problematic
or inapplicable at a general level.

As regards emergencies (1) and knowledgeable patients (2), it is easy to agree with Kirby. In the emergency case, especially if the patient is unconscious, the disclosure would obviously be futile. Similarly, if a patient possesses expert medical knowledge concerning her own illness, it is hard to see the significance of further attempts to inform her. However, the remark permitting confinement to disclosure only in 'general terms' (3) is more problematic. What Kirby seems to mean by this permission is not, namely, that specific medical language can be omitted – which would be reasonable from the viewpoint of patient autonomy – but rather that physicians are allowed to restrict their disclosure to the immediate effects of the suggested procedure. Kirby himself expresses the matter thus:

> Certainly, the medical practitioner is not under an obligation to describe in detail all of the remotely possible consequences of treatment. . . . There is no obligation to go over with the patient anything more than the 'inherent implications' of the particular procedure proposed for treatment.[16]

In the light of what has been stated above, one must object to this on two accounts. First, Kirby seems to have forgotten all about the *alternatives* to the proposed procedures: it is, after all, quite impossible for the patient to make well-thought-out and well-informed decisions, if medical experts are permitted to conceal all choices but the one they themselves are suggesting. From a strictly legal viewpoint this is not necessarily a problem, since the patient can always refuse the treatment on its own merits, but it is definitely an ethical problem if autonomy is considered important. Second, it also remains unclear why the practitioner could not, after explaining the alternatives that are available, and their 'inherent implications', go on to summarize the 'remotely possible consequences' as well. Even granted that it would take too much time and effort to fully describe all possible combinations, there is hardly anything to prevent the doctor from providing a more general statement.

The artificial nature of these restrictions becomes even more apparent when they are compared with Kirby's views on the non-availability of alternatives (4) and the non-harmfulness of the treatment (5) as potential exceptions to the rule requiring informed consent. Reasonably enough, Kirby rejects these suggestions, in the former case because, alternatives or no alternatives, the patient needs knowledge in order to accept or refuse the proposed treatment, in the latter case because it would not cause any difficulties for the doctor to let the patient know that no harm is forthcoming, and then leave the decision to him. I find no cause for disagreement in these inferences. But if knowledge is given when this can be done without overwhelming effort, I cannot understand why Kirby would wish to defend the physician's right to 'confinement to general terms'.

As to appeals to the patient's best interest (6), Kirby sensibly maintains that cases where the patient's right to know about his condition can be overridden by paternalistic reasons are very rare. It is sometimes possible that any amount of information could trigger a disastrous mental process, and indirectly inflict irreparable harm on an individual, but no overall policies can be founded upon these exceptional instances. The situation is entirely different, of course, when patients themselves do not wish to know about their condition (7). In such cases, it is often appropriate and humane to respect the patients' wishes, especially if the knowledge would no longer serve any medical or otherwise relevant purposes. However, there may also be cases in which it is an individual's duty to know about his own medical condition. Notably, this may be the case where the disclosure can be expected to have a considerable positive effect on the wellbeing of others. Thus, the doctor's duty to inform the patient is sometimes supplemented by the patient's respective duty to know.

A DUTY TO TELL, A DUTY TO KNOW?

The medical practitioner's obligation to disclose information concerning the patient's condition has not, however, historically been recognized for long, and it is certainly not universally recognized even today. Many theorists tend to think that medical work can only be efficient if the traditional, strongly paternalistic *medical values*, allegedly based on the best interest of the patient in the spirit of the Hippocratic Oath, are restored and respected.[17] These 'traditional medical values', according to those who rely on them, seem to support quite straightforward utility calculations with regard to disclosure and non-disclosure: the patients should hear the truth if, and only if, in the physician's judgement, they will be benefited rather than harmed by it. The defenders of this view do not usually consider patient autonomy as being primary to medical ethics – instead, they maintain that the doctors' primary duties in their work are, first, to abstain from harming their patients, and second, to try to benefit them.[18] As a recent formulation puts the matter, autonomous choice is just 'one biological function' among others, 'not the only one, or always the overriding one, or a function having preferred formal status'.[19] And as the autonomy of free and informed choices and decisions in this model ceases to be a major value, disclosure loses its importance as well.

There are, however, at least two ways of challenging the 'traditional medical values' approach to the question of truth-telling in medicine and health care. First, the *empirical* claim can be made that honesty still is, in the majority of cases, the best policy even for doctors. It is, according to this view, probable that telling the truth most often brings about a minimum of harm and a maximum of happiness in medical situations. And second, it can be stated that even if the effects of truth-telling were sometimes adverse, patients would still, *ethically* speaking, have a right to know about their own condition. Even if autonomy is not the only value, it is still one of the values to be considered in medical decision-making, and thus the burden of proof rests on the side of paternalistic physicians, who in fact are mostly unable to tell whether particular patients would be harmed by the truth or not.

As regards the empirical argument, a number of sceptical remarks have been made concerning the alleged benefits of lying or withholding the truth in bedside situations. It has been argued, for instance, that contrary to the doctors' beliefs patients usually want to hear the truth even if it is unpleasant;[20] that patients do not normally withdraw or deny their consent to proposed procedures when the risks are revealed to them;[21] that truth-telling as a part of a careful informed consent procedure does not harm patients;[22] and that, on the contrary, it is when patients are lied to or information is withheld that patients may suffer serious harm.[23] The difficulty with an appeal to these observations is, however, that they remain controversial as grounds for universal truth-telling in medicine. Although 95 per cent of patients may wish to be told the truth, and 80 per cent of them may bear it well, there will always be cases in which patients react to the truth in ways which are directly or indirectly harmful and possibly even fatal to them. Consequently, the defender of strong medical paternalism can maintain that the observations cited above in fact support rather than undermine her view: if telling the truth sometimes, no matter how rarely, leads to the premature death of a patient, then it is hard to see how a good case could be made in favour of universal disclosure.

This is where the ethical – as opposed to the empirical or 'scientific' – argument can be introduced. As Allen Buchanan points out in his article 'Medical paternalism', those who appeal to harm prevention usually forget that the assessment of harm should, of course, be *comparative* and not absolute.[24] The (alleged) fact that a patient will be harmed by the truth does not in itself prove that the truth should not be told: physicians must also ask themselves how much harm is to be expected from a policy of lying and withholding information. Only a thorough comparative evaluation would enable them to choose with any confidence the alternative which, in terms of preventing harm, is the best. And as Buchanan also notes, there is an additional problem in that the 'harm' to be assessed is not readily measurable, or even definable. Especially the claim that seriously ill patients are driven to suicide by the truth about their illness involves three difficulties: first, it is probably an unfounded psychiatric generalization; second, even if it were a sound psychiatric generalization, ordinary physicians would have no competence in applying it to their patients; and third, suicide is not necessarily an irrational choice for the terminally ill patient.[25] What these points add up to is that the 'harm caused by truth' by no means provides unequivocal support to the policy of selective non-disclosure.

Another argument for withholding the truth from patients is based on the idea that the physician–patient relationship is predominantly contractual. A common understanding of this idea among physicians is that the contract in question is *implicit*, and that simply by seeking professional medical assistance patients assent to any procedures the doctor may find beneficial to them. And as medical practices in the patient's alleged best interest may sometimes include lying, deceiving and withholding information, the patient has freely consented to all these possibilities in entering the doctor–patient relationship.[26] Furthermore, since the proposed basis for decisions is what *doctors expect* to be beneficial, not what the patients think about the matter, this approach evades the critique concerning definitions and assessments. Although comparative judgements may be difficult to make, they are not impossible when the values involved are medical and thus readily definable.[27]

Buchanan in his article attacks this view on two accounts.[28] First, if the contractual nature of physician–patient relationships is intended as a descriptive generalization, it is most certainly a false one: although there may be people who accept the idea of implicit authorization, there are surely also people who do not recognize its validity. And if the patient does not view his relationships with physicians as including an implicit permission to withhold information from him, then the model is descriptively unsound. Second, Buchanan also argues that it is not reasonable for patients to accept the authorization suggested by the contractual model, even if they had the opportunity to decide about the matter themselves. Buchanan's argument is that rational agents always set some limits at least to their explicit contractual relationships with other agents, thereby retaining the possibility of modifying or terminating the relationship if it becomes dangerous or unpleasant. This method of self-protection, however, would be unworkable in the medical authorization scheme: the information that the doctor withholds can be vital to the patient's decision-making, and if and when it is, lack of relevant knowledge will undermine any attempts that the patient may make to control the situation.

As far as the descriptive interpretation of the implicit contract between physician and patient is concerned, Buchanan is obviously correct: not every patient wishes to permit lies or half-truths 'in his own best interest'. But as regards the acceptability of explicit authorizations to the same effect, the situation is more complicated. Donald VanDeVeer, in an article entitled 'Withholding medical information', has criticized Buchanan's view by pointing out that the permission to conceal facts, given by the patient, does not necessarily extend as widely as Buchanan seems to think. VanDeVeer writes:

> I might want certain information revealed to me and other information not revealed. Recognizing the benefits frequently associated with the 'placebo effect' I may reasonably prefer not to be told when a placebo has been prescribed as part of my treatment. Also, I may recognize my penchant for undue anxiety and worry over the fact that certain of my symptoms are suggestive but not conclusive evidence of the presence of some dreaded disease. Hence, I may choose to remain ignorant of such matters until the physician is certain of its presence. Further, if my affairs are in order, I may even prefer to live out my last days falsely hopeful of recovery even when the physician is certain that I have terminal cancer. These preferences for ignorance with regard to a certain range of information may be made clear to the physician in a contract. . . . The nature of the contract would

obviously depend on one's preferences and one's degree of trust and confidence in the judgment [of] one's physician.[29]

Within the kind of contractual context sketched by VanDeVeer, indeed, Buchanan's worries about the patient losing control of the situation seem rather far-fetched. If there is an explicit contract between the patient and the doctor, the conditions can surely be formulated in a manner which will allow maximum autonomy for the patient's decision-making. Since the patient can obviously call the contract off if this becomes necessary, he can, at any time, obtain all the information the physician can give. And while the contract is on, his autonomy is probably best respected by withholding the facts he has chosen to be ignorant about.

But although VanDeVeer is probably correct in that an explicit contract would under certain circumstances legitimate the non-disclosure of unpleasant truths, it is by no means clear that such contracts or circumstances exist in contemporary health care systems. In reality, the procedure of finding out what a patient wishes to know is far more complicated. In the words of Raanan Gillon:

> There is, of course, an important practical difficulty here: how is the doctor to find out a patient's views without disclosing any unpleasant facts to those patients who would rather not know such information? There is no simple answer to this, but by sensitive questioning or by simply (but genuinely and at different times) offering to answer any questions, and giving adequate time for this, skilful doctors can often master this difficult medical art.[30]

In practice, Gillon's advice may be difficult to follow, just as explicit contracts between doctors and patients may be rare, but the important thing here is that the moral message of these two exceptions to the ban of medical deception is essentially the same. Non-disclosure is ethically acceptable only if it parallels or supports rather than violates the patient's autonomous decision-making.

John Harris in his book *The Value of Life* combines the topics of this section and the foregoing one by raising the issue of *informed consent to non-disclosure*. He argues, against a view expressed by Michael Kirby, that a patient who waives his right to information – and the doctor's corresponding obligation to disclose it – does not know what he is consenting to, and thereby is in no position to validly assent to any medical procedures the doctor may suggest.[31] This remark is, of course, essentially correct: if 'valid consent' is taken to mean consent based on information that the medical profession judges important, a sufficiently informed consent is not possible unless the patient knows all the relevant facts about his condition. But the situation is different if it is stated, as in the above, that the doctrine of informed consent only requires the doctor to disclose what 'the patients can reasonably be expected to find material to their decision-making'. A patient's explicit wish not to know about certain details concerning his own physical health excludes, within this kind of theory, such details from the scope of valid informed consent. The only remaining question, then, is whether one should talk about 'informed' or simply 'valid' consent in these cases. But this is rather a matter of stipulation than a matter of serious argumentation.

Harris, however, also raises another question which is important in the context of disclosure and non-disclosure, namely, whether or not 'the patients have a *right to remain in ignorance* if they so wish, or if, in the judgment of the doctor, full disclosure would somehow harm the patient'.[32] Harris himself takes a sceptical stand on the issue, contending that even if the patient clearly does not wish to be told about her condition, it is difficult to see what the basis for a *right* not to know would be. He writes:

> There are all sorts of unpleasant things in life that we might prefer not to know about, but it does not follow that anyone infringes our rights if they inform us. I might well wish to remain blissfully ignorant of the plight of the poor, or of the starving, or of victims of disease or of accidents, and to hear about such things might distress me greatly, but it does not follow from this that I possess a right that no one tells me about them.[33]

After these remarks, Harris goes on to assert that here, as in his view elsewhere, the language of 'rights' is unhelpful in tackling the ethical problems of medical practice.

But even though I agree with Harris in that mere talk about rights often leaves the fundamental questions of medical ethics unanswered, I also believe that the right to remain in ignorance – meaning the doctor's duty not to disclose information against the patient's wishes – cannot be universally rejected by using the particular examples he introduces for the purpose. A person's ignorance concerning the plight of the poor and the starving is not necessarily her business alone, since the unpleasant information that she has so far managed to evade could, when finally conveyed, well lead to a desire to do something for those in need. To put the matter in slightly different terms, the fact that one does not care to know about other people's misery may well be other-regarding in a sense in which ignorance concerning one's own physical condition is not. Of course, there are cases in which these categories get mixed, as in the Case of the Determined Doctor, involving the patient who wants to ignore a possible HIV infection (Case (4) introduced in chapter 1, p. 5). In addition to the possible self-regarding benefits of non-disclosure for the patient, ignorance of one's HIV infection could, at least arguably, encourage unsafe sexual habits which, in turn, could further spread the disease.[34] Mixed or unmixed, however, the point is that a patient's prima-facie right to remain in ignorance cannot be legitimately overridden by strongly paternalistic considerations alone – disclosure against the patient's explicit wishes can only be justifiable if harm to others is to be expected, as in fact is the case in Harris' examples.

It must be noted here that the borderline between weak and strong paternalism is extremely fuzzy when the duty or permission to disclose information in medical contexts is discussed. Lack of knowledge is, after all, one of the legitimate grounds for weakly paternalistic intervention, and it would therefore seem that disclosure is always permissible. So far at least Harris seems to be correct. But if the patient's consent is an important factor, and if one can validly consent to remain in ignorance, as I have argued, then disclosure against the patient's wishes turns into strong, unjustifiable paternalism. In reality, when the doctor tries to find out what the patient wants – and does not want – to know, the distinction between strong and weak paternalism becomes no doubt in many cases blurred. However, this is not to say that there is no distinction, or that it lacks ethical relevance. Although it may frequently be difficult to distinguish between autonomy-respecting and autonomy-violating behaviour, the difference does exist, and it should be taken into account whenever it can be clearly recognized.

Cases (1) – (4), introduced in chapter 1 above (pp. 4–5), all involve either a duty to tell or an alleged duty to know, and it is therefore appropriate to conclude this part of the discussion by briefly summarizing some of their ethically relevant features.

(1) In the Case of the Dying Mother, Mrs *A*'s doctor knows that her son has recently died during criminal activities, but the doctor hides this from the mother, allegedly to secure her peaceful demise. There are at least two major difficulties with such deceptive behaviour under the circumstances of the case. First, the doctor's choice shows that he regards and treats Mrs *A* as an example of the imaginary category 'Sweet Old Ladies' rather than as an individual with her own thoughts and feelings: the way the situation is described, there is nothing to guarantee that Mrs *A*'s peaceful demise would in fact be furthered by the doctor's lies. After all, it is quite possible that Mrs *A*, who has always been convinced that her son is a genuine rotten egg, has survived for so long merely by clinging on to the hope that she will live to see the disgrace of the family wiped off permanently. If so, then what the doctor secures for her by his lies is a death overshadowed by an unnecessary sense of disappointment and defeat. Second, even if the doctor happened to estimate Mrs *A*'s mood correctly, it would remain unclear whether his lie is designed to benefit the patient or, rather, to spare the medical personnel from inconvenience. Even assuming that the news would be distressing, it does not seem in any way obvious that Mrs *A* herself would be better off without the information: only truthful disclosure can give her a fair chance to settle things in her mind and take stock of her life as it really is. Such a process is not necessarily peaceful, and it may often be disturbing to medical personnel – who would be saved from the potential unpleasantness only by lying to the patient in the first place. Bearing these remarks in mind, and being convinced that the anguish of doctors and nurses should never override the needs of the patient, I would hesitate to judge the doctor's lie to Mrs *A* as ethically acceptable as such.

(2) In the Case of the Man with Lung Cancer, the doctor with-holds from her 75-year-old patient the information that a shadowed area probably indicating lung cancer has been detected in his chest x-ray examination. Fortunately for the doctor, the patient dies two-and-a-half years later of other causes, never knowing about the professional suspicions, and thereby never being able to challenge the doctor's deception. It is alleged in the description of the case that the patient is happy until the end, and that his happiness in fact is the factor that justifies withholding the truth from him. But the situation is not as simple as all that. To begin with, the contingent fact that the patient never comes to know about the

doctor's suspicions, and therefore 'dies happily', does not justify morally dubious choices even within a rough-and-ready utilitarian model. Consider, as a point of comparison, the following case which is structurally similar:

> A casual passer-by happens to see a blind beggar sitting on the pavement. Instead of simply walking on, the passer-by steps aside and kicks the beggar in the head. When the beggar wakes up in hospital, his sight has miraculously returned, and he is immeasurably happy.

Despite the unexpected twist in the course of events, the subsequent happiness of the beggar hardly justifies the attack against him: it is the expected rather than the actual outcome that determines the moral value of the action. In a similar manner, the physician is unable to legitimate her duplicity by referring to the accidental happiness of the patient, as it is clear that the knowledge concerning the disease, obtained through other channels, could easily have tipped the balance during the two-and-a-half years following the initial deception. The patient could then have been rendered considerably more desperate by the hiding of information than he would have been by a straightforward professional disclosure at the very beginning. Furthermore, there are the patient's dignity and autonomy to be considered as well. If one does not want to accept deception of people in general, it is hard to see how qualities such as age, illness and dependency could make such a radical difference. Such factors do not justify keeping information from elderly men who are not in the best of their health any more.

(3) The Case of the Fatal Urography concerns informed consent and highlights one of the problems of telling the truth: the experienced radiologist does not disclose the remote possibility of death caused by intravenous urography, and when the worst happens, he is accused of acting without a valid consent. Under these circumstances, the important thing is whether or not a less than 1 in 20,000 risk of death is to be considered 'material' to the patient. Obviously, this will depend on the preferences and attitudes of the patient herself, and the radiologist clearly makes a mistake by assuming a rigid policy of non-disclosure regardless of the patient's opinions. Here again, one of the doctor's motives is reported to be 'to facilitate things' – presumably for himself – and it is thus not necessarily the patient's best interest that the physician has in mind in deciding about the withholding of information. In the name of

fairness, it must also be said that when the risk is as small as it is in this case, the doctor's choice is quite understandable. However, understanding the doctor's behaviour cannot imply accepting it, if he has not taken all the steps in his power to secure that the procedures taken are not likely to violate the patient's autonomy.

(4) The Case of the Determined Doctor differs from the first three examples in that a duty to know rather than a duty to tell is at issue. A middle-aged man returns from Central Africa and wants to be tested for every sexually transmissible disease except AIDS – he tells the doctor that since there is no cure, he does not want to know about his possible HIV infection. Against the patient's wishes, however, the doctor tests his blood for HIV antibodies, and, finding the result positive, informs the patient about the contagion. The ethically problematic question here is not, I believe, the one concerning the paternalistic disclosure itself: once it has been established that the patient wishes to remain in ignorance, it cannot be the physician's business to force information on him on the pretence that it is 'in his own best interest'. It may be the case that those who learn about their HIV infection at the earliest stages will during the actual illness be better off both physically and psychologically, but it does not follow from this that a forcible intervention is justified. Neither is it possible to defend the disclosure by appealing to harm inflicted on other people, since the connection between knowledge on the one hand and protective action on the other is far too complicated to be judged with any confidence by the physician.[35]

Consequently, the only question which has real ethical significance here is whether the validity of *uninformed consent* not to be tested ought to be recognized, or should the patient be informed about the implications of an HIV infection before his request for (only) selective testing is fulfilled. It seems that *in situations like this* John Harris may, after all, be correct in maintaining that patients cannot validly consent to something they do not know anything about. By this I do not mean to deny the possibility of a voluntary and competent decision to remain in ignorance – the point is, rather, that the physician cannot necessarily evade her professional responsibilities simply by doing what the patient in the example asks her to do. Although the link between knowing about one's HIV infection and protecting others is too fragile to justify deceptive testing and compulsory telling, it may nevertheless be solid enough to obligate the doctor to inform her patient about the risks of contagion before accepting the consent not to be tested.

After informing the patient, however, the doctor should not prolong fulfilling his request any more. And it must be remembered that even though this kind of compulsory AIDS education may indeed be justifiable, it is only justifiable because it may protect others from harm, not on the grounds that the 'patient's own best interest' could legitimate the practice.

REFUSALS AND COMPULSION: THE DRAMATIC CASES

I have examined at some length the relatively undramatic issues of benevolent bedside lying, medical deception for the patient's own sake, and attempts to extract the patient's consent without properly informing her or him. The reason for this emphasis is that instances of quiet and unnoticeable withholding of information presumably constitute a major part of the day-to-day medical paternalism in clinics and hospitals, and thus they are, from a practical viewpoint at least, as important as the philosophically more intriguing medico-ethical decisions involving life, death and human reproduction. I shall now turn my attention to the latter category, which at the level of clinical practice consists of refusals to treat, refusals not to treat and (other) compulsory medical procedures, intertwined with and complicated by an array of religious and ideological considerations.

When 'ordinary' ailments such as headaches, bone fractures or appendicitis are concerned, the physician usually has little reason to refrain from giving treatments – likewise, the patient seldom has good grounds for refusing to be treated. In emergency situations, Jehovah's Witnesses are probably the only group to have systematic problems: for religious reasons, a member of this sect cannot accept blood transfusions even if her medical condition was otherwise fatal. In some countries the medical professionals are appropriately safeguarded against litigation in these situations, and they can respect the patient's wishes if no one else is involved; in other countries (e.g. in Finland) the policy is to wait until the patient has lost consciousness, and then proceed to administer the blood transfusion according to the decision-making powers that physicians normally have during emergencies. The latter solution is, of course, more often than not outrageously autonomy-violating, since in the name of self-determination and valid consent, physicians in fact have no right to tamper with the patient's choices after she cannot alter them herself. But here again the doctor's decision may seem quite understandable, particularly when one reminds oneself of the fact that the policy of life-saving, if known to all within the religious community, may well function as a safety-net for individuals who really want to have the vital transfusion but who do not want to lose face in the eyes of the rest of the sect. The situation is perhaps analogous to duelling and its prohibition: public authorities should carefully assess whether the influence of traditions and ideologies in such cases is 'undue' – if it is, then weak paternalism is all that is needed to justify compulsory practices. The additional problem with giving blood transfusions to Jehovah's Witnesses is, however, that if religious belief is considered contradictory to 'real' autonomy, the vast majority of humankind ought to be defined as non-autonomous, and this, in turn, would be quite destructive to the general liberal position.

In non-emergencies, people sometimes grow tired of the inability of 'official' or 'school medicine' to offer relief, and they may then turn to the practitioners of 'alternative medicine' instead. Homeopathy, acupuncture, herbalist healing and many other methods whose therapeutic value from the viewpoint of Western medical science is either dubious or inexplicable are often employed as last chances when major operations or massive medication have proved ineffective.[36] Alternative healing methods sometimes help and sometimes do not help the patient, much in the same way as school medicine can fail as well as succeed in curing people's illnesses – after all, a major factor in any healing is and always has been the 'placebo effect' of caring human contact combined with reassuring medical rituals. The difficulty for the public authorities who more readily rely on modern science-based medicine is that sometimes its alternatives may seem positively dangerous to the patients, either directly (as in 'letting out the bad blood' of a patient who is anaemic to start with), or indirectly (as in trying to 'cure' cancer with homeopathic products while tumours in the patient's body keep fatally spreading). If the patient really knows what she is doing, and is capable of making autonomous decisions without undue pressures, the case from the ethical viewpoint is clear: even assuming that there are apparently irrational risks present, the choice of treatment is the patient's own decision, and should not be interfered with. Furthermore, from the fact that a patient decides to rely on scientifically dubious procedures it should not be automatically inferred that she is lacking in relevant knowledge. Nor is it acceptable to argue that the illness itself is always a pressure which decreases the patient's decision-making abilities. On the other hand, of course, the mixture of religion, ideology and economic competition characteristic of many branches of alternative medicine render illegitimate pressures quite possible when desperate people seek help from whoever offers it. But all one can deduce from this possibility is that consumer protection is an extremely important matter in controlling the risks of unofficial as well as official healing practices.

A particularly tricky problem which manifests itself both in the blood transfusion issue and in licensing unorthodox therapies is the question of who gets to make the ultimate decisions concerning the treatment of *children* whose consent cannot yet be considered valid. Existing legislation in many countries seems to hand down this power to parents by letting them, in the non-medical field at least, decide about most things that concern their child's welfare before he reaches maturity. There are exceptions, however, to this parental decision-making power, one of them stating that parents are not allowed to inflict harm on the child by their choices – thus it may seem as if lethal refusals of blood or dangerous commitments to probably ineffective methods could easily be overridden by what one would perhaps like to call more responsible decision-making by public authorities. But the situation is not all that simple. If the only foundation for arguments on both sides is the best interest of the child, it is not at all clear which one of the paternalistic agencies is employing the right criteria in its choices. Granted that premature death and aggravated illness are great evils, those defending the alternative positions might argue that even greater evils are to be expected from the interference of the authorities. Jehovah's Witnesses, in particular, can maintain that natural death in their axiology is relatively unimportant as compared to the prospect that the survival of one's eternal soul may be compromised by letting foreign blood into one's veins.

The most intuitive solution to the problem is, I believe, an appeal to the child's *future autonomy*. When it comes to protection of individuals who have not yet developed a capacity to make (sufficiently) consistent and self-determined choices, legitimate paternalistic authority is held by the agency who possesses the strongest potential of raising the child to the level of autonomous decision-making. What such an authority ideally ought to do amounts to two rules which should be applied in a lexical order.[37] First, future autonomy should be recognized as the primary goal to be aimed at: any policy which is harmful to the individual's development towards self-determination ought to be strongly discouraged. And second, if this is not against the first rule in the situation in question, the fragments of autonomy the individual already possesses should be protected and cultivated: to put it roughly, whenever there is no fatal danger in letting the child decide for himself, this should be allowed. In the two examples examined above, the application of these rules may well imply mutually different results. As regards the issue of blood transfusions and Jehovah's Witnesses, parents clearly prevent their children from becoming autonomous human beings by refusing the treatment, and these parents should therefore be ignored in the decision-making. Admittedly, there may be difficulties with the socialization of the children later on, as the sect may consider them outsiders, and their development towards firm self-determination may be hindered. But whichever way one looks at the matter, survival is a necessary precondition of independent decision-making in the future, and must be respected as such. Alternative medicine, in turn, is an entirely different matter in that the lives of children are seldom in greater direct risk from unofficial healing methods than they are from officially accepted procedures. When terminally ill children are concerned, survival is no option anyway, and when milder illnesses are in question, irreparable harm through even the most blatant quackery is rare. Thus the intervention by public authorities is justified only if severe but curable conditions are ignored and children may otherwise die owing to their parents' dedication to an 'alternative' medical ideology – in other words, if the circumstances closely resemble those of the blood transfusion case.

Turning now to even more hotly debated issues, non-therapeutic abortions and voluntary euthanasia have both been resisted on strongly paternalistic grounds by professional physicians. The abortion discussion has in our day drifted into other directions, as the main argument has for the last few decades been that by terminating pregnancies women and abortionists alike inflict harm on 'others', i.e. the foetuses, and violate their 'sanctity of life'.[38] It is, however, useful to remember that, for instance, the medical profession in nineteenth-century America consistently maintained that terminations were extremely dangerous to women and should therefore be prohibited, when in fact the actual risks of abortion were – as they still are in countries where restrictive policies prevail – mostly due to the physicians' own efforts to outlaw the practice. What the American doctors really worried about was not so much the well-being of women as their own professional and financial status in comparison with 'non-regular' abortionists – or, in the case of more idealistic doctors, a fear that the native Puritan population would be outnumbered by Catholics, who did not permit abortions.[39] This example is a good reminder of the fact that allegedly protective attitudes at the level of public policy most often disguise other motives, based on self-interest and ideological commitments.

As direct harm to others has been more difficult to detect in proposals concerning voluntary euthanasia than in the abortion debate, conservative theorists have had to invent more ingenious explanations for defending their restrictive attitudes. In the light of what has been stated in the preceding chapters, genuine requests for a good and easy death, whether to be induced actively or passively, are unproblematic as far as justified medical paternalism goes.[40] When a patient expresses a wish to die rather than to continue living, the authenticity of the wish must, of course, be carefully checked. But if the decision proves to be autonomous and considered, refusals allegedly appealing to the 'patient's own best interest' surely reflect fear of public opinion and legal sanctions rather than true concern for the patient's ailment. It is an entirely different matter whether or not additional considerations, like the fact that active euthanasia requires that someone actually *kills* the patient, alter the situation. Strictly in the context of the patient's own good, respect for her autonomy speaks loudly in favour of fulfilling her considered and reasonably self-determined wishes.

Alexander Morgan Capron in an article entitled 'Right to refuse medical care' has lucidly analysed the reasons conservative theorists usually put forward against euthanasia, and against fatal refusals of treatment.[41] As Capron notes, in addition to the aspects that create paternalistic tension – autonomy and self-regarding harm – there are at least six competing principles and claims to be taken into account, namely:[42]

(1) that the refusal of treatment is a violation of societal norms related to health care;

(2) that the refusal of treatment may (cumulatively) threaten the maintenance of a healthy and sufficient population which is needed to preserve society;

(3) that the refusal of treatment may indirectly inflict harm on identifiable third parties when the result is serious injury or death;

(4) that the refusal of treatment threatens to increase unnecessarily health care and other costs;

(5) that the refusal of treatment presents a threat against public morality and decency; and

(6) that the refusal of treatment is a violation of the basic moral principle that life is sacred.

All these reasons can, however, be challenged on closer analysis, as Capron in fact does.

(1) By the first point Capron refers to social expectations which are related to the workings of the health care system. Citing Talcott Parsons, he writes:

> A person who is ill is accorded the many special privileges that go with the sick role but is expected to reciprocate by devoting himself or herself to the task of regaining health by seeking out and cooperating with technically competent assistance. On its face, a refusal of indicated treatment means that the individual has violated societal norms. For protection of the errant individual, society can thus be seen as having legitimate reasons to countermand those choices.[43]

The idea that persons who are sick ought to behave in a certain inoffensive manner and participate in the professionals' efforts to regain health may seem rather attractive with regard to ordinary illnesses which are believed to be curable. Suppose, for instance, that a patient refuses to take his prescribed medication, and the result (which was clearly predictable from the beginning) is that he develops certain additional unpleasant symptoms. Under such circumstances, there is a definite temptation to think that as the patient has violated the accepted rules, he will have to bear the consequences as well: it is not the doctor's duty to relieve 'self-inflicted' symptoms, especially if there are also 'genuine' patients to be attended to. (I shall return to this question below, in examining Capron's fourth point.) But these considerations cannot be applied very well to *incurable* conditions or *fatal* refusals of treatment, since sooner or later the expected outcome in these cases is the patient's death. Unless posthumous degradation – as the burying of suicides in unsanctified ground – is considered a proper and effective sanction, there is no method of reaching the patients afterwards for correction.

(2) The point concerning the cumulative effect of refusals reintroduces the topic discussed at the end of chapter 5 above, i.e. the circumstances that Joel Feinberg called *garrison threshold situations*. Assuming that 'an organized society has an interest in its own preservation', as Capron states,[44] it does indeed seem possible to condemn individual decisions to die as being potential elements in the breakdown of society: if too many individuals decide to depart life voluntarily and prematurely, the vanishing of a healthy and dynamic population can threaten the very continuity of social life. But this argument against refusals of treatment is, as also pointed out by Capron, flawed both empirically and conceptually.[45] To start with, there is no reason whatsoever to believe that refusals of lifesaving treatment would in the near future accumulate sufficiently so as to threaten the survival of any presently existing society. In fact, only the terminally ill and the suffering can be expected to take an interest in the possibility of dying quickly and easily, and as they are presumably not a part of the 'healthy and dynamic population' anyway, their voluntary demise would hardly make a crucial demographic difference. And even if it did, one would have to question the nature and spirit of a society which would have to protect its existence by forcing treatments upon people and preventing them from killing themselves *en masse*. All organised societies may have an *interest* in preserving themselves, but not all of them are morally *entitled* to it.

(3) The third of the competing claims is that refusals of treatment and decisions to die may inflict economic or psychological harm on third parties such as friends, business associates, medical advisers, spouses and children. This claim can perhaps best be analysed in three stages. As regards *psychological effects* in general, it is hardly plausible to defend lifesaving treatment against the patient's wishes on the ground that the professional or familial feelings of some adult human beings will otherwise be hurt. The doctor's pride and the cousin's grief may deserve some attention but they are, after all, minor factors when compared to the patient's freedom of choice. *Economic loss*, when it is grave, could in some cases be

a more serious consideration, but since people can only be kept alive, not economically productive, against their own wishes, the utility of regulations to this effect would be questionable. The harm the patient is about to inflict by refusing treatment can no doubt be produced in other (legitimate) ways if the refusal is ignored. Finally, the case of *minor dependants* seems to be the most problematic: parents dying of their own free will and leaving their children behind without adequate support could sometimes, in principle at least, be accused of neglect. But two observations reduce the relative weight of this point. First, one must recall that patients requesting voluntary euthanasia are mostly in a terminal phase, and seldom have long to live – the neglect, then, would only be worth mentioning in the exceptional circumstances where, say, the fortnight that the patient can be kept alive would make a drastic difference in the children's financial position or emotional balance. Second, even if the death was premature or the loss otherwise voluntarily brought about, it should be noted that authorities do not usually interfere with the dealings of parents with their children in matters related to economy, health or habits. It would not, therefore, seem fair to force helpless patients to undergo predicaments which are not imposed on their fellow human beings who happen to be healthy.[46]

(4) Fairness is also a key word in rejecting a claim which states that refusals of treatment unnecessarily increase health care costs. What those presenting this claim characteristically believe is that 'declining efficacious treatment often worsens the patient's condition and may even lead to permanent disability and the need for further care for the patient and for his or her dependants'.[47] The idea seems to be that this state of affairs would be regrettable, because the need for 'further care' would create an unnecessary burden on the public medical system. But the division of health care services into 'necessary' and 'unnecessary' like this is not at all unproblematic. Capron draws attention to two major difficulties: first, counting the actual loss in real life cases is by no means easy, as the non-monetary burden will be mostly carried by families and friends, and as the monetary cost is often partly covered by private resources; second, as those with private means will automatically have the health care they need even after the refusals, it would be unjust to discriminate against those who have to rely on publicly funded services. In addition, why should clinical refusals be treated any differently from all the other methods of 'voluntarily' acquiring illnesses, such as mountain-climbing, smoking, breathing in Western

capitals and jogging? When one looks at the matter impartially, the only possible conclusion is that refusals of treatment do not lead to 'unnecessary' health care needs any more or any less than other high-risk activities do.

(5) The fifth point against fatal refusals of treatment and requests for voluntary euthanasia is that these choices, even though strictly speaking harmless to others, will pose a threat to public morality and decency. Capron formulates this accusation in slightly more concrete terms by stating that if it is accepted, then prohibitions of self-destructive behaviour can be based 'on the moral and aesthetic revulsion felt by many people for an act that goes contrary to social mores and the instinct of self-preservation'.[48] As this kind of attempt to justify coercive practices was considered at some length – and finally refuted – in chapter 5, I believe that it is not necessary to return to the question again. Even the most rudimentary respect for values such as freedom, autonomy and personal privacy requires that self-regarding human activities are not constrained merely because they arouse indignation and disgust in people who have nothing to do with these activities or the people who practise them.

(6) The final argument against giving up one's life is that all life is, in some indefinable – yet to many people persuasive – sense *sacred*. Insofar as the 'sacredness of life' does not merely refer to the inarticulate 'moral' or 'religious feelings' that people sometimes have, there are four basic messages that the phrase may be intended to imply, namely: (i) that (human) life is always absolutely valuable; (ii) that every human being ultimately wants to live; (iii) that it is strictly forbidden to use human beings as a means to an ulterior end; (iv) that every human being possesses an inalienable right to live. The difficulty with these maxims is that they are, each and every one of them, either invalid, ambiguous or at least inapplicable to the purpose they are set to serve in the argument. The only valid principle which can be formulated concerning the 'sacredness of life', on the basis of these maxims or otherwise, is in fact the one stating that *if* a person wants to live, then she ought not to be killed by others. And while this is no doubt a sound principle when one wishes to defend the prohibition of murdering people, i.e. *taking lives* against the victim's will, it does not make much of an argument against *giving up lives* when that is what people want to do. Thus the 'sacredness of life' does not directly justify the societal regulation of refusals of treatment and voluntary euthanasia.

Some theorists maintain, however, that the required justification is in fact indirect: that although even active euthanasia could be accepted in itself, the real problem is that the liberation of voluntary procedures would inevitably lead to pressures which would support non-voluntary and involuntary killing as well. The prime example for proponents of this view is the development which led from 'euthanasia programmes' to mass murder and genocide in National Socialist Germany during the 1930s.[49] The problem with this so-called *slippery slope* (or 'thin end of the wedge' or 'snowball effect' or 'camel's nose') argument is that the German experiment never had anything to do with permitting euthanasia at the patient's free and deliberated request – rather, 'euthanasia' was a euphemism for doing away with those who were racially or politically suspect, or whose ability to work was reduced.[50] So there was never any development in Germany from what was acceptable and just to what was not, only a steady accumulation of injustice. And in the absence of further evidence concerning fatal slippery slopes, it is difficult to see how the argument could seriously be defended, or indeed where its alleged worth lies.

Capron's six points provide a useful framework for assessing many instances of strong medical paternalism, not only refusals of treatment and requests for voluntary euthanasia. One contentious issue that can be analysed by Capron's tools is the doctor's refusal to sterilize a healthy young person on her own request (Case (5) in chapter 1, p. 5). If all the foregoing remarks concerning freedom and autonomy are to be taken seriously, it is at once clear that a physician who refuses to operate by appealing to the patient's best interest is violating the patient's right to self-determination and is therefore acting wrongly. But the physician can also decline to use the explicitly paternalistic argument and employ a combination of Capron's points (1), (2) and (4) instead. Patients who ask their doctors to operate on healthy and functioning organs are, according to this view, transgressing the rules of medical interaction, which are aimed at removing illness and preventing future disease, not at satisfying the patients' random whims. In the particular case of sterilization, moreover, the patients' refusal to propagate presents a potential threat against the survival of society, and the operation itself unnecessarily increases health care costs. The upshot of all this is that, minimally, people who want to be sterilized in publicly funded hospitals for no clinical reason should be told that if they really want the operation they can have it, but that societal health care services after the operation will not be made available to them any more, since they have broken the generally accepted rules of medical care and refused to contribute to the survival of society.

There may be a certain initial appeal in this argument, but closer scrutiny reveals serious flaws. To begin with, propagation is hardly the only way to benefit society – a fact which becomes especially clear if one thinks in terms of the Case of the Refused Sterilization (Case (5)), where the patient requesting tubal ligation is herself a young medical practitioner. Surely it is imaginable that in her capacity as a doctor she will do more for the survival of society than the mother of a dozen healthy bank robbers. And there are, of course, additional considerations which increase the difficulties facing the argument, such as attitudes towards contraception, infertility and total chastity. Should all these methods and conditions somehow be regulated? Should everybody using contraceptives be excluded from the health care provision because society is in danger? If the proponent of the view does not want to commit himself to absurdities like these, he must also reject his own original claims about regulating voluntary childlessness.

Refusals to operate on people at their own request seem all the more bizarre when attention is drawn to the favourable opinions medical professionals often hold regarding *compulsory* sterilizations for the mentally retarded. The same people who cannot bring themselves to tie the tubes of someone who wishes it and clearly expresses the wish, can quite lightheartedly sterilize a retarded person who does not even know what is happening, on the alleged ground that 'it makes his or her life easier'.[51] In a majority of cases, the actual reason for sterilizing a mentally retarded person is that his or her parents want it to be done: the fertility of a retarded child is threatening and burdensome *to the parents themselves*, symbolically as well as concretely. There are persistent taboos, such as those regarding contraception and masturbation, which often prevent discussion and other less drastic solutions, and create an unnecessary pressure towards invasive surgery. It is most likely, therefore, that a better solution to the problems of both the child and the parents would usually be reached by providing the family with financial, social and psychological support which would enable the parents to be open in discussing sexual matters with the child *and* which would give the child room to express him or herself both physically and emotionally without getting involved in potentially exploitative sexual relations.[52] Doctors who deny this, and insist on compulsory sterilizations without the patient's consent as a standard solution, may find that the only justification open to them is an appeal to eugenics and racial hygiene, previously employed in pre-war Germany, where up to 50,000 people were sterilized yearly against their own will.[53] And somehow one is inclined to think that physicians would not like to encompass the National Socialist medical ideals in this matter.

The treatment of persons who are mentally retarded or ill is also at issue in the Case of the Lady with Mnemic Problems (Case (6) in chapter 1, pp. 5–6). In this case, Mrs L, a 60-year-old woman, was involuntarily committed in an institution, because she had memory lapses during which she neglected herself and periodically wandered in the streets without a clear conception of her own identity or the passing of time.[54] The confinement was continued even though Mrs L was expected to inflict harm on no one but herself, and during her more lucid moments understood and preferred the risks she would take by leaving the hospital. As it turned out, it seems that Mrs L was ultimately correct about what was good for her: she died, still confined in the institution against her will, a few years later, and during the last year she had had no visitors. What can be learned from the clearly condemnable court ruling of this real-life case is that even temporary flashes of autonomy must be fully respected, when the individual displaying them has once been perfectly capable of self-determined decision-making. Although partial autonomy in the case of children implies only partial freedom of choice, the situation is different with people like Mrs L: as it is impossible to justify constraints by referring to future autonomy and its protection, the decisions reached during the better moments should be regarded as if they were made by someone who is continuously in control of her own actions.

An intermediary case between children and Mrs L is the possibility of compulsory withdrawal programmes for persons addicted to 'hard drugs' such as heroin, cocaine and opium. As far as *past autonomy* is concerned, an adult drug addict (i.e. a person who has only started the use of drugs as an adult) is in the same boat as Mrs L: they have both been fully autonomous decision-makers once, and this fact lends certain respectability to their present choices, even if they decided to engage themselves in dangerous activities. With regard to *future autonomy*, however, the case of the drug addict can be seen to come closer to that of small children: the fragments of self-determination that presently manifest themselves in the individual's behaviour could, with proper treatment over a period of time, be transformed (again) into permanent and full autonomy. The question, then, is which one of the two aspects should take precedence in the matter – the choice determines whether compulsory treatment for drug addicts is justifiable.

In answering the question, it is important to note that the latter approach to the drug addict's predicament embodies two assumptions, neither of which can in fact be taken for granted.[55] First, it is assumed that drug addiction somehow renders the individual unfree and his choices non-autonomous. This idea is, no doubt, popular enough both among the general public and among medical authorities, but its validity can be questioned simply by referring to the possibility of spontaneous withdrawals from taking 'hard drugs'. If people really lost their ability to self-determination due to drug addiction, such spontaneous cases would have to be impossible – yet they exist in great numbers, and are well documented in the literature.[56] Second, those who put their faith in compulsory programmes seem to believe that it is indeed possible to forcibly 'cure people from drug addiction'. All available evidence, however, seems to indicate that unless the drug taker himself makes a self-generated decision to quit, treatments seldom have any permanent effect.[57] The point of these remarks is that either the autonomy of drug addicts needs no saving in the first place, or that if it does, it cannot be saved unless the initiative comes from the addicts themselves. Although the actual withdrawal programme can be as constraining and coercive as need be, the patient must freely consent to the procedure to secure its success – and, consequently, its legitimacy.

PREVENTIVE MEDICINE AND THE WELFARE OF THE POPULATION

In addition to face-to-face clinical and courtroom paternalism in matters related to medicine and health care, the population of industrialized societies is also subject to more delicate and far more extensive forms of possibly paternalistic intervention. These include, most notably, laws regulating dangerous behaviour in everyday life, regulations concerning the manufacture, advertising, sale and consumption of drugs and intoxicating substances, and preventive medical and socio-political measures such as quarantines, vaccinations, plumbing and health education. In fact, a surprisingly large part of these regulations and activities are ethically unproblematic,

either because there are good non-paternalistic grounds for uphold-
ing and approving them, or because their paternalism is, measured
by the standards of freedom and autonomy, clearly legitimate or
clearly illegitimate, as the case may be. A brief survey will elucidate
the situation.

As regards laws regulating *dangerous everyday behaviour*, there
are two examples which have often dominated philosophical discussions on the topic, namely driving a car without using a seat
belt and riding a motorcycle without wearing a crash helmet.
The liberal assessment of regulating these practices is simple:
unless the motorists can be expected to inflict harm on other
people by their behaviour, there are no legitimate grounds for
constraint. Minors excluded, individuals are entitled to apparently
stupid, reckless and irresponsible choices, such as the rejection of
simple safety precautions in traffic, if the risk taken is mainly or
entirely self-regarding.

Three kinds of argument can be put forward, however, to prove
that the seemingly self-regarding nature of unsafe motoring is an
illusion, and that other people are, after all, harmed as a result of fatal
accidents. First, according to the threshold argument, people driving
without seat belts and safety helmets present a threat against society
as a whole, since in fatal accidents the social fabric will be deprived
of able-bodied citizens, whose future contribution will be lost, and
who will possibly create an unnecessary burden for the health
care system. Second, there is the argument from indirect harm,
stating that families and friends will be disturbed and economically
inconvenienced by a refusal to take all the necessary precautions.
And third, it can also be suggested that harm will be inflicted on
other motorists, who have to see the crushed skulls and twisted
bodies, and on the people who are responsible for washing away
the blood and cleaning up the debris.

But all these attempts to justify restrictions are inadequate. The
main difficulty, and one which the three attempts have in common,
is that almost all serious traffic accidents have the effects listed here,
quite regardless of the use of helmets, and often regardless of the
use of seat belts as well. In fact, it could well be claimed against the
first two arguments that the helmet is a particularly controversial
device, as it covers the skull but leaves the spine unprotected. The
'unnecessary health care costs' increase considerably if the patient
survives with serious spinal damage instead of bashing her head
in and passing quietly away, and the 'psychological burden on the

family and friends' will also be prolonged. It may, of course, be that the patients themselves would prefer being alive even if it meant permanent paralysis, but such a preference would be self-regarding rather than other-regarding, and therefore could not be utilized in non-paternalistic argumentation.

Moving on to regulations and practices which are more conspicuously medical in nature, *quarantines* – as traditional and recognized instruments of preventing disease – draw their justification from the general good instead of the good of those whose freedom is restricted or autonomy violated. It was definitely not for the sailors' sake that the ships arriving in port and suspected of carrying contagious diseases were held in isolation from the shore for a period of forty days, nor is it for their own best interest that AIDS patients in Sweden are transported into an isolated nursing home on an island. Quarantines and quarantine-like measures such as home arrest, electronic surveillance, compulsory hospitalization and imprisonment are justifiable, if and when they are justifiable, by an appeal to harm inflicted on other people by carriers of communicable diseases.[58]

There are, of course, many qualifications which reduce the ethical acceptability of isolation policies in real-life situations: the threat posed to others may be symbolic rather than concrete (as is often the case with 'mental illness');[59] the isolation can amount to the life imprisonment of a person who has never committed any crime (as in the notorious case of 'Typhoid Mary' in the early 1900s);[60] the identification of those to be isolated would sometimes require violations of civil liberties in the process (AIDS patients are a case in point);[61] and finally, compulsory hospitalizations lack medical purpose when no actual cure is available (as was the case with AIDS all through the 1980s). By these remarks I am not trying to say that quarantine is always condemnable. If by the temporary isolation of one individual many other individuals can be directly saved from serious health hazards, the use of compulsory means is sometimes no doubt legitimate. What I am saying, however, is that the promotion of general good in the medical sense is not the only ethical consideration when coercive isolation and imprisonment policies are discussed.

Even more complicated problems arise with regard to the legitimacy of *vaccination programmes*. Although mass inoculation is usually a very effective way of preventing dangerous and fatal diseases, it is also often the cause of a few vaccine deaths among the population, and sometimes a source of bitter ideological opposition against the public health authorities.[62] As long as the programmes are organized without coercion and force, the problems are not necessarily insurmountable: if adult citizens are sufficiently informed about the risks involved and no one actually makes them take the vaccine, they can be seen as freely and knowingly – albeit implicitly – giving their consent to the procedure. (That the condition of sufficient information is seldom fulfilled in the real world should give the medical authorities something to think about, but does not refute the argument itself.) Where children are concerned, the validity of the proxy consent or dissent given by parents or guardians depends on the facts of the case – whether or not the child, if inoculated, has a better chance of surviving and developing into adulthood and full autonomy than without artificial immunization. But the introduction of coercion and constraint changes the situation radically. An individual who refuses the vaccination does not directly harm anyone but himself and other dissenters, and indirect harm to other people does not under the circumstances seem unproblematic as a ground for coercion either. The threshold argument could in principle be employed to support the programmes, as society might well collapse as a result of too many refusals, but it is perhaps not quite acceptable to argue that the present 'pro-vaccinal' form of society ought to be forcefully protected, if in the future the majority of citizens came to express their support to an alternative, 'anti-vaccinal' society by refusing the offered shot.

One of the methods frequently used by medical authorities to persuade people into cooperation in matters such as undertaking vaccination, is the *offering of rewards*. The bait may be anything from food and medical equipment to lollipops for children, but the ethical framework remains largely the same in all situations. If what the authorities 'offer' as a reward for compliance is something that in the moral sense already belongs to the people and seems essential to their survival, the authorities are wrongfully taking advantage of the coercive situation they have themselves created, and their behaviour should be condemned. On the other hand, if the offers presented are genuine – i.e. the goods do not morally belong to the people and are not needed quite that badly – then there is no denying that the authorities are acting in a legitimate manner. The difficulty in the latter case is, however, that offers which are not made under coercive circumstances are probably not, from the official point of view, tempting enough.

Preventive measures which influence the population as a whole even more clearly than vaccinations and quarantines do, include the *installation of plumbing* and the *fluoridation of drinking water*. These societal practices are quite pervasive in the sense that if they are effected by the public authorities, practically everyone living in an industrialized society will have to face them in one form or another. The individual can, in a manner of speaking, freely decide whether or not to utilize the plumbing or to drink fluoridated water, but the pipes and the fluoride nevertheless influence one's daily routines – a refusal to drink 'official' water, for instance, would force the city dweller into buying all his drinking water from the supermarket. These constraints, brought about in the name of general hygiene and the reduction of tooth decay, have most often been regarded as instances of paternalism, since the best interest of the population obviously is at stake here. This interpretation would, however, presuppose that public health authorities ought to be seen as benevolent physicians who are doing all in their power to 'cure' a sick community or to prevent it from catching unpleasant diseases. And the problem with this presupposition is that, according to their professional ethical codes as well as more general moral principles, doctors usually have no right to act as distributive agents – which is what the authorities of preventive medicine frequently do by removing illnesses from one part of the population (in the issue at hand, the majority developing stronger teeth) at the expense of another part (the minority developing fluoride-related diseases).

In fact, the actual justification of fluoridation and plumbing comes from other quarters, namely from the requirements of democracy and social justice. If the majority of citizens in a democratic country prefer plumbing and fluoridated drinking water to more 'natural' conditions, and express this preference through the appropriate political procedures, respect for majority rule implies, prima facie, that the opposing minority will also have to comply with the decision and, for their own part, suffer its consequences. Exceptions to the rule are possible, of course, if the human rights of the minority would otherwise be violated, but this is hardly the case with plumbing and fluoridation: pipes presumably do not harm anybody, and although fluoride may statistically increase morbidity in the long run, this does not amount to a violation of human rights as long as there is no legal obligation to drink the 'official water'. However, if the authorities of a given country are *not* justified in putting chemicals in the drinking water, this is because they have not kept the alternatives available widely enough among the population.

The methods of medical prevention introduced thus far have all been designed to make people do something that they would not do by themselves. Regulations concerning *drugs and intoxicating substances*, in their turn, usually work in the opposite direction: the purpose of the sanctions is to prevent or deter people from doing what they would or could have done had not the sanctions been set up and enforced.

Public *anti-smoking policies* provide a good illustration of the fact that most regulations related to intoxicating substances are, from the viewpoint of freedom and autonomy, unproblematic – the rights and wrongs of smoking control have to do with other-regarding harm and justice rather than strong paternalism.[63] Let me use as my example Finland – the country which since the enactment of the Tobacco Act in 1976 has presumably possessed the strictest legal regulations in the Western world concerning tobacco production, marketing and consumption. Based on the 1976 law, the official Finnish anti-smoking policy has during the late 1970s and all through the 1980s consisted of three major categories, namely: (1) health education; (2) price policy; and (3) restrictions on marketing and smoking.[64] By examining these more closely one can see where the true ethical weight of the different control policies lies.

(1) Health education in schools and via the mass media do not create even initial problems, since informing school children about the dangers of smoking belongs to the category of weak paternalism, and the spreading of information through the mass media is an instance of soft paternalism. Due to the possibility of switching channels and selecting one's reading, the general propagation of knowledge is not even prima facie autonomy-violating, and as schoolchildren do not yet possess the full adult right to self-determination, the prima-facie violation of their autonomy is automatically excused. Anti-smoking propaganda in clinics and hospitals is a different matter, because people who seek help from the physician are in an especially vulnerable position, and should not be terrorized into making less than autonomous decisions. A good demarcation line in this matter is whether the patient's symptoms indicate a tobacco-related disease or not: if they do, then informing the patient about the risks of smoking is the doctor's duty, if they do not, the patient should not be unnecessarily harassed.[65]

(2) Price policy by differential taxation has been defended by Joel

Feinberg on the grounds that smokers cumulatively and indirectly inflict harm on other people by placing on the rest of society a burden of hospitalization, medical care and lost productivity.[66] But Feinberg, and those who agree with him, tend to forget at least two considerations which may well alter the picture. First, it has nowhere been shown that smokers would actually burden the rest of society more than the average non-smokers do – arguments like the one presented by Feinberg are mainly based on gut feeling and prejudice, and the all-important comparative element of policy judgements is entirely missing. Although smokers may die young of tobacco-related diseases, the burden they place on the national economy should at least be compared to the corresponding costs caused by non-smokers who, surviving long after their retirement, may spend a good twenty years in idle consumption and non-productiveness. Second, unless cigarette prices can be stratified according to the prevailing differences in income, an issue of economic injustice will arise here. Without such an arrangement, any rise in consumer prices will inevitably hit the poor harder than the rich, and assuming that smoking is a self-regarding and – for the smokers themselves – a pleasurable activity, it does not seem fair to discriminate among smokers by differences of income.

(3) Restrictions on smoking in public premises, in schools and nurseries, in public transport and in work premises can all be justified by an appeal to the harm inflicted on other people: although the risks of 'passive smoking' have not yet been conclusively studied, it is at least clear that cigarette smoke is not healthy for children or asthmatics.[67] It is also easy to find justifications for the total ban on advertisement and sales promotion, as well as for the prohibitions against selling tobacco products to minors and – which amounts to the same thing – in unguarded slot machines. These regulations are all aimed at protecting minors from the dangers of persuasion and undue influence. Furthermore, health warnings on packages stating the tar, nicotine and carbon monoxide contents of the product can hardly be disputed on anti-paternalistic grounds, as no one is forced to read them. Subsequently, only one of the restrictions presently employed in Finland can be condemned as strongly paternalistic, and this one is the ban on manufacturing and selling brands which would contain too many harmful substances measured by the standards of the Tobacco Act. There are no reliable studies indicating that 'stronger' brands would be any more dangerous to smokers than 'mild' brands, and even if there were, the prohibition, which would

have to be founded on purely self-regarding grounds, would clearly be autonomy-violating. However, as the ban on 'strong' brands is the only instance of unavoidably strong paternalism in this rather extensive set of regulations, it is perhaps appropriate to conclude that smoking control is not essentially the fortress of wrongful paternalism that the tobacco industry and its lobbyists often try to make it out to be.

Slightly different considerations are required when the control over *medicinal and narcotic drugs* instead of the traditionally accepted recreational substances is discussed. It is not the aim of public authorities to prevent people from curing themselves or others by the use of pharmaceuticals, only to protect them from any harmful side effects that many of these may, quite unexpectedly, have. To secure the protective effect, medicinals and narcotics have been divided in most Western countries into three categories: *non-prescription* drugs, which are available to anybody on request; *prescription* drugs, which can only be obtained by a doctor's written permission; and *illegal* drugs, the possession and sale of which is always prohibited and often punishable.

I have already addressed the question of 'hard' illegal drugs above (pp. 170–1), when discussing compulsory treatment and violations of autonomy. If what I stated in that context is true, i.e. if drug addicts can be as autonomous as any other people, then weakly paternalistic grounds cannot possibly justify constraints on drug sale or use. Moreover, as regards harm inflicted on other people, the situation is similar: the most serious drug-related threat that the authorities can point out is organized crime, but this, of course, has more to do with the illegality of the business than with any intrinsic danger emanating from the use of opium, heroin or cocaine. The only valid reason for keeping narcotics illegal that I can think of is that where they are already illegal, an uncontrolled liberalization might lead to instances of injustice which could not be tolerated. If those using 'hard drugs' are mostly unemployed, uneducated youths from the lowest social classes, then a sudden free flow of drugs might kill some of them and otherwise worsen the situation for many others. But this argument stating that drugs should not be liberated at one blow is at best only a partial one. And even as such, it is an argument that cannot be supported by any reliable data, because none of these matters has been studied extensively and without prejudice.[68] The issue is complicated by many ideological and political disputes, and it sometimes seems, as two Scandinavian social scientists have recently put it, that illegal drugs are for most public authorities 'too good an enemy' to be lost – waging endless drug wars is often a good way to conceal really important social problems such as poverty, unemployment and the unequal distribution of civil rights.[69]

But let me move on to an apparently less dramatic case, which nevertheless raises interesting ethical questions – the case of *prescription drug laws* and their justification. Many liberal theorists have believed that weakly paternalistic grounds can be found for accepting such laws, since ordinary people do not know enough about the side effects of various medicinal drugs to make sufficiently voluntary and autonomous decisions concerning their use.[70] Other liberal theorists, notably J.S. Mill, have disagreed with this view, arguing that if 'voluntariness' and 'autonomy' are defined too strictly, many other activities besides the sale of dangerous drugs would have to be prohibited as well, in a spirit that would be quite illiberal.[71] And recently a third approach has been introduced by George W. Rainbolt, who has argued[72] that prescription drug laws are justifiable but *strongly paternalistic*.[73] If this third view is correct, prescription laws in fact constitute a counterexample against liberal views like the one I have been sketching in the above, since my claim has been that strong paternalism is never justified, and that it is always illegitimate to constrain fully autonomous behaviour 'in the agent's own best interest'.

Rainbolt's argument is based on a distinction between two levels of knowledge concerning drugs, originally presented by Joel Feinberg.[74] An ordinary citizen who takes drugs either for medicinal or recreational purposes does not as a rule know much about the substances themselves, but he does know about his own ignorance in the matter and about the implications of his ignorance. The ordinary citizen, then, lacks *first-level knowledge* about drugs, but possesses relevant *metaknowledge* which, according to Rainbolt, enables him to make hazardous decisions with his 'eyes wide open', or to put the matter in more technical terms, with sufficient voluntariness and autonomy. Thus weakly paternalistic grounds cannot be employed to justify intervention, and if the laws in question are justifiable, as Rainbolt believes they are, then their ethical basis must be strongly paternalistic.

C.L. Ten criticizes Rainbolt by arguing that metaknowledge concerning one's own ignorance does not, as such, make an agent's decision's voluntary.[75] He writes:

Very much depends on what the relevant metaknowledge is supposed to include. If all that is required is that people know that they are ignorant about drugs, then indeed we can attribute such metaknowledge to them. But metaknowledge of this kind is compatible with first-level ignorance which cancels voluntariness in risk-taking. Thus an ignorant drug-user might be unaware of the high risk that she is taking because she does not know that the drug can cause very grave harm. She does not therefore voluntarily take the risk of grave harm.[76]

Ten concludes that weak paternalism, based on concrete first-level ignorance, is what – despite the existence of the vague metaknowledge – justifies prescription laws for some drugs.[77]

As Rainbolt correctly points out in a reply, however, Ten by his comment raises the difficult issue of setting limits to (weakly) paternalistic interventions: if first-level ignorance always implied legitimate constraint, then there should be, for instance, laws prohibiting unknowledgeable persons from fixing their own car brakes.[78] Moreover, I am not entirely convinced that Ten is right in his analysis of the relationship between the two kinds of knowledge in the drug-user example. It is certainly true that an ignorant decision-maker might 'not know that the drug can cause very grave harm' – but this is only crucial if she lacks *both* the first-level knowledge *and* the metaknowledge concerning her own ignorance. The relevant metaknowledge would simply be that the agent consciously knows that she *does not know whether or not the drug in question is seriously harmful*. If she knows this, there is nothing to stop her from making relatively voluntary and autonomous choices.

Keeping these remarks in mind, it is interesting to consider one further retort that a consistent 'weak' paternalist could make in defence of his own position. What he could claim, namely, is that ordinary citizens who have not had medical training do not, in fact, know about their own ignorance concerning drugs, and do not, therefore, in the real world possess the relevant metaknowledge attributed to them by Rainbolt. As this is an empirical claim, not a conceptual argument, the 'weak' paternalist is free to agree with Rainbolt's theory of metaknowledge – all that is stated is that the theory does not apply to the prevailing social reality.

There is obviously a grain of truth in this counterargument, and it is therefore quite possible that weakly paternalistic grounds could, after all, be employed to justify some prescription drug laws for potentially harmful medicinals. But granted that this is true one must, at this point, start looking for explanations: *why* is it that ordinary drug-consuming citizens do not even know that their ignorance may be fatal? One popular answer to this question is that because the variety of drugs is so great nowadays, people simply cannot master even the most elementary pharmacological questions concerning the drugs they use. But this response is, in our present context, beside the point: regardless of the variety and diversity, it is surely possible to inform people about the general risk. After all, it was not required in Mill's famous bridge example,[79] that the person crossing should be given a course in construction engineering before he can be allowed to cross the river.

The only other explanation that comes readily to mind connects the legal requirement of prescriptions with the role and status of the medical profession in Western societies. Prescription drug laws are extremely important and useful to physicians, who through the power of the legal system are given the monopoly to control what drugs people use, and when. This arrangement naturally opens channels for them in the direction of the medical industry as well, and it is understandable that doctors would not like to lose their key position in the presumably quite profitable prescription drug game.

Explanations of this kind, however, are for sociologists rather than philosophers to tackle, and I must return to the conceptual issues. From this point of view, the foregoing considerations seem to imply that although prescription drug laws may at the moment be justifiable, owing to the prevailing lack of metaknowledge, it does not follow from this that the laws ought to be upheld indefinitely. Rather, the ethical implication is that people ought to be provided with health education and drug information so that they could become masters of their own lives in using drugs as well as in accepting or refusing other treatments. Incidentally, this latter point also means that Rainbolt is ultimately more correct than his critic Ten on the issue of metaknowledge and its significance. Fortunately, however, it cannot be inferred from this that Rainbolt is right in his other claim: he does not actually prove the legitimacy of prescription drug laws in his article, and thus his argument concerning the moral status of strong paternalism remains unsubstantiated. Consequently, I am once again left free to conclude that strong paternalism never provides valid grounds for restricting people's liberty and violating their autonomy 'in their own best interest'.

CONCLUDING REMARKS

Finally, let me sum up some of the foregoing issues, and present a few remarks about what has and what has not been proven in this study.

Using the theoretical framework sketched in chapters 2 and 3, I have in the present chapter analysed some of the most important cases of what has been called in the literature 'medical paternalism'. The analysis shows that medically motivated interventions into citizens' lives can be roughly divided into three categories:

(1) those that either need no justification or can be justified by an appeal to the recipient's own good;
(2) those that can be justified only by an appeal to other reasons, mainly to harm inflicted on other people; and
(3) those that cannot be justified at all.

Practices belonging to the first category have been called here *soft* or *weak* medical paternalism, and they include, for instance, non-threatening health education, and blood transfusions to the children of Jehovah's Witnesses. Interventions belonging to the second category are not, strictly speaking, paternalistic at all, but they have often been so called, because the other-regarding grounds that ultimately justify the practices are inconspicuous and defy attempts at disclosure. Vaccination and fluoridation programmes may sometimes be regarded as instances of this category. The third set of activities, finally, is what gives 'medical paternalism' its bad name among almost all liberal theorists. Restrictions and deception that cannot be justified by referring to other-regarding harm, justice or incompetence in decision-making, can only be defended by appeals to utility, morality or rationality, regarded as separate from the self-chosen happiness of individual human beings. Insulting bedside lies, compulsory treatments, refusals to treat, prohibitions on pleasurable activities and involuntary confinements often belong to this category.

In analysing the cases, I have not always reached – or even attempted to reach – final external solutions to the problems that have emerged on the way. Real-life medical situations are often factually and emotionally so complex that it is not, I believe, possible to formulate general moral principles which would adequately direct all relevant bedside behaviour. Thus, there will always be troublesome – or 'hard' – cases which must be solved more or less intuitively and case by case in their proper medical context. And as these difficult decisions are often inevitably made by the doctors in charge of the treatment, there are situations in which the doctors simply must know best.

What I have tried to show, however, is that the extent of the category of 'hard' cases is not indefinitely large – and that physicians are not, therefore, justified in claiming that their professional competence and experience is *always* needed when choices concerning treatments, medications and their withdrawals are being made. The majority of decision-making situations in hospitals and clinics are quite ordinary, and thus do not require emergency procedures – except perhaps in the technical medical sense. This implies that there cannot be standard policies requiring violations of patients' autonomy in the name of their own best interest – or, in other words, that there cannot be legitimate medical working procedures which are based on *strong* paternalism. The only standard policy within modern medicine and health care which is ultimately acceptable is the policy of moderate anti-paternalism, based on firm respect for the freedom and autonomy of the patient.

NOTES

1 THE PROBLEM OF PATERNALISM IN MODERN MEDICINE AND HEALTH CARE

1 Parsons 1951, 428–79; 1975. Parsons's position is discussed in Childress 1982, 10–12.
2 For discussions on the sexist nature of the metaphor 'paternalism', see, e.g., Benjamin and Curtis 1981, 50–8; Childress 1982, 8–9; Kleinig 1983, xii–xiii; Soble 1976, 49.
3 Kleinig 1983, 3–4
4 An expression of this new way of seeing individuals' role in society can be found in Locke 1690, bk II, ch. 6.
5 Kleinig 1983, 3.
6 'The Hippocratic Oath', in Edelstein 1967. The Oath and other important codes are reprinted, e.g., in Beauchamp and Childress 1983, 329ff.
7 Gert and Culver 1976, 46.
8 Achté, Autio and Tammisto 1982, 153.
9 Allen 1976; Childress 1982, 219–20 (Case (6)).
10 The case was originally presented in Basson (ed.) 1981, 135–6. The present formulation, however, is more or less directly quoted from Childress 1982, 233 (Case (19)), except for the solution, expressed in the last two sentences, which derives from Cassell 1981. Cf. Beauchamp 1981.
11 Beauchamp and Childress 1983, 294–5 (Case (9)).
12 E.g. Häyry and Häyry 1987; M. Häyry and H. Häyry 1989.
13 Basson (ed.) 1981, 133.
14 As for the last item on my list, the battle between the sexes, the gender of the doctor was not specified in the original case. However, Eric Cassell's contribution (see below pp. 7–11) does rest on the assumption that the gynaecologist is male.
15 Cassell 1981.
16 Cassell 1981, 145.
17 Cassell 1981, 145–6.
18 Cassell 1981, 146.
19 Cassell 1981, 145–6. Parenthesis omitted.
20 For various definitions of euthanasia, see, e.g., Kluge 1975, 173; Foot 1981, 34–5; Glover 1977, 182; Bok 1975, 1–4. Euthanasia in itself does

not necessarily involve only *persons*, but the voluntariness of voluntary euthanasia obviously does.

21 On the differences and (moral) similarities between active and passive euthanasia, see, e.g., Foot 1981, 45–51; Grisez and Boyle 1979, 86–7; O. Russell 1975, 19–20; Singer 1979, 147–53; Kuhse 1987. The terms 'direct' and 'indirect' refer to the Roman Catholic distinction between intentional and unintentional evildoing. The sense in which I use the concept here is more fully explained in H. Häyry and M. Häyry, 1989.

22 On divisions of medical euthanasia according to the patient's will, see, e.g., Devine 1978, 168; Fletcher 1978, 14; Foot 1981, 51–5; Glover 1977, 182; Grisez and Boyle 1979, 86–7; B. Russell 1978, 278; O. Russell 1975, 19, 21; Singer 1979, 128–30.

23 The only outstanding exception is the Netherlands – see, e.g., Gevers 1987; Final report of . . . 1987.

24 I am assuming here that the 'evil for oneself' is not an instrument for some further purposes, say, for protecting other people from even greater evils. It is generally considered morally permissible to make sacrifices for others' sake – presumably this can also be considered rational in some circumstances. But here the evil to oneself is the sole result.

25 Cf. Childress 1982, 221–2 (Case (8)).

26 Foot 1981, 42.

27 Foot 1981, 42–3.

28 Foot 1981, 43.

29 For a critique, see Rachels 1986, 70–1. A non-theistic version of this view is presented and criticized in Feinberg 1978, esp. pp. 113–14.

30 The term 'traditional theory' comes from Rachels 1986, 3–4. For the justifications and their critique, see, e.g., Kuhse 1987.

31 These arguments are introduced and criticized, e.g., in Singer 1979; Glover 1977.

32 J.S. Mill, *Collected Works*, vol. xiv, 294 – quoted from Ten 1980, 159.

2 FREEDOM, CONSTRAINT AND THE VALUE OF LIBERTY AND AUTONOMY

1 Mill 1859, 14–15. All references are to R. Wollheim's 1975 edition.

2 G. Dworkin 1972, 64.

3 See, e.g., Feinberg 1973, 33.

4 Feinberg 1984, 45–51.

5 Feinberg 1984, 37–45.

6 Feinberg 1984, 47.

7 Feinberg 1973, 33.

8 Feinberg 1973, 33.

9 Bentham 1789.

10 This tradition begins with Dworkin 1972.

11 Kleinig 1983, 19 (italics deleted). The following account of the modes of freedom draws heavily on Kleinig's discussion (1983, 19–21).

12 Parent 1974; M. Häyry and Airaksinen 1988a, b. Cf. Benn and Weinstein 1971, 1974; Steiner 1975–6; Day 1977; Miller 1983.

13 Green 1964, 51–3; Ritchie 1894, 138–9 – referred to in Kleinig 1983, 20. See also Berlin 1958; MacCallum 1967; Gray 1984.
14 Feinberg 1973, 13; Feinberg 1980, 30–44.
15 Feinberg 1973, 13.
16 Feinberg 1973, 13–14.
17 Feinberg 1973, 13.
18 Mill 1859, 71 ff.
19 Benn 1975–6, 112–17; Kleinig 1983, 20–1; Benn 1989; Ryan 1989.
20 Benn 1989 – quoted from Ryan 1989. For a rival account of autarchy and autonomy, see D'Agostino 1982, 324ff.
21 Rousseau 1762. Also Rousseau 1755, 73n.
22 Kant 1786; 1788. See, e.g., Engelhardt 1978, 204–8. Cf. Komrad 1983, 38–40; Gillon 1985a, 1807.
23 Rousseau 1762, 192 (italics deleted). On the point of being constrained and yet not free, see Rousseau 1762, 278n.
24 *Webster's* s.v. 'constraint'.
25 *Webster's* s.v. 'constrain'.
26 Locke 1690, bk II, xxi, 10.
27 Miller 1983.
28 Rousseau, as cited by Berlin 1958, 123. Miller 1983, 69. Also Taylor 1979, 182.
29 Miller 1983, 72.
30 Miller 1983, 73.
31 Miller 1983, 74
32 Miller 1983, 75; Davis 1980–1.
33 Miller 1983. 70–2.
34 M. Häyry and Airaksinen 1988a, 35, b, 387.
35 Miller 1983, 70–2.
36 Miller 1983, 74.
37 Spinoza 1677. Cf. R.G. Collingwood's ideas concerning the 'corruption of consciousness' (1938, 219, 282–5).
38 Heidegger 1927; Sartre 1943.
39 See, e.g., McLellan 1980a, 156ff., 1980b, 117ff.; Hegel 1821.
40 Bayles 1972; Nozick 1972; Frankfurt 1973; McCloskey 1980; Ryan 1980; Airaksinen 1988a, b.
41 Airaksinen 1988b, 214.
42 Kleinig 1983, 5.
43 Kleinig 1983, 5. On threats and offers, see, e.g., M. Häyry and Airaksinen 1988a, 36–42, b, 388–93.
44 Nozick 1972, 115–16.
45 Nozick 1972, 116.
46 Nozick 1972, 112, 116.
47 Nozick 1972, 116.
48 Airaksinen 1988b; 215ff.
49 The list comes from Day 1977, 265.
50 Day 1977, 265ff.
51 *Webster's* s.v. 'coercion' and 'coerce'. The quotations are exact in content but not literal.
52 The list comes from Day 1977, 265. Day himself includes 'deterring' in

the list of non-coercive modes of influence, but since this deterrence in his opinion seems to imply 'tacit threatening', I cannot see how deterring could fail to be coercive within his view.

53 Hart and Honoré 1959, 71, 173; Day 1977, 265.
54 Steiner 1974–5.
55 Steiner 1974–5, 36.
56 Cf., Day 1977, 258; M. Häyry and Airaksinen 1988a, 40ff., b, 391ff.
57 Day 1977.
58 M. Häyry and Airaksinen 1988a, b.
59 M. Häyry and Airaksinen 1988a, 38 ff., b, 390ff.
60 Day 1990. See also M. Häyry and Airaksinen 1990.
61 See M. Häyry and Airaksinen 1988a, 39.
62 See, e.g., Feinberg 1973, 18–20; and other sources referred to in Raz 1986, 8n.1.
63 Raz 1986, 8ff.
64 Raz 1986, 8–9.
65 Raz 1986, 9–10.
66 Raz 1986, 11.
67 Feinberg 1980, 40ff.; Kleinig 1983, 51.
68 Feinberg 1984, 212.
69 Mill 1859, 22ff.
70 Rawls 1972, 224ff.
71 McCloskey 1970. Cf. however, Monro 1970.
72 Feinberg 1980, 40ff., 1984, 211–12.
73 Huxley 1932.
74 Kleinig 1983, 50.
75 None of this is intended to deny: (1) that some animals may be autonomous; (2) that pleasure without autonomy is intrinsically valuable both in human and non-human beings; and (3) that non-human values may extend even further than individuality and pleasure. These points are discussed, respectively, in T. Regan 1984, Singer 1975 and Taylor 1986. All I am trying to say is that from a purely anthropocentric point of view, human life is richer if its pleasures are accompanied by autonomous choices than if they are experienced automatically, as a result of somebody else's decisions.

3 PATERNALISM, COERCION AND CONSTRAINT

1 Feinberg 1973, 45.
2 G. Dworkin 1972, 65.
3 Murphy 1974, 465.
4 Arneson 1980, 471.
5 Gert and Culver 1976, 45. Gert and Culver explicitly criticize the views of G. Dworkin 1972; Bayles 1974; and D.H. Regan 1974.
6 Gert and Culver 1976, 46–7.
7 Gert and Culver 1976, 48.
8 Gert and Culver 1979, 199. I have used this formulation instead of the one given in Gert and Culver 1976, 49–50, because the wording of feature (4) in the earlier paper was slightly unfortunate.

9 Gert and Culver 1979, 200n.4. Also Gert and Culver 1976, 51–2.
10 Gert and Culver 1976, 49.
11 Gert and Culver 1976, 49 (italics added).
12 Gert and Culver 1979, 199 (italics added).
13 Gert and Culver 1976, 51 (the example is originally presented on p. 46).
14 Steven Lee 1981, 193.
15 Steven Lee 1981, 193.
16 Lindley 1983. Since the paper is hitherto unpublished, I shall give no reference to page numbers in the quotations below.
17 Feinberg 1986, 28 (the italics in (i), (ii) and (iii) are original, in (iv) added). The sovereignty of political states is an original meaning, which is of no direct interest to me here.
18 Feinberg 1986, 31–44.
19 Feinberg 1986, 46.
20 Feinberg 1986, 46.
21 Arneson 1980, 477–8.
22 Huxley 1932.
23 At this point, cf. Raz 1986, ch. 14.
24 Feinberg 1986, 30.
25 Feinberg 1986, 380n.8.
26 Feinberg 1986, 30.
27 Feinberg 1986, 48.
28 Feinberg 1986, ch. 19.
29 Mill 1859, 16.
30 Arneson 1980, 482–3.
31 Cf. McCloskey 1970; Monro 1970.
32 Mill 1859, 141.
33 Berlin 1958, 128.
34 On the possibility of developing a utilitarian theory which could be faithful to the original Benthamite ideals *and* endorse the best aspects of the Millian liberal approach, see H. Häyry and M. Häyry 1990a.
35 Fotion 1979, 191.
36 Fotion 1979, 193–6.
37 Fotion 1979, 194.
38 G. Dworkin 1978, 164–6.
39 Mill 1859, 118.
40 Lindley 1983.
41 Both levels described by Lindley belong to the condition and ideal dimensions of autonomy in Feinberg's classification presented above.
42 Lindley 1983; G. Dworkin 1972. Dworkin discusses liberty instead of autonomy, but the basic idea remains the same.
43 Mill 1859, 15 (italics added).
44 Ten 1971, 61–2.
45 Ten 1971, 60.
46 Ten 1971, 61.
47 Ten 1971, 61.
48 Ten 1971, 61.
49 Ten 1971, 61.

50 Ten 1971, 62.
51 Ten 1971, 63.
52 An interpretation of what it means that someone else is 'substantially involved' can be found in H. Häyry and M. Häyry 1990a.
53 My usage of the terms *soft*, *hard*, *weak* and *strong* paternalism differs from that of Feinberg 1986, but the division between *weak* and *strong* conforms with the earlier usage of terms in, for instance, Feinberg 1973 and Beauchamp 1976.
54 C.E. Harris 1977, 88 (italics added).
55 C.E. Harris 1977, 89; Feinberg 1973.
56 Bayles 1988, 113; Feinberg 1986.
57 G. Dworkin 1978, 168–9.
58 G. Dworkin 1978, 168.

4 THE UTILITARIAN CASE FOR STRONG PATERNALISM

1 See M. Häyry and H. Häyry 1990, 2–4.
2 Characterization by Hart 1963, 16.
3 All references are to a 1967 reprint, edited with an introduction and notes by R.J. White, of the second edition, which originally appeared in 1874 (a). Stephen's work is occasionally referred to in the literature (Hart 1963; Cowling 1963, xv n. 1; Ten 1971; G. Dworkin 1972; Golding 1975, 56), but on the whole his criticism has been neglected lately in favour of more contemporary views.
4 Sidgwick 1874.
5 Moore 1903; 1912.
6 Hare 1981.
7 Brandt 1959.
8 This is true, e.g., of most articles in Sen and Williams (eds) 1982.
9 Hart 1963.
10 Devlin 1965.
11 Golding 1975, 56, 63, 87.
12 Stephen 1874a, 53–64. See also White 1967, 11–15.
13 Stephen 1874b, 274. Cf. Stephen 1874a, 228.
14 Stephen 1874a, 57, 67–8.
15 Stephen 1874a, 58.
16 Stephen 1874a, 67. The quotation from Mill's *On Liberty*: Wollheim's edition, 1975, 16.
17 Stephen 1874a, 67–8.
18 Stephen 1874a, 68.
19 Stephen 1874a, 68.
20 Morley 1873. See also Stephen 1874c, 26 notes.
21 Morley 1873. Quoted from Stephen 1874a, 68n.
22 Stephen 1874a, 68–9; 68n.
23 Stephen 1874b, 274.
24 Stephen 1874a, 227.
25 Stephen 1874a, 228.

26 Stephen 1874b, 275.
27 Stephen 1874c, 32.
28 Roberts 1979, 259.
29 Roberts 1979, 4.
30 Stephen 1874a, 85–6.
31 Stephen 1874b, 272.
32 Stephen 1874b, 276.
33 Stephen 1874b, 277.
34 Stephen 1874b, 277.
35 See, e.g., Stephen 1874a, 86–7.
36 Stephen 1874a, 97–8.
37 Stephen 1874a, 228.
38 Stephen 1874a, 228.
39 Stephen 1874a, 231.
40 Stephen 1874c, 36.
41 Stephen 1874c, 35.
42 Stephen 1874c, 36–9; Stephen 1874a, 232–5; Stephen 1874b, 282–3.
43 Harrison 1873. See also Stephen 1874c, 26n.4, 33–4, 33 notes.
44 Stephen 1874c, 33.
45 Stephen 1874c, 36.
46 Stephen 1874c, 36.
47 Stephen 1874c, 36.
48 Stephen 1874a, 244–5.
49 Stephen 1874a, 249–50.
50 Stephen 1874a, 250–1 (italics added).
51 Stephen 1874a, 152.
52 Stephen 1874a, 250–1.
53 Cf. Stephen 1874a, 262.
54 Stephen 1874a, 228.

5 MORALS AND SOCIETY

1 The *Report of the Committee on Homosexual Offences and Prostitution* is hereafter referred to as Wolfenden 1957.
2 *The Street Offences Act* 1959. Månsson 1985, 336.
3 Wolfenden 1957, para. 62.
4 Wolfenden 1957, para. 62.
5 Wolfenden 1957, para. 13.
6 Wolfenden 1957, para. 224.
7 Wolfenden 1957, para. 13.
8 First published in 1959, reprinted with other essays in 1965. Both editions carry the title *Enforcement of Morals*. All references here, however, are to Devlin, in R. Dworkin (ed.) 1977, where the 1965 version of the article is reprinted. Hereafter referred to as Devlin 1959.
9 Devlin 1959 in R. Dworkin (ed.) 1977, 68–9. Devlin borrows the definition of 'sin' from the *Oxford English Dictionary*.
10 Devlin 1959 in R. Dworkin (ed.) 1977, 69.

11 Devlin 1959 in R. Dworkin (ed.) 1977, 71.
12 Devlin 1959 in R. Dworkin (ed.) 1977, 70–1.
13 Devlin 1959 in R. Dworkin (ed.) 1977, 69.
14 Devlin 1959 in R. Dworkin (ed.) 1977, 73.
15 Devlin 1959 in R. Dworkin (ed.) 1977, 73 (italics added).
16 Devlin 1959 in R. Dworkin (ed.) 1977, 73–5.
17 Devlin 1959 in R. Dworkin (ed.) 1977, 80.
18 Devlin 1959 in R. Dworkin (ed.) 1977, 78.
19 See, e.g., S. Lee 1986, ch. 9.
20 S. Lee 1986, 48–9.
21 Wollheim 1959.
22 Wollheim 1959, 38–9.
23 Wollheim 1959, 38.
24 Wollheim 1959, 39.
25 Wollheim 1959, 39.
26 Wollheim 1959, 40.
27 Wollheim 1959, 40.
28 Devlin 1959 in R. Dworkin (ed.) 1977, 77n.20.
29 All references here are to R. Dworkin (ed.) 1977, where the article is reprinted.
30 R. Dworkin 1977, ch. 10.
31 Hart 1959 in R. Dworkin 1977; R. Dworkin (ed.) 1977, 245–6.
32 Devlin 1959 in R. Dworkin (ed.) 1977, 80.
33 Hart 1959 in R. Dworkin (ed.) 1977, 87–8.
34 R. Dworkin (ed.) 1977, 246.
35 Hart 1963, 48–50. The expressions 'extreme thesis' and 'moderate thesis' are Hart's.
36 Devlin 1959 in R. Dworkin (ed.) 1977, 80. Devlin is hopelessly unclear at this point: right after the quoted passage he goes on to say that 'society cannot be denied the right to eradicate' homosexuality, if 'the genuine feeling of the society' is that it is 'a vice so abominable that its mere presence is an offence', thus falling back on the extreme thesis.
37 Devlin 1959 in R. Dworkin (ed.) 1977, 80.
38 Hart 1963, 48–9.
39 S. Lee 1986, 15–17.
40 Hart 1961, ch. 9.
41 S. Lee 1986, 15.
42 S. Lee 1986, 15–16.
43 See, e.g., Raz 1986, chs 14, 15.
44 Feinberg 1986, 21–3.
45 Feinberg 1986, 22.
46 Feinberg 1986, 22.
47 Feinberg 1986, 22.
48 Feinberg 1986, 22.
49 Feinberg 1986, 22–3.
50 Feinberg 1986, 23.
51 The following is based on Schonsheck 1988.
52 Implied by Schonsheck 1988.

53 Feinberg 1986, 23.

6 APPEALS TO RATIONALITY: THE VARIETIES OF PRUDENTIALISM

1 G. Dworkin 1972.
2 G. Dworkin 1972, 77.
3 G. Dworkin 1972, 77.
4 G. Dworkin 1972, 78.
5 G. Dworkin 1972, 78 (italics added).
6 G. Dworkin 1972, 78.
7 G. Dworkin 1972, 83.
8 G. Dworkin 1972, 84.
9 Hodson 1977.
10 Hodson 1977, 67.
11 Cf. the four classes of cases in which weak paternalism is justifiable, introduced in chapter 3 above.
12 Hodson 1977, 67.
13 Hodson 1977, 68.
14 Besides, although Dworkin is not absolutely clear at this point, he does seem to reject the idealistic 'real will' theories in 1972, 77.
15 See, e.g., G. Dworkin 1972, 76–7; Carter 1977. Cf. VanDeVeer 1979.
16 Kleinig 1983, 61; Husak 1981, 33; VanDeVeer 1980a, 194.
17 VanDeVeer 1986, 69.
18 Kleinig 1983, 62–3; VanDeVeer 1979, 638; Murphy 1974, 482–3n.29; Elster 1979, 47.
19 Carter 1977, 136–8.
20 Rawls 1972, 249.
21 Rawls 1972, 248–9.
22 Rawls 1972, 249 (italics added).
23 Rawls 1972, 92–3 (italics added).
24 Rawls 1972, 250.
25 Rawls 1972, 250.
26 See Radcliffe Richards 1981, 36ff., esp. 39, for a rational account of the matter.
27 E.g. Golding 1975, 56–7.
28 Parfit 1986.
29 Parfit 1986, chs 13–15.
30 Parfit 1986, 319–20.
31 Parfit 1986, 321.
32 Parfit 1986, 321.
33 Parfit 1986, 321.
34 See chapter 5 above.
35 Parfit 1986, 199–201.
36 Parfit 1986, 199–200.
37 Parfit 1986, 201.
38 Parfit 1986, 201.
39 Parfit 1986, 279, 280.

40 Wording from Parfit 1986, 270.

7 THE LIMITS OF MEDICAL PATERNALISM

1 *Slater* v. *Baker & Stapleton* 1767 – cited in Kirby 1983, 70.
2 Appelbaum, Lidz and Meisel 1987, 36–7.
3 See, e.g., Katz 1978, 771ff.; Doudera 1981, 101–2; Kirby 1983, 70; Appelbaum, Lidz and Meisel 1987, 37ff.
4 Doudera 1981, 101.
5 *Schloendorff* v. *Society of New York Hospital* 1914 – cited in Doudera 1981, 102.
6 *Natanson* v. *Kline* 1960 – cited in Katz 1978, 772.
7 My reasons for mentioning the codes of nurses and other health care workers only parenthetically are twofold. First, professional medical ethics has until quite recently almost exclusively tackled the rights and duties of physicians – the duties of 'their staff' have been considered subordinate, derivative and unimportant. And second, in a demanding sense, only physicians constitute a profession within the health care system: they are, for instance, the only group within the medical field who can autonomously decide about the recruitment and training of new members in their profession.
8 Annas 1975, 57.
9 Doudera 1981, 103. See also Kirby 1983, 69; Herbert 1980.
10 Doudera 1981, 110n.9.
11 The three approaches presented in this paragraph derive from Doudera 1981, 104–5. See also Skegg 1975; Thomson 1979.
12 *Canterbury* v. *Spence* (1972) and *Cobbs* v. *Grant* (1972) – both cited in Doudera 1981, 104–5.
13 It seems obvious, for instance, that the American court which boldly stated that a risk below 0.75 per cent is, as a rule, 'immaterial' (*Mason* v. *Ellsworth*, 1970 – cited in Doudera 1981, 105) cannot very well claim universal validity for its ruling. Why 0.75 per cent? Why not 5 or 0.5 per cent? And in medical matters, who can accurately estimate which risks would meet any of these demands?
14 Doudera 1981, 105; Curran 1979, 482. Also Cassell 1978; Ingelfinger 1980.
15 Kirby 1983, 71–2.
16 Kirby 1983, 71, 72.
17 E.g. Ingelfinger 1980; Clements and Sider 1983. Cf., however, Gillon 1985b.
18 E.g. Meyer 1969.
19 Clements and Sider 1983, 2015. See also Churchill and Cross 1984; Steffen 1984; Howe 1984; Sider and Clements 1984.
20 L. Harris *et al.* 1982, 138; Gillon 1985c, 1557; Goldfield and Rothman 1987, 484.
21 Bok 1982, 179.
22 Boverman 1983, 232.
23 Boverman 1982.
24 Buchanan 1978, 377–9. Buchanan uses as his empirical source of

information Donald Oken's study 'What to tell cancer patients: A study of medical attitudes' (1976).
25 I shall return to this point in discussing voluntary euthanasia below.
26 Buchanan 1978, 383–4.
27 VanDeVeer 1980b, 200–1.
28 Buchanan 1978, 384–5.
29 VanDeVeer 1980b, 202–3; also VanDeVeer 1986, 201.
30 Gillon 1985c, 1556. Cf. Guiora 1982.
31 J. Harris 1985, 207; Kirby 1983, 71.
32 J. Harris 1985, 207 (italics mine).
33 J. Harris 1985, 208.
34 I have dealt with this problem in more detail in Häyry 1991. Also M. Häyry and H. Häyry 1989.
35 H. Häyry and M. Häyry 1987; M. Häyry and H. Häyry 1989.
36 The differences between 'official' and 'alternative' medicine are analysed in a useful manner in Aakster 1986.
37 I employ the term 'lexical' (which is, in fact, short for 'lexicographical') in the sense defined by Rawls 1972, 42–3.
38 This has by no means been the only argument or motive in the history of medical abortions – see, e.g., J. Mohr 1978 for a lucid account of the anti-abortion movements in nineteenth-century America. On the many versions of the 'sanctity-of-life doctrine', see Kuhse 1987.
39 J. Mohr 1978, chs 6 and 7.
40 The sense in which I use the concept of 'euthanasia' is more fully explained in M. Häyry and H. Häyry 1990, 156ff.
41 Capron 1978. Capron in fact explicitly examines only dangerous or fatal refusals of treatment, and thus implicitly the possibility of *passive* euthanasia. Until an ethically significant difference between active and passive, direct and indirect euthanasia is shown, however, there is no reason not to include all kinds of euthanasia in the discussion.
42 Capron 1978, 1499–503. Capron himself regards the first point below as part of the self-regarding harm principle, not as an independent point.
43 Capron 1978, 1500; Parsons 1951, 436–7.
44 Capron 1978, 1500.
45 Capron 1978, 1500–1.
46 Capron 1978, 1501.
47 Capron 1978, 1501.
48 Capron 1978, 1502.
49 E.g. Grisez and Boyle 1979, 170–6, 242–7.
50 For discussions, see Devine 1978, 184ff.; Singer 1979, 153ff.
51 Norio 1982, 143–4.
52 Kleinig 1983, 134ff.; Law Reform Commission of Canada 1979, 75.
53 See, e.g., Seidelman 1985. Cf., however, the ruling of Justice Holmes in *Buck* v. *Bell* (1927).
54 *Lake* v. *Cameron* (1966); Katz, Goldstein and Dershowitz 1967, 552–4, 710–13; Kleinig 1983, 139.
55 Graham 1988.
56 Caplin and Woodward 1986, 59.
57 Caplin and Woodward 1986, 74; Stewart 1987, ch. 7.

58 E.g. Mayo 1988; M. Häyry and H. Häyry 1989.
59 See, e.g., Szasz (1971, 182ff.) on 'masturbatory insanity' as an alleged cause of hereditary diseases and ground for isolation of the 'patient' in a madhouse.
60 Mary Mallon, aka 'Typhoid Mary', was an Irish-born cook who in her work in New York accidentally infected several people with typhoid fever. In 1925 she was imprisoned indefinitely, because the authorities wanted to protect the general public from the innocent threat posed by her cooking. She died twenty-three years later, still imprisoned, without ever having committed a punishable crime.
61 R. Mohr 1987; Mayo 1988.
62 E.g. Last 1987, 354; H. Häyry and M. Häyry 1989.
63 The question in the Finnish context has been discussed in Häyry, Häyry and Karjalainen 1989.
64 Leppo and Vertio 1986. Leppo and Vertio in fact present a fourth category as well: (4) research, planning and evaluation. But since this set of activities is obviously subsidiary to the first three groups, I shall not examine it separately. The same applies, incidentally, to a subactivity within the third category, namely quality control.
65 This demarcation line was suggested to me by Dr Sakari Karjalainen.
66 Feinberg 1984, 23–5.
67 O'Connel and Logan 1974; Tager, Weiss, Rosner and Speizer 1979; Knight and Breslin 1985.
68 A good philosophical survey of problems related to 'hard' drugs is Graham 1988.
69 Christie and Bruun 1985.
70 Feinberg 1986, 127–33; Ten 1989.
71 Mill 1859, 118–19; Arneson 1980, 482.
72 Rainbolt 1989 a.
73 To be exact, Rainbolt discusses 'hard paternalism' here, following Feinberg's later terminology and definitions, but his argument can equally well be directed against 'strong paternalism' in the sense I have defined it in chapter 3 above.
74 Rainbolt 1989a, 50ff.; Feinberg 1986, 161.
75 Ten 1989.
76 Ten 1989, 136.
77 Ten 1989, 138–9.
78 Rainbolt 1989b, a, 52–3.
79 Mill 1859, 118.

BIBLIOGRAPHY

Aakster, C.W. (1986) 'Concepts in alternative medicine'. *Social Science and Medicine* 22: 265–73.

Achté, K., Autio, L. and Tammisto, T. (1982) 'Elämän ja kuoleman peruskysymyksiä' [Basic questions concerning life and death, in Finnish], K. Achté *et al.* (eds), *Lääkintäetiikka* [Medical ethics]. Vaasa: Suomen Lääkäriliitto.

Airaksinen, T. (1988a) *Ethics of Coercion and Authority: A Philosophical Study of Social Life.* Pittsburgh: University of Pittsburgh Press.

Airaksinen, T. (1988b) 'An analysis of coercion'. *Journal of Peace Research* 25: 213–27.

Allen, R.W. (1976) 'Informed consent: a medical decision'. *Radiology* 119: 233–4.

Annas, G. (1975) *Rights of Hospital Patients.* New York: Avon Books.

Appelbaum, P.S., Lidz, C.W. and Meisel, A. (1987) *Informed Consent: Legal Theory and Clinical Practice.* New York and Oxford: Oxford University Press.

Aristotle (1976) *Nicomachean Ethics*, revised edition, H. Tredennick (trans.). Harmondsworth: Penguin.

Arneson, R.J. (1980) 'Mill versus paternalism'. *Ethics* 90: 471–89.

Basson, M.D. (ed.) (1981) *Rights and Responsibilities in Modern Medicine.* New York: Alan R. Liss, Inc.

Bayles, M. (1972) 'A concept of coercion', J.R. Pennock and J.W. Chapman (eds), *Coercion – Nomos XIV.* Chicago: Aldene-Atherton.

Bayles, M. (1974) 'Criminal paternalism', J.R. Pennock and J.W. Chapman (eds), *The Limits of Law – Nomos XV.* Chicago: University of Chicago Press.

Bayles, M. (1988) Book review on Joel Feinberg's 'Harm to self'. *Law and Philosophy* 7: 107–22.

Beauchamp, T.L. (1976) 'Paternalism and bio-behavioral control'. *The Monist* 60: 67.

Beauchamp, T.L. (1978) 'Paternalism', W.T. Reich *et al.* (eds), *Encyclopedia of Bioethics,* vol. 4. New York: The Free Press.

Beauchamp, T.L. (1981) 'Paternalism and refusals to sterilize', M. D. Basson (ed.), *Rights and Responsibilities in Modern Medicine.* New York: Alan R. Liss, Inc.

Beauchamp, T.L. and Childress, J.F. (1983) *Principles of Biomedical Ethics*, second edition. New York and Oxford: Oxford University Press.

Benjamin, M. and Curtis, J. (1981) *Ethics in Nursing*. New York: Oxford University Press.

Benn, S.I. (1975–6) 'Freedom, autonomy and the concept of a person'. *Proceedings of the Aristotelian Society* **76**: 109–30.

Benn, S.I. (1989) *A Theory of Freedom*. Cambridge: Cambridge University Press.

Benn, S.I. and Weinstein, W.L. (1971) 'Being free to act, and being a free man'. *Mind* **80**: 194–211.

Benn, S.I. and Weinstein, W.L. (1974) 'Freedom as the non-restriction of options: a rejoinder'. *Mind* **83**: 435–8.

Bentham, J. (1982) *An Introduction to the Principles of Morals and Legislation* (1789), J.H. Burns and H.L.A. Hart (eds). London and New York: Methuen.

Berlin, I. (1969) 'Two concepts of liberty' (1958). *Four Essays on Liberty*. Oxford: Oxford University Press.

Bok, S. (1975) 'Euthanasia and care of the dying', J.A. Behnke and S. Bok (eds), *The Dilemmas of Euthanasia*. Garden City, NY: Anchor Press/Doubleday.

Bok, S. (1982) 'Lies to the sick and dying', T.L. Beauchamp and L.R. Walters (eds), *Contemporary Issues in Bioethics*. Belmont, Cal.: Wadsworth Publishing Company.

Boverman, M. (1982) 'Truth telling in medicine' (letter to the editor). *Journal of the American Medical Association* **248**: 1307.

Boverman, M. (1983) 'Mental health aspects of the informed consent process', K. Berg and K.E. Tranøy (eds), *Research Ethics*. New York: Alan R. Liss.

Brandt, R.B. (1959) *Ethical Theory: The Problems of Normative and Critical Ethics*. Englewood Cliffs, NJ: Prentice-Hall.

Brandt, R.B. (1979) *A Theory of the Good and the Right*. Oxford: Clarendon Press.

Buchanan, A. (1978) 'Medical paternalism'. *Philosophy and Public Affairs* **7**: 370–90.

Buck v. *Bell* (1927) 274 US 200, at 208.

Canterbury v. *Spence* (1972) 464 F.2d 722 (DC Cir.).

Caplin, S. and Woodward, S. (1986) *Drugwatch: Just Say No!* London.

Capron, A.M. (1978) 'Right to refuse treatment', W.T. Reich (ed.), *Encyclopedia of Bioethics*, vols 1–4. New York: The Free Press.

Carter, R. (1977) 'Justifying paternalism'. *Canadian Journal of Philosophy* **7**: 133–45.

Cassell, E.J. (1978) 'Informed consent in the therapeutic relationship: I. Clinical aspects', W.T. Reich (ed.), *Encyclopedia of Bioethics*, vols 1–4. New York: The Free Press.

Cassell, E.J. (1981) 'The refusal to sterilize Elizabeth Stanley is not paternalism', M. D. Basson (ed.), *Rights and Responsibilities in Modern Medicine*. New York: Alan R. Liss, Inc.

Childress, J.F. (1982) *Who Should Decide? Paternalism in Health Care*. New York and Oxford: Oxford University Press.

Christie, N. and Bruun, K. (1985) *Den gode fiende* [The Good Enemy, in Norwegian]. Oslo: Universitetsforlaget.

Churchill, L.R. and Cross, A.W. (1984) 'Medical ethics' assault upon medical values' (letter to the editor). *Journal of the American Medical Association* 251: 2791.

Clements, C.D. and Sider, R.C. (1983) 'Medical ethics' assault upon medical values'. *Journal of the American Medical Association* 250: 2011–15.

Cobbs v. *Grant* (1972) 8 Ca. 3d 229, 502 P.2d 1.

Collingwood, R.G. (1958) *The Principles of Art* (1938). Oxford: Oxford University Press.

Cowling, M. (1963) *Mill and Liberalism*. Cambridge: Cambridge University Press.

Curran, W.J. (1979) 'Informed consent, Texas style: disclosure and nondisclosure by regulation'. *New England Journal of Medicine* 300: 482.

D'Agostino, F. (1982) 'Mill, paternalism and psychiatry'. *Australasian Journal of Philosophy* 60: 319–30.

Davis, N. (1980–1) 'Utilitarianism and responsibility'. *Ratio* 22: 15–35.

Day, J.P. (1977) 'Threats, offers, law, opinion and liberty'. *American Philosophical Quarterly* 14: 257–72.

Day, J.P. (1990) 'Comments on "Hard and soft offers as constraints" by Matti Häyry and Timo Airaksinen'. *Philosophia* 20: 321–3.

Devine, P.E. (1978) *The Ethics of Homicide*. Ithaca and London: Cornell University Press.

Devlin, P. (1977) 'Morals and the criminal law' (1959), R.M. Dworkin (ed.), *The Philosophy of Law*. Oxford: Oxford University Press.

Devlin, P. (1965) *Enforcement of Morals*. Oxford: Oxford University Press.

Doudera, A.E. (1981) 'Informed consent: how much should the patient know?' M. D. Basson (ed.), *Rights and Responsibilities in Modern Medicine*. New York: Alan R. Liss, Inc.

Dworkin, G. (1972) 'Paternalism'. *The Monist* 56: 64–84.

Dworkin, G. (1978) 'Moral autonomy', H.T. Engelhardt, Jr and D. Callahan (eds), *Morals, Science and Sociality. Vol. III, The Foundations of Ethics and Its Relationship to Science*. New York: The Hastings Center.

Dworkin, G. (1976) 'Autonomy and behavior control'. *Hastings Center Report* 6, No. 1 (February): 23–8.

Dworkin, R. (ed.) (1977) *The Philosophy of Law*. Oxford: Oxford University Press.

Dworkin, R. (1977) *Taking Rights Seriously*. London: Duckworth.

Edelstein, L. (1967) *Ancient Medicine*, O. Temkin and C. Lillan Temkin (eds). Baltimore: Johns Hopkins University Press.

Elster, J. (1979) *Ulysses and the Sirens: Studies in Rationality and Irrationality*. Cambridge: Cambridge University Press.

Engelhardt, H.T. Jr (1978) 'Moral autonomy and the polis: response to Gerald Dworkin and Gregory Vlastos', H.T. Engelhardt, Jr and D. Callahan (eds), *Morals, Science and Sociality*. New York: The Hastings Center.

Feinberg, J. (1973) *Social Philosophy*. Englewood Cliffs, NJ: Prentice-Hall.

Feinberg, J. (1978) 'Voluntary euthanasia and the inalienable right to life'. *Philosophy and Public Affairs* 7: 93–123.

Feinberg, J. (1980) *Rights, Justice, and the Bounds of Liberty*. Princeton: Princeton University Press.

Feinberg, J. (1984) *Harm to Others*. Oxford: Oxford University Press.

Feinberg, J. (1985) *Offense to Others*. Oxford: Oxford University Press.

Feinberg, J. (1986) *Harm to Self*. Oxford: Oxford University Press.

Feinberg, J. (1988) *Harmless Wrongdoing*. Oxford: Oxford University Press.

'Final report of the Netherlands state commission on euthanasia: an English summary'. (1987) *Bioethics* 1: 163–74.

Fletcher, J. (1978) 'Infanticide and the ethics of loving concern', M. Kohl (ed.), *Infanticide and the Value of Life*. Buffalo, NY: Prometheus Books.

Foot, P. (1981) *Virtues and Vices and Other Essays in Moral Philosophy*. Berkeley and Los Angeles: University of California Press.

Fotion, N. (1979) 'Paternalism'. *Ethics* 89: 191–8.

Fowler, M. (1982) 'Coercion and practical reason'. *Social Theory and Practice* 8: 329–55.

Frankfurt, H. (1973) 'Coercion and moral responsibility', T. Honderich (ed.), *Essays on Freedom of Action*. London: Routledge & Kegan Paul.

Gert, B. and Culver, C.M. (1976) 'Paternalistic behavior'. *Philosophy and Public Affairs* 6: 45–57.

Gert, B. and Culver, C.M. (1979) 'The justification of paternalism'. *Ethics* 89: 199–210.

Gevers, J.K.M. (1987) 'Legal developments concerning active euthanasia on request in the Netherlands'. *Bioethics* 1: 156–62.

Gillon, R. (1985a) 'Autonomy and the principle of respect for autonomy'. *British Medical Journal* 290: 1806–8.

Gillon, R. (1985b) 'Paternalism and medical ethics'. *British Medical Journal* 290: 1971–2.

Gillon, R. (1985c) 'Telling the truth and medical ethics'. *British Medical Journal* 291: 1556–7.

Glover, J. (1977) *Causing Death and Saving Lives*. Harmondsworth: Penguin.

Goldfield, N. and Rothman, W.A. (1987) 'Ethical considerations of informed consent: a case study'. *Social Science and Medicine* 24: 483–6.

Golding, M. (1975) *Philosophy of Law*. Englewood Cliffs, NJ: Prentice-Hall.

Graham, G. (1988) 'Drugs, freedom and harm'. Plenary paper presented at the Fourth International Conference on Social Philosophy, Oxford, England, August 16–19.

Gray, J. (1984) 'On negative and positive liberty', Z. Pelczynski and J. Gray (eds), *Conceptions of Liberty in Political Philosophy*. London: Athlone Press.

Green, T.H. (1964) *The Political Theory of T.H. Green: Selected Writings*, J.R. Rodman (ed.), New York: Appleton-Century-Crofts.

Grisez, G. and Boyle, J.M. (1979) *Life and Death with Liberty and Justice:*

A Contribution to the Euthanasia Debate. Notre Dame, IN: University of Notre Dame Press.

Guiora, A.Z. (1982) 'Freedom of information vs. freedom from information', T.L. Beauchamp and L.R. Walters (eds), *Contemporary Issues in Bioethics*. Belmont, CA: Wadsworth Publishing Company.

Hare, R.M. (1981) *Moral Thinking: Its Levels, Method and Point*. Oxford: Clarendon Press.

Harris, C.E. (1977) 'Paternalism and the enforcement of morality'. *Southwestern Journal of Philosophy* 8: 85–93.

Harris, J. (1985) *The Value of Life: An introduction to medical ethics*. London: Routledge & Kegan Paul.

Harris, L. *et al.* (1982) 'Views of informed consent and decision making: parallel surveys of physicians and public in making health care decisions'. *President's Commission for the Study of Ethical Problems in Medical and Biomedical and Biobehavioral Research*, vol. 2, *Making Health Care Decisions*. Washington, DC: US Government Printing Office.

Harrison, F. (1873) 'The religion of inhumanity'. *Fortnightly Review*, June.

Hart, H.L.A. (1977) 'Immorality and treason' (1959), R.M. Dworkin (ed.), *The Philosophy of Law*. Oxford: Oxford University Press.

Hart, H.L.A. (1961) *The Concept of Law*. Oxford: Clarendon Press.

Hart, H.L.A. (1963) *Law, Liberty and Morality*. London: Oxford University Press.

Hart, H.L.A. and Honoré, A.M. (1959) *Causation in the Law*. Oxford: Oxford University Press.

Häyry, H. (1991) 'Human immunodeficiency virus (HIV) and the alleged right to remain in ignorance', Y. Hudson and C. Peden (eds), *Selected Papers for the Fourth International Conference on Social Philosophy*. Lewiston, NY: Edwin Mellen Press.

Häyry, H. and Häyry, M. (1987) 'AIDS now'. *Bioethics* 1: 339–56.

Häyry, H. and Häyry, M. (1989) 'Utilitarianism, human rights and the redistribution of health through preventive medical measures'. *Journal of Applied Philosophy* 6: 43–51.

Häyry, H. and Häyry, M. (1990a) 'Liberty, equality, utility – classical to liberal utilitarianism', T. Campbell (ed.), *Law and Enlightenment in Britain*. Aberdeen: Aberdeen University Press.

Häyry, H. and Häyry, M. (1990b) 'Euthanasia, ethics and economics'. *Bioethics* 4: 154–61.

Häyry, H., Häyry, M. and Karjalainen, S. (1989) 'Paternalism and Finnish anti-smoking policy'. *Social Science and Medicine* 28: 293–7.

Häyry, M. and Airaksinen, T. (1988a) 'Elements of constraint'. *Analyse und Kritik* 10: 32–47.

Häyry, M. and Airaksinen, T. (1988b) 'Hard and soft offers as constraints'. *Philosophia* 18: 385–98.

Häyry, M. and Airaksinen, T. (1990) 'In defence of "hard" offers – a reply to J.P. Day'. *Philosophia* 20: 325–7.

Häyry, M. and Häyry, H. (1989) 'AIDS, society and morality – a philosophical survey'. *Philosophia* 19: 331–61.

Häyry, M. and Häyry, H. (1990) 'Health care as a right, fairness and medical resources'. *Bioethics* 4: 1–21.

BIBLIOGRAPHY

Hegel, G.W.F. (1967) *The Philosophy of Right* (1821), T.M. Knox (trans.), Oxford: Oxford University Press.

Heidegger, M. (1953) *Sein und Zeit* (1927). Tübingen: Max Niemeyer Verlag.

Herbert, V. (1980) 'Informed consent – a legal evaluation'. *Cancer* 46: 1042–3.

Hodson, J. D. (1977) 'The principle of paternalism'. *American Philosophical Quarterly* 14: 61–9.

Howe, K. R. (1984) 'Medical ethics' assault upon medical values' (letter to the editor). *Journal of the American Medical Association* 251: 2792.

Husak, D. N. (1981) 'Paternalism and autonomy'. *Philosophy and Public Affairs* 10: 27–46.

Huxley, A. (1983) *Brave New World* (1932), M. S. Ellis (ed). Harlow, Essex: Longman.

Ingelfinger, F.J. (1980) 'Arrogance'. *New England Journal of Medicine* 303: 1507–11.

Kant, I. (1983) *Grundlegung zur Metaphysik der Sitten* (1786), M. Thom (ed.), Leipzig: Reclam.

Kant, I. (1983) *Kritik der praktischen Vernunft* (1788), M. Thom (ed.), Leipzig: Reclam.

Katz, J. (1978) 'Informed consent in therapeutic relationship: II. Legal and ethical aspects', W.T. Reich (ed.), *Encyclopedia of Bioethics*, vols 1–4. New York: Free Press.

Katz, J., Goldstein, J. and Dershowitz, A. (1967) *Psychoanalysis, Psychiatry, and Law*. New York: Free Press.

Kirby, M.D. (1983) 'Informed consent: what does it mean?' *Journal of Medical Ethics* 9: 69–75.

Kleinig, J. (1983) *Paternalism*. Manchester: Manchester University Press.

Kluge, E.–H.W. (1975) *The Practice of Death*. London: Yale University Press.

Knight, A. and Breslin, A.B. (1985) 'Passive cigarette smoking and patients with asthma'. *Medical Journal of Australia* 142: 194–5.

Komrad, M.S. (1983) 'A defence of medical paternalism: maximising patients' autonomy'. *Journal of Medical Ethics* 9: 38–44.

Kuhse, H. (1987) *The Sanctity-of-Life Doctrine in Medicine: A Critique*. Oxford: Oxford University Press.

Lake v. *Cameron* (1966) 364 F.2d, 657 (DC Cir.).

Last, J.M. (1987) *Public Health and Human Ecology*. Ottawa: Appleton & Lange.

Law Reform Commission of Canada (1979) *Sterilization: Implications for Mentally Retarded and Mentally Ill Persons*. Working Paper no. 24. Ottawa. Partly reprinted in 'Sterilizing the mentally handicapped: who can give consent?' *Canadian Medical Association Journal* 122: 234–9.

Lee, Simon (1986) *Law and Morals*. Oxford: Oxford University Press.

Lee, Steven (1981) 'On the justification of paternalism'. *Social Theory and Practice* 7: 193–203.

Leppo, K. and Vertio, H. (1986) 'Smoking control in Finland: a case study in policy formulation and implementation'. *Health Promotion* 1: 5–16.

Lindley, R. (1983) 'Paternalism and caring'. Hitherto unpublished paper.

Locke, J. (1970) *Two Treatises of Government* (1690), a critical edition with an introduction and apparatus criticus by P. Laslett, second edition. Cambridge: Cambridge University Press.

MacCallum, G. (1967) 'Negative and positive freedom'. *Philosophical Review* 76: 312–34.

Mason v. Ellsworth (1970) 474 P.2d 909 (Wash. App.).

Mayo, D. (1988) 'AIDS, quarantines, and non-compliant positives', D. VanDeVeer and C. Pierce (eds), *AIDS: Ethics and Public Policy*. Belmont, CA: Wadsworth).

McCloskey, H.J. (1970) 'Liberty of expression. Its grounds and limits'. *Inquiry* 13: 219–37.

McCloskey, H.J. (1980) 'Coercion: its nature and significance'. *Southern Journal of Philosophy* 18: 335–51.

McLellan, D. (1980a) *Marx before Marxism*, second edition. London: Macmillan.

McLellan, D. (1980b) *The Thought of Karl Marx*, second edition. London: Macmillan.

Meyer, B.C. (1969) 'Truth and the physician'. *Bulletin of the New York Academy of Medicine* 45: 59–71.

Mill, J.S. (1975) *On Liberty* (1859). *Three Essays*, R. Wollheim (ed.). Oxford: Oxford University Press.

Mill, J.S. (1979) *Utilitarianism* (1861), M. Warnock (ed.). Glasgow: William Collins Sons & Co.

Mill, J.S. (1900) *Principles of Political Economy*. New York: P.F. Collier and Sons.

Miller, D. (1983) 'Constraints on freedom'. *Ethics* 94: 66–86.

Mitchell, B. (1968) *Law, Morality and Religion in a Secular Society*. Oxford: Oxford University Press.

Mohr, J.C. (1978) *Abortion in America: The Origins and Evolution of National Policy, 1800–1900*. New York: Oxford University Press.

Mohr, R.D. (1987) 'AIDS, gays and state coercion'. *Bioethics* 1: 35–50.

Monro, D.H. (1970) 'Liberty of expression. Its grounds and limits'. *Inquiry* 13: 238–53.

Moore, G.E. (1959) *Principia Ethica* (1903). Cambridge: Cambridge University Press.

Moore, G.E. (1965) *Ethics* (1912). New York: Oxford University Press.

Morley, J. (1873) 'Mr Mill's doctrine of liberty'. *Fortnightly Review*, August.

Murphy, J.G. (1974) 'Incompetence and paternalism'. *Archiv für Rechts-und Sozialphilosophie* 60: 465–86.

Månsson, U. (1985) 'Synti, rikos, ihmisoikeus – oikeustaistelun historiaa ja nykypäivää' [Sin, crime, human rights, in Finnish], K. Sievers and O. Stålström (eds), *Rakkauden monet kasvot: Homoseksuaalisesta rakkaudesta, ihmisoikeuksista ja vapautumisesta* [The Many Faces of Love: On Homosexual Love, Human Rights and Liberation]. Helsinki: Weilin & Göös.

Natanson v. Kline (1960) 186 Kan. 393, 350 P.2d 1093; 187 Kan. 186, 354 P.2d 670.

Norio, R. (1982) 'Kliinisen genetiikan etiikka' [The ethic of clinical genetics, in Finnish], K. Achté *et al.* (eds), *Lääkintäetiikka* [Medical ethics]. Vaasa: Suomen Lääkäriliitto.

Nozick, R. (1972) 'Coercion', P. Laslett, W.G. Runciman, Q. Skinner (eds.), *Philosophy, Politics and Society*, fourth series. Oxford: Basil Blackwell.

O'Connel, E. and Logan, G.B. (1974) 'Parental smoking in childhood asthma'. *Annales of Allergy* 32: 142–5.

Oken, D. (1976) 'What to tell cancer patients: a study of medical attitudes', S. Gorovitz *et al.* (eds), *Moral Problems in Medicine*. Englewood Cliffs, NJ: Prentice-Hall.

Parent, W.A. (1974) 'Freedom as the non-restriction of options'. *Mind* 83: 432–4.

Parfit, D. (1986) *Reasons and Persons*. Oxford: Oxford University Press.

Parsons, T. (1951) *The Social System*. Glencoe, IL: Free Press.

Parsons. T. (1958) 'Definitions of health and illness in the light of American values and social structure', E.G. Jago (ed.), *Patients, Physicians and Illness*. New York: Free Press.

Parsons, T. (1975) 'The sick role and role of the physician reconsidered'. *Millbank Memorial Fund Quarterly* 53: 257–78.

Rachels, J. (1986) *The End of Life: Euthanasia and Morality*. Oxford: Oxford University Press.

Radcliffe Richards, J. (1981) *The Sceptical Feminist: A Philosophical Inquiry*. Harmondsworth: Penguin.

Rainbolt, G.W. (1989a) 'Prescription drug laws: justified hard paternalism'. *Bioethics* 3: 45–58.

Rainbolt, G.W. (1989b) 'Justified hard paternalism: a response to Ten'. *Bioethics* 3: 140–1.

Rawls, J. (1972) *A Theory of Justice*. Oxford: Oxford University Press.

Raz, J. (1986) *The Morality of Freedom*. Oxford: Clarendon Press.

Regan, D.H. (1974) 'Justifications for paternalism', J.R. Pennock and J.W. Chapman (eds), *The Limits of Law – Nomos XV*. Chicago: University of Chicago Press.

Regan, T. (1984) *The Case for Animal Rights*. Berkeley: University of California Press.

Report of the Committee on Homosexual Offences and Prostitution (1957) Cmnd. 247.

Ritchie, D.G. (1894) *Natural Rights*. London: Allen & Unwin.

Roberts, D. (1979) *Paternalism in Early Victorian England*. London: Croom Helm.

Rousseau, J.J. (1986) *A Discourse on the Origin of Inequality* (1755). *The Social Contract and Discourses*, G.D.H. Cole (trans.), J.H. Brumfitt and J.C. Hall (eds). London: J.M. Dent & Sons Ltd.

Rousseau, J.J. (1986) *The Social Contract or Principles of Political Right* (1762). *The Social Contract and Discourses*, G.D.H. Cole (trans.), J.H. Brumfitt and J.C. Hall (eds). London: J.M. Dent & Sons Ltd.

Rudinow, J. (1978) 'Manipulation'. *Ethics* 88: 338–47.

Russell, B. (1978) 'Still a live issue'. *Philosophy and Public Affairs* 7: 278–81.

Russell, O.R. (1975) *Freedom to Die*. New York: Human Sciences Press.

Ryan, A. (1989) 'A law unto oneself'. *Times Literary Supplement*, August 4–10: 855.
Ryan, C.C. (1980) 'The normative concept of coercion'. *Mind* **89**: 481–98.
Sartre, J.-P. (1943) *L'Etre et le Néant*. Paris: Gallimard.
Schloendorff v. *Society of New York Hospital* (1914) 105 NE 92, 93 (New York).
Schonsheck, J. (no date) 'Legal paternalistic intervention'.
Schonsheck, J. (1988) 'Concerns about Feinberg's "Garrison Situations"'. Paper presented at the American Philosophical Association Central Division Eighty-Sixth Annual Meeting, Cincinnati, Ohio, April 27–30.
Seidelman, W.E. (1985) 'The professional origins of Dr Joseph Mengele'. *Canadian Medical Association Journal* **133**: 1169–71.
Sen, A. and Williams, B. (eds) (1982) *Utilitarianism and Beyond*. Cambridge: Cambridge University Press.
Sider, R.C. and Clements, C.D. (1984) 'Medical ethics' assault upon medical values' (in reply). *Journal of the American Medical Association* **251**: 2792–3.
Sidgwick, H. (1907) *The Methods of Ethics* (1874). London: Macmillan.
Sinclair, K. and Ross, M. (1985) 'Consequences of decriminalization of homosexuality: a study of two Australian states'. *Journal of Homosexuality* **12**: 119–27.
Singer, P. (1975) *Animal Liberation*. New York: Random House.
Singer, P. (1979) *Practical Ethics*. Cambridge: Cambridge University Press.
Skegg, P.D.G. (1975) '"Informed consent" to medical procedures'. *Medicine, Science and Law* **15**: 124–8.
Slater v. *Baker & Stapleton* (1767) **95** Eng. Rep. 860 (K.B.).
Soble, A. (1976) 'Legal paternalism', unpublished Ph.D. dissertation. State University of New York in Buffalo.
Spinoza, B. (1957) *The Ethics. The Road to Inner Freedom* (1677), D.D. Runes (ed). Secaucus, NJ: The Citadel Press.
Steffen, G.E. (1984) 'Medical ethics' assault upon medical values' (letter to the editor). *Journal of the American Medical Association* **251**: 2791–2.
Steiner, H. (1974–5) 'Individual liberty'. *Proceedings of the Aristotelian Society* **75**: 33–50.
Stephen, J.F. (1874a; 1967) *Liberty, Equality, Fraternity* (second edition 1874a), R.J. White (ed.). Cambridge: Cambridge University Press.
Stephen, J.F. (1874b) 'Note on utilitarianism', in Stephen 1874a.
Stephen, J.F. (1874c) 'Preface to the second edition', in Stephen 1874a.
Stewart, T. (1987) *The Heroin Users*. London.
Szasz, T.S. (1971) *The Manufacture of Madness: A Comparative Study of the Inquisition and the Mental Health Movement*. London: Routledge & Kegan Paul.
Tager, I.B., Weiss, S.T., Rosner, B. and Speizer, F.E. (1979) 'Effect of parental cigarette smoking on the pulmonary function of children'. *American Journal of Epidemiology* **110**: 15–26.
Taylor, C. (1979) 'What's wrong with negative liberty?', A. Ryan (ed.), *The Idea of Freedom*. Oxford: Oxford University Press.
Taylor, C. (1986) *Respect for Nature: A Theory of Environmental Ethics*. Princeton, NJ: Princeton University Press.

Ten, C.L. (1969) 'Crime and immorality'. *Modern Law Review* **32**: 659–61.

Ten, C.L. (1971) 'Paternalism and morality'. *Ratio* **13**: 56–66.

Ten, C.L. (1980) *Mill On Liberty*. Oxford: Clarendon Press.

Ten, C.L. (1989) 'Paternalism and levels of knowledge: a comment on Rainbolt'. *Bioethics* **3**: 135–9.

The Street Offences Act, England (1959).

Thomson, J.H. (1979) 'Informed consent to medical treatment in the United States'. *Medical Journal of Australia* **2**: 412–15.

VanDeVeer, D. (1979) 'Paternalism and subsequent consent', *Canadian Journal of Philosophy* **9**: 631–42.

VanDeVeer, D. (1980a) 'Autonomy respecting paternalism'. *Social Theory and Practice* **6**: 187–207.

VanDeVeer, D. (1980b) 'The contractual argument for withholding medical information'. *Philosophy and Public Affairs* **9**: 198–205.

VanDeVeer, D. (1986) *Paternalistic Intervention: The Moral Bounds of Benevolence*. Princeton, NJ: Princeton University Press.

Webster's Ninth New Collegiate Dictionary (1983). Springfield, MA: Merriam-Webster Inc.

Weinstein, W.L. (1965) 'The concept of liberty in nineteenth century English political thought'. *Political Studies* **13**: 145–62.

White, R.J. (1967) 'Editor's Introduction', J.F. Stephen, *Liberty, Equality, Fraternity*, R.J. White (ed.). Cambridge: Cambridge University Press.

Williams, G. (1966) 'Authoritarian morals and the criminal law'. *The Criminal Law Review*.

Wolfenden: see *Report of the Committee on Homosexual Offences and Prostitution* (1957).

Wollheim, R. (1959) 'Crime, sin, and Mr Justice Devlin'. *Encounter* **13**: 34–40.

NAME INDEX